OFF THE BEATEN PATH® MARYLAND AND DELAWARE

Help Us Keep This Guide Up to Date

We would love to hear from you concerning your experiences with this guide and how you feel it could be improved and kept up to date. Please send your comments and suggestions to:

editorial@GlobePequot.com

Thanks for your input, and happy travels!

OFF THE BEATEN PATH® SERIES

NINTH EDITION

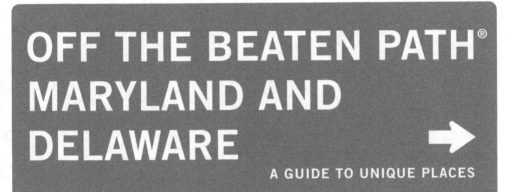

OFF THE BEATEN PATH®
MARYLAND AND
DELAWARE

A GUIDE TO UNIQUE PLACES

JUDY COLBERT

gpp®
travel

Guilford, Connecticut

All the information in this guidebook is subject to change. We recommend that you call ahead to obtain current information before traveling.

Editor: Amy Lyons
Project Editor: Lynn Zelem
Layout: Joanna Beyer
Text Design: Linda R. Loiewski
Maps: Equator Graphics © Rowman & Littlefield

ISSN 1538-5485
ISBN 978-0-7627-5730-5

Distributed by NATIONAL BOOK NETWORK

About the Author

Judy Colbert is a longtime resident of Maryland. An award-winning freelance writer and photographer, Judy's more than 800 articles and photographs have appeared in such publications as *Howard County Times, Chesapeake Life, Grapevine, Spinsheet, Maryland Life, SouthernTravelNews.com, SouthernCruising.com, Fredericksburg Free Lance-Star, Forward, Meetings Media,* and dozens of other publications. She has appeared on television and radio programs, including *Good Morning America* and *Arthur Frommer's Almanac of Travel.*

Other titles that Judy has authored include *Virginia Off the Beaten Path* and *Insiders' Guide to Baltimore,* published by Globe Pequot Press; *Country Towns of Maryland and Delaware,* published by Country Roads Press; and *Fun Places to Go with Children in Washington, D.C.,* published by Chronicle Books.

Acknowledgments

Travel guidebook information is difficult to maintain. Businesses open and close. Operating hours and admission fees change. If nothing else, keeping up with Web site URLs could be a full-time job. Being up-to-date and accurate is essential because if you read something that is incorrect, you may wonder about the next entry and the next. Similarly, you may delight in a restaurant or attraction I suggested even though the operation may be "wet behind the ears" and still working out the kinks when I write about it. "If she's right on that, she must be right on the other suggestions," you think. I love telling you that I think this is worth your time and that is worth your effort, particularly when it does take you off the beaten path. It's why I don't tell you where not to go or that a particular restaurant hasn't passed a health inspection in the last three years. (Ugh!)

With that introduction, and with more appreciation than I can begin to express, thanks go to the people at the county and city DMOs (Destination Marketing Organization), convention and visitor bureaus, and chambers of commerce of Maryland and Delaware. They send information to me, show me around when I visit for a few days, and—in the figurative sense—keep me on my toes with what I should know. Publicists and business owners, and regular users of these *Off the Beaten Path* guides who send suggestions and updates, are all invaluable.

Knowing I will omit someone and apologizing ahead of time, extra thanks go to: (alphabetically)

Bobby Abner, Tiffany C. Ahalt, Marc Apter, Joyce Baki, Paul and Lisa Bales, Rachelina Bonacci, Nikki Boone, Bill Clark, Martha Clark, Tina Common, Robin Coventry, Jeff Crider, Jennifer de la Cruz, Rob DeFord, Sue duPont, Rae Emerson, Michael Evitts, Sue and Rick Farrell, Jill Feinberg, Jazzlyn Flores, Tim Gallagher, Amie Gorrell, Jim Grube, Steele Hardy, Kelly Housen, Barry Kessler, Carolyn Laray, Richard Lewis, Kathleen Mackel, Aubrey Manzo, Ken Mellgren, Captain Ed O'Brien, Hannah Olanoff, Rebecca Pawlowski, Eliot Pfanstiehl, Michele Robinette, Karen Rosage, Jack Russell, Vicki Saltzman, James and Gina Schillinger, Ann Shumard, Barbara Siegert, Louise Soroko, Alan Spence, Susan Steckman, Frank and Recy Tatum, Michael Tersiguel, Laurie Verge, Sue Wilkinson, Connie Yingling, Nina Wahl, and Chief Ranger Sam Zambon.

Contents

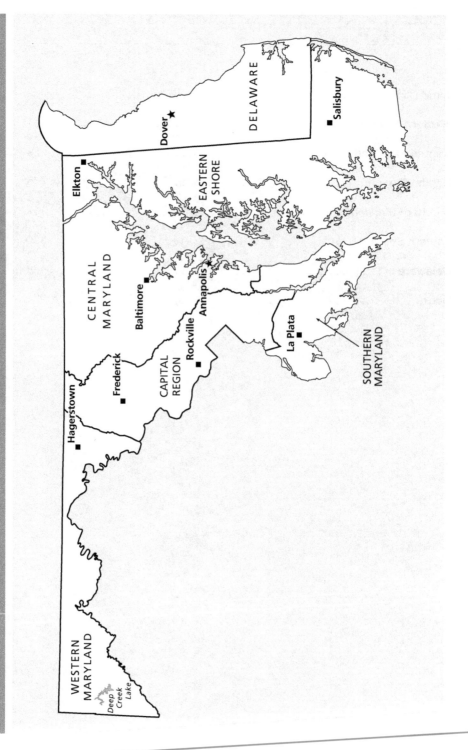

Introduction

Welcome to *Maryland and Delaware Off the Beaten Path*, ninth edition, two states where you'll find some of the best food, the friendliest people, the most incredible history, amazingly unusual attractions, wonderful scenery and natural resources, and enough interesting ways to spend a few hours off the interstate to keep you busy for years.

Maryland is often called America in Miniature because the state goes from the seashore (the Atlantic Ocean and the Chesapeake Bay) on the east to the mountains (the Appalachians) on the west. The mountains are not high compared to the Rockies (Backbone Mountain in Garrett County is the tallest, at 3,360 feet), but they provide fair downhill and excellent cross-country skiing. The seashore is among the finest in the East. In one day you can go from one to the other and theoretically ski in the morning and the afternoon; snow skiing one direction, water skiing the other. About the only clime we don't have here is desert, yet there are sand quarries.

Not everything in Maryland, however, is miniature. The National Aquarium in Baltimore is one of the world's largest. The collection at the Walter's Art Museum, also in Baltimore, is world renowned. Maryland also has one of the nation's largest hydroelectric generating stations at Conowingo (Cecil County), the largest colony of African black-footed penguins in the United States (Baltimore City Zoo), one of the largest and finest public libraries in the United States at the Enoch Pratt Free Library (Baltimore City), and the largest wooden dome in the country built without nails (Annapolis). Well, the list continues, but you get the idea.

Maryland is also called the Free State (road signs say KEEP THE FREE STATE LITTER FREE), and if you ask residents, they'd probably cite the freedom of worship advocated by the state's founders. Others might point to Maryland's alliance with the northern states during "the war" and its intolerance of slavery (at least in some parts of the state). These historical facts are true, but the nickname dates from 1917, when the state opposed Prohibition on the grounds that it was a states' rights issue.

And a third nickname is the Old Line State, which honors Maryland's regular line troops who served courageously in the Revolutionary War.

In the summer of 2000, Maryland introduced its Scenic Byways program, celebrating the "roads less traveled." From the mountains to the seashore, nineteen scenic byways have been designated, encompassing 2,487 miles. The average length of a byway is 60 miles and takes seventy minutes to drive, but lots of side trips are possible. The shortest is five miles, along the Historic National Seaport route, and the longest is 170 miles along the Historic National

Road route. As part of this program, 800 new SCENIC BYWAYS signs were erected, a state map was created, and a free 192-page book titled *Maryland Scenic Byways* was published. For information, contact the state highway administration communications office at (410) 545-0303 or (800) 323-6742. You can download a PDF version of the scenic byways map at www.marylandroads .com/oed/MarylandScenicByways.pdf. The Chesapeake Country Byway, the only National Scenic Byway in Maryland and one of only seventy-five in the country, runs from Stevensville (through Chestertown) to Chesapeake City, with legs to Rock Hall and the Eastern Neck National Wildlife Refuge.

officialfossil

The state's official fossil, the four-ribbed snail, is an extinct invertebrate that ranged in size from microscopic to three or four inches in diameter. Fossils can be found at the Cliffs of Calvert, in the Choptank and St. Mary's areas.

Two historic trails let you explore some of the highlights of the Civil War and the War of 1812. The ***Civil War Trail*** includes carefully mapped driving tours that explore the Antietam campaign, John Wilkes Booth's escape from Ford's Theatre after assassinating President Abraham Lincoln, and Baltimore. The ***Star Spangled Banner Trail & The War of 1812*** is a 100-mile scenic and historic trail that follows the route taken by the British Marines as they invaded the Chesapeake Bay area in 1814.

Maryland is also involved with the Gateways Network, coordinated by the National Park Service in partnership with the Chesapeake Bay program. A Gateway is an entrance to the byways and water trails in the National Park Service program. Among the first Chesapeake Bay Gateways in Maryland, Washington, D.C., Virginia, Pennsylvania, and New York, are twelve Gateway sites, one Gateway hub, two regional information centers, seven water trails, and one land trail. And, that's just the beginning. Pick a Maryland Gateway and you may visit the Barge House Museum (Annapolis), the Blackwater National Wildlife Refuge (Cambridge), Jefferson Patterson Park and Museum (St. Leonard), and the Monocacy River Water Trail. For additional information, stop by www.baygateways.net.

Maryland toll roads are part of the E-Z Pass system (all of New England except Vermont and Connecticut, and west to Chicago, Illinois and south to Virginia and West Virginia) that lets you through toll booths by collecting tolls electronically. Maryland and DRBA (Delaware River and Bay Authority) collect a monthly account maintenance fee ($1.50) and an initial fee.

Maryland has four area codes divided in an overlay pattern. Generally, 301 and 240 codes are for the western, suburban Maryland (around Washington, D.C.), and southern Maryland counties. Similarly, 410 and 443 are for Annapolis, Baltimore, and Eastern Shore areas. All local calls require the entire ten-digit number (area code and phone number). Only long-distance calls require the number 1 before the ten-digit number.

Although much of Maryland is urban, you can find open countryside within a few miles of wherever you are. You can also find campgrounds and the National Association of RV Parks and Campgrounds recognized Jellystone Park Camp-Resort in Williamsport with its "Plan-It-Green" Award and the Maryland Association of Campgrounds won an award for producing the best statewide campground direction in the small state category in 2009. Deb Carter of the Maryland Association of Campgrounds was selected as the "State Executive Director of the Year." For additional information, call (303) 681-0401 or visit www.GoCampingAmerica.com.

howtoflytheflag

The Maryland flag was adopted in 1904. The red and white section is the coat of arms of the Crossland family, the first Lord Baltimore's relatives on his mother's side. The black and gold design is the coat of arms for the Calvert family, Lord Baltimore's relatives on his father's side. When hanging the flag, the black and gold quadrant is uppermost and closest to the pole.

In addition to showcasing Maryland's attractions, this book also explores Delaware, which has been called Small Wonder for its diminutive size and its natural beauty. Only 96 miles in length, the state is bordered by the Atlantic Ocean and Delaware Bay on the east and Maryland to the west and south. Delaware proudly boasts the fact that there is no sales tax. That's why you'll find so many outlet stores and other good shopping venues, from small shops to sprawling malls, throughout the state.

The area code for Delaware is 302, and you needn't dial it for local calls within Delaware.

I hope you enjoy reading and using this book as much as I enjoy discovering *Maryland and Delaware Off the Beaten Path*.

WESTERN MARYLAND →

Western Maryland's three counties—Garrett, Allegany, and Washington—are a combination of farmlands, rugged mountains, sedate streams, and white-water rivers.

The products of farms and iron furnaces needed to be transported to customers between Wheeling, West Virginia, and the East Coast. So through this territory came the National Pike, which now is Alternate Rte 40. It was the first road across the country funded by the federal government. Along the road are many of the original mile markers, white metal (although they look like stone) obelisks that stand about 3 feet high.

People used to travel to this area to escape the heat and humidity of a city summer. Now, they flock here for the year-round outdoor activities from white-water rafting to downhill and cross-country skiing. Former summer cottages have been modified for year-round living or torn down and replaced with vacation or primary housing. Condos have sprung up like dandelions. (You know, some people like dandelions because of the wine and salad potential. Others hate dandelions because they're annoying weeds.) Artsy and New Age people have moved here, as certain a harbinger of a "real" community

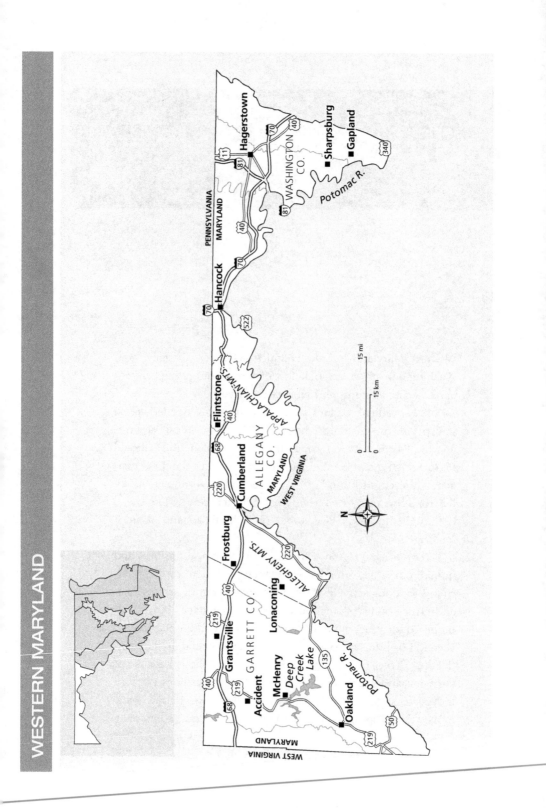

WESTERN MARYLAND

developing as spotting the first robin of spring. We will not discuss the fact that some robins winter over in Maryland.

Garrett County

Garrett County is known for the Wisp four-season resort and **Deep Creek Lake,** the largest lake in the state (all Maryland lakes were made by humans). The dam (1,300 feet long and 62 feet high) creating the lake was built in 1925 to provide hydroelectric power. In 1999 Maryland bought the lake for $7.8 million to ensure that the area remained available as a recreation site. The lake is great for boating, fishing, swimming, and just about any other water-based activity you can want. The boats and floating docks and piers are removed in early winter and the water level is dropped. This allows for winter freezing, snow accumulation, and the runoff of the spring thaw. It does receive about 120 inches of snow a year, more than Anchorage, Alaska. Deep Creek Lake State Park, 898 State Park Rd., Oakland, is open daily from sunrise to sunset. Contact (301) 387-5563 or www.dnr.state.md.us/publiclands/western/deepcreeklake.html.

Railroads were once an efficient means of transportation in this area (the county was named for John Work Garrett, president of the B&O Railroad). Today Interstates 81, 68, and 70 provide the lifelines connecting this part of the state with the rest of the country.

Some areas and attractions are still in remote places and **The Nature Conservancy's Cranesville Sub-Arctic Swamp** is about as off the beaten path as you're going to find. It's about 10 miles out of Oakland off Cranesville Rd., and covers more than 500 acres in Maryland (plus more in West Virginia). This natural phenomenon is a remnant of a boreal forest that produces growth normally found in arctic regions. So, you geologists, biologists, and nature lovers can see many rare species of flora and fauna, at least rare for this area. You may see the tamarack or larch and the tiny, round-leaved sundew, an insectivorous plant. You may also see the northern water shrew or the golden-crowned kinglet or the saw-whet owl.

AUTHOR'S FAVORITES WESTERN MARYLAND

Antietam Battlefield

Garrett County Historical Museum

LaVale Toll Gate House

Washington County Museum of Fine Arts

Western Maryland Scenic Railroad

MARYLAND WEB SITES AND INFORMATION

Farmers Markets; www.mda.state.md
.us/mdproducts/farmers_market_dir.php

**Maryland Department of Natural
Resources;** www.dnr.state.md.us

Maryland Fall Foliage Hotline; (800)
LEAVES-1; www.dnr.state.md.us/
outdoors/fallfoliage

In 1965 Cranesville Swamp became one of the first National Natural Land-marks to be designated by the National Park Service. It's open to the public for photography, nature study, birding, and walking, with four color-coded marked trails (with interpretive signs) through the woods to a 500-foot boardwalk. The trails start from either the drive into the swamp or from the parking lot, and all trails lead to the boardwalk. Please stay on the trails and the boardwalk so you don't take a chance of harming the plants. Officials suggest you start with a visit to their Web site and download the brochure and the trail guide. Bring plenty of drinking water, and wear sensible shoes, sunblock, insect repellent, and socks pulled up over your pants' cuffs. Call (301) 897-8570 to let them know you're coming. Visit them on the Web at www.nature.org.

In late 2008, Maryland became the twenty-eighth state to start a ***Barn Quilt program*** when the Barn Quilt Association of Garrett County saw the placement of its first quilt. This organization celebrates the designs and dedication to creating these family heirlooms. So far, four barns are adorned with 8' by 8' quilt patterns and you can take a self-guided drive to see them. The first barn quilt, a Lemoyne Star, done in the Maryland state flag colors, went up on November 25, 2008 on a barn owned by Gary and Kate Fratz at 27599 Garrett Hwy., Accident. You can see it along Rte 219 between McHenry and Accident

PUBLIC TRANSPORTATION

Amtrak, (800) USA-RAIL; www.amtrak
.com.

**Baltimore Washington International
Airport (BWI),** (410) 519-0000, (301)
261-1000, (800) 435-9294; www
.bwiairport.com.

**Washington Metropolitan Area Transit
Authority (WMATA),** (202) 637-7000;
www.wmata.com.

on the western side of the ride (on the right if you're traveling south). An Ohio Star quilt, done in red, white, and blue, is on a barn owned by Delegate Wendell and Ruth Beitzel at 7644 Rock Lodge Rd., between Bittinger and McHenry. A Delectable Mountains quilt, dedicated to Greg Hinebaugh's mother was mounted in May 2009 and is on a whitewashed barn owned by Hinebaugh at 5440 Sang Run Rd., McHenry. The most recent quilt, Turkey Tracks (done in red and blue on a white background) was mounted in July 2009, and is on Sue Logan's barn, 2515 Boiling Springs Rd., Deer Park.

The association says they think there are 600 barns in Garrett County and they anticipate 50 to 75 barns will have quilt blocks within the next few years. When you want to know more about these pieces of our past and how to participate, you can contact the association, 809 Memorial Dr., Oakland, 21550; (301) 616-1074; www.garrettbarnquilts.org.

Another reminder of times gone by is the **Drane House,** built by the town's first permanent settler, James Drane in 1797. Walking through the one-and-a-half story home and inspecting the recreated garden gives history buffs (and others) a feel for life as it was at one of the few original frontier plantation homes remaining in this area. For a free tour, call the Accident Town Hall.

A key to Accident's past, the one-and-a-half-story log and frame house has been restored by the Garrett County Historical Society and is open for free tours upon request. The Drane House is on Accident-Bittinger Rd., Accident. Call the Accident Town Hall, Mon, Wed, or Fri, at (301) 746-6346.

Climate Overview

Maryland enjoys, if that's the word, hot and humid summers (temperatures are sometimes in the 90s) and cold and snowy winters. An average of 16 inches of snow falls each year in the Baltimore–Washington, D.C., corridor. In 1997–1998, there was only 0.1 inch of snow, while a few years earlier there were 70 inches of the white stuff (if this is Friday it must be snowing, or if it's snowing, it must be Friday).

Keep in mind, of course, that there's more likely to be snow in the mountainous western part of the state (Garrett County gets an average of 120 inches), while the Eastern Shore is almost snowless. Summer temperatures will usually be ten to twenty degrees cooler in the mountains than at the beach.

Actually, the weather can be quite pleasant most of the year, and the state has at least its share of seasons, with beautiful spring blossoms, showy summers, fall foliage, and winter wonderlands. The Chesapeake Bay is large enough to create its own weather systems.

home sweet home

Just 13 feet from the shores of Deep Creek Lake is the **Lake Pointe Inn**, a bed-and-breakfast inn. It is the oldest house on the lake, dating from the late 1800s. 174 Lake Pointe Dr., McHenry; (301) 387-0111, (800) 523-LAKE; www.deepcreekinns.com.

The **Wisp Resort** in McHenry is known for its four-season appeal, so think golf, the **Sewickley Spa** (301-387-7000, www.sewickleyspa.com), fly fishing, skate park (20,000-square-foot paved and wood facility), paintball, downhill mountain biking, disc golf, chairlift rides (great for fall foliage viewing), bonfires, nature program, horseback riding, day camps, and other individual and family activities (296 Marsh Hill Rd.; 301-387-4911; www.wisp resort.com or www.skiwisp.com).

Wisp is the only downhill ski facility in the state. In 2006 they opened its North Camp, offering ten more trails and two quad chairlifts. **Bear Claw Snow Tubing Park** at Wisp has trails for snow tubing, with a lift to pull you and your tube back up the mountain so you don't have to waste time and energy trekking and schlepping back up the hill. Another winter activity is the annual Beachin' Weekend, in March, with music, swimsuit slalom, and games.

The **Mountain Coaster** that opened at Wisp in August 2007 was only the fourth one built in the United States and the second on the East Coast. Popular in Europe, the Mountain Coaster is a hybrid of an alpine slide and a roller coaster. Riders travel 1,300 feet uphill before descending, twisting, turning, dipping and rolling for 3,500 feet downhill. The attraction is open year-round, and operates at night as well.

history lesson

The town of McHenry was settled about 1805 by Col. James McHenry, aide to Gen. George Washington, signer of the Declaration of Independence, and the man for whom the Baltimore fort was named.

Never let it be said that Wisp isn't on the cusp of everything innovative for they now offer hour-long Segway tours. Those are the two-wheel personal transportation devices that have become popular in airports and tourist hotspots.

When you want to try white-water canoeing for the first time or if you want to perfect your skills, then head to the **Adventure Sports Center International (ASCI).** Featuring a 1,600-foot recirculating white-water course, located on Marsh Mountain in McHenry (at the top of the Wisp Resort), the course can be changed, the rocks moved, and who knows how many other adaptations they can make? It's said to more closely replicate the conditions of a natural river than any other in the world. The 2009 USRA Rafting Nationals competition were held here. Matt Taylor, an Olympic whitewater competitor, is ASCI's Director of Operations. This flexibility means it will be great for those who want to try these sports and those who defy them. A streamside amphitheater seating 600 allows spectators a front-row seat from a dry perspective. Visit Adventure Sports Center at 685 Mosser Rd.; call (301) 387-3250 or (877) 300-2724; or visit www.adventuresports center.com.

sweettoothtime

Garrett County is the southernmost place in the country where maple syrup is produced. Syrupmaking demonstrations are held at Swallow Falls State Park each March and include pancake-and-syrup tastings.

Within the more than 90,000 acres of public land, Garrett County has cleared and marked trails in New Germany State Park, six miles of maintained trails around Herrington Lake, and an additional six miles of primitive trails. Deep Creek and Swallow Falls State Parks have marked hiking trails that are suitable for cross-country skiing. Ski rentals are available at Herrington Manor State Park (301-334-9180; www.dnr.state.md.us/publiclands/western/ herringtonmanor.html) and New Germany State Park (301-895-5453; www.dnr .state.md.us/publiclands/western/newgermany.html).

Reportedly Western Maryland has the only town in the country named **Accident,** about 10 miles north of Deep Creek on U.S. Hwy. 219. The story is that King George II gave George Deakins a land grant for 600 acres in Western Maryland in 1751. Deakins sent two engineers on separate missions to find his paradise. By accident each selected the same plot, starting at the same tall oak tree. Deakins called this plot "The Accident Tract," and the name endures; locals wouldn't have it any other way. Most noted by visitors are the Accident Garage, the Accident Fire Department, and the Accident Professional Building.

Vacationers have been seeking respite in Garrett County for hundreds of years, and traces of that history can be found throughout the county. The Shawnee Indians summered here. People from the sun-baked, humid cities of Washington and Baltimore came here to enjoy the cool mountain climate as early as 1851. That is when the Baltimore and Ohio Railroad ran its line to Oakland, which would become the county seat. The train no longer stops in Garrett

fitforthe president(s)

Presidents Grant, Garfield, Harrison, and Cleveland attended services in the St. Matthew's Episcopal Church in Oakland. (301) 334-2510.

ANNUAL EVENTS IN WESTERN MARYLAND

FEBRUARY

State Police Deep Creek Dunk
Deep Creek
(301) 387-5898

MARCH

Turning Sap into Syrup
Herrington Manor State Park
(301) 334-9180
www.dnr.state.md.us/publiclands/
western/herringtonmanor.html

APRIL

**Maryland House and Garden
Pilgrimage**
Statewide
(410) 821-6933
www.mhgp.org

MAY

**National Pike Festival and Wagon
Train**
Various locations
(301) 791-3246
www.nationalpikefestival.org

Sharpsburg's Memorial Day Parade
Town Square
(301) 432-4428

JUNE

George's Creek Days
Lonaconing
(301) 463-2189

Grantsville Days
Grantsville
(301) 895-5387
(301) 387-4386

Heritage Days
Cumberland
(301) 722-0037
www.heritagedaysfestival.com

McHenry Highland Festival
Garrett County Fairgrounds, McHenry
(301) 387-3093
(800) 313-0811
www.highlandfest.info

Western Maryland Blues Fest
Hagerstown
(301) 739-8577, ext.116
www.blues-fest.org

County, but the Oakland station, an outstanding and picturesque Queen Anne structure built in 1884, remains.

The *Oakland Post Office mural* at 22 South Second St, Oakland, was created by Robert Gates in 1942; it portrays a buckwheat harvest. Gates also did the mural in the Bethesda Post Office, which depicts the Montgomery County Farm Woman's Cooperative Market.

Walk along Second St. a little more and you'll come across the *Garrett County Historical Museum,* with its exhibits portraying the history of the county's residents, from Native American to Civil War, and enough genealogical information to keep a family of history buff busy for days or years. There is no admission fee to the museum (contributions are accepted, though), which is located at 107 South Second St., Oakland. Generally, it's open in the summer

JULY

**Maryland Symphony Orchestra
Antietam Sparkle
Independence Celebration**
Sharpsburg
(301) 797-4000
www.mdsymphony.com

AUGUST

Augustoberfest
Downtown Hagerstown
(301) 739-8577, ext. 116
http://augustoberfest.org

Garrett County Agriculture Fair
Garrett County Fairground
McHenry
(301) 533-1010
www.garrettcountyfair.org

SEPTEMBER

Apple Butter Boil
Swallow Falls State Park
Oakland
(301) 334-9180

OCTOBER

Alsatia Mummers' Parade
Hagerstown
(301) 739-2044
www.hagerstownmd.org

Autumn Glory Festival
Garrett County
(301) 387-4386
www.visitdeepcreek.com

DECEMBER

Christmas in the Village
Grantsville
(301) 895-3332
www.spruceforest.org

Christmas Model Train Open House
Allegany Fairgrounds
(301) 777-5905

from Mon through Sat from 11 a.m. to 4 p.m. and Thurs through Sat in the winter. Call to confirm that the museum will be open for visitors at (301) 334-3226; or visit www.deepcreeklake.com.

Take a few more steps down Second St. and walk into Judy Devlin's **Book Mark'et & Antique Mezzanine.** It's a cozy yet spacious independent bookstore with a definite focus on regional and local titles. They have a special children's room for young readers, and the mezzanine has antiques and vintage collectibles. Judy's had this store at this location since the late 80s or early 90s and she was at another location for a half-dozen years before that. In other words, if there's anything you want to know about this town (or its people), you may as well start with Judy. The store is open Mon through Fri from 9:30 a.m. to 5:30 p.m. (6 p.m. on Wed and Fri), Sat from 9 a.m. to 5

waytoshow somebackbone

Garrett County has the state's highest mountain (Backbone, at 3,360 feet), the longest waterfall (Muddy Creek Falls, at 52 feet), and the largest lake (Deep Creek, with a length of 12 miles and a 65-mile shoreline). Backbone Mountain has another distinction as the location of the first wind farms in the state. Synergics Wind Energy of Annapolis is building a 50-megawatt wind farm with up to 20 turbines and Constellation Energy is building a 70-megawatt complex with 28 turbines that should provide enough power for 23,000 households.

The historical marker for the 3,360-foot highest point in the state is on Backbone Mountain; take U.S. Hwy. 50 east of Redhouse and you'll be at the crest of the Alleghenies.

p.m., and Sun from 11 a.m. to 4 p.m. Located at 111 South Second St.; call (301) 334-8778.

Walk to the traffic light and turn left as you're walking through historic downtown Oakland and you're sure to realize the mountain air must be good at getting the creative juices flowing. Stop by the **Garrett County Arts Council** where you can learn about upcoming events (exhibits, concerts, demonstrations, and workshops), see the works of more than 100 artists and artisans, and learn about the annual Art in the Park festival at the Discovery Center. Located at 206 East Alder St.; call (301) 334-6580 or visit www.garrettarts.com.

Garrett County is home to numerous artists and there is joy in visiting each and every one of them. For those who don't have that kind of time, stop by the **Shoppe at Heritage Square,** the 1884 B&O Railroad Station in Oakland, to buy items made in the county. The store carries apparel, soaps, stained glass, and pottery from local craftspeople. The farmers provide salsa and pepper jellies and honey. Trains, books, and puzzles, dolls, and dollhouse furniture will delight the child in all of us. Yes, the antiques that are used to display all these items are for sale. The Shoppe is open Wed through Sat from 10 a.m. to 4 p.m. Call (301) 334-1243 or visit www.garrettchamber.com.

Just behind the main drag is the Mt. Fresh Pavilion on the Town Parking Lot where you can find public restrooms, the Little Youghiogheny Music Festival on Friday summer nights, seasonal farmers' market stands, and other events. Behind the parking lot is the Asa M. McCain, Jr. Bridge that leads to a tree-lined walking path to the Lighthouse, past Safe Harbor, and around the Yough Glades Housing Complex.

Those who know me know the **Deep Creek Lake Discovery Center** is my kind of place. I love learning how things work or why things do what they do. The Center is run by the Maryland Department of Natural Resources as an interpretive environmental center and it's a fun place to take the children so they can touch fossils, put their hands in a black bear paw print (compare that to the plaster of Paris hand mold they made in kindergarten), see underwater ecology through a microscope, and participate in such programs as hiking and boating safety. Within the 6,000-square-foot building are a classroom, an a/v-equipped conference area for educational programs, and a gift shop with environmental and educational toys, souvenirs, field guides, and books. The Discovery Center is open daily from 10 a.m. to 5 p.m. in the summer, and on weekends the rest of the year; 898 State Park Rd., Swanton; (301) 387-7067; www.dnr.state.md.us/public lands/western/discovery.html.

For years, dining options around Deep Creek Lake and Wisp have been down-home family type places where multiple generations of several families have worked over the years. Then, as the seasonal and year-round population grew, so did the dining options from fast-food chains to slow food that is almost fine dining with white tablecloths. If you're an oenophile who insists on the properly deep bowled glass for your red wine, you'll probably be disappointed. If you're a wine geek who just enjoys a nice glass of wine for a modest price, then you'll be happier than a kid in a candy store. The dress code is still extremely casual and, for the most part, the food is still good and relatively inexpensive, whether it's a pizza or fresh seafood. The big decision may be do you want a view of the mountains or the lake or both?

One of the more scenic lake locations is the **Four Seasons** restaurant at the **Will o' the Wisp** condo complex on the lake. It's open for breakfast, lunch, and dinner during warm weather and dinner only during the winter. Chef

nativeillustrators

Garrett County has drawn even more artistic talent with illustration work of Mark and Laura Stutzman, who operate Eloqui studio. You've seen left-handed Mark's work on numerous McDonald's packages (*Batman, Jurassic Park*), and *Mad* magazine covers, but he's best known for designing the Elvis Presley postage stamp for the "Legends in American Music" series. Laura's clients include PBS, MCI, CBS, Simon & Schuster, Sleeping Bear Press, and many others. Look for activities sponsored by the Garrett Lakes Arts Festival and you'll probably find both Mark and Laura in attendance. Their studio is at 100 G St., Oakland; call (301) 334-4086 or visit www.eloqui.com.

bubblebubble notoilortrouble

Yes, there is a connection between the name Deer Park and Deer Park bottled water. The water comes from a spring that's 3,000 feet above sea level, in the midst of hundreds of acres of woodlands. The water is moved directly from the source through gravity-fed pipes to the bottling plant.

Jason likes to mix the expected with the unexpected, although one of the more popular items is his signature balsamic BBQ burgers. The floor-to-ceiling windows overlook trees down to the lakeside and there are boat slips if you'd rather go by water than by land, again during warm weather. Located at 20160 Garrett Hwy., Oakland; call (888) 590-7283 or (301) 387-5503; or visit www .willothewisp.com.

As you drive east out of Oakland, you'll find your way to **Mountain Lake Park,** established in 1881. There's a small museum, set in the Ticket Booth that was built in 1900 in conjunction with the Bashford Amphitheater. It has exhibits showing how the town was established as a Chautauqua-style summer resort and thrived until the early years of World War II. A statue of seven children playing on a jungle-gym type structure is dedicated to the seven children who died on September 10, 1959, at the Mountain Lake Park railroad crossing on their way to school. The museum is open regularly on monthly occasions or by appointment. Call (301) 334-2250 or (301) 334-4314 or visit www .mtnlakepark.com.

maryland mysteries

If you read Martha Grimes mysteries, then this area might "feel" familiar to you. Her mother, June, owned the Mountain Lake Hotel and Martha and her brother spent a lot of their childhood here. She went on to receive undergraduate and graduate degrees at the University of Maryland and has taught locally at Frostburg State University and Montgomery College. The Hotel Paradise reflects on experiences she had here. The hotel was torn down in 1967.

There may be more Victorian homes in one place than you'll see anywhere else in the state. Of course, if you're a tennis player, then you probably know the town as the home of the **Western Maryland Clay Court Tennis Championships,** held every Aug. For more information about Mountain Lake Park, contact the town staff at 1007 Allegheny Dr., Mountain Lake Park, 21550; (301) 334-2250.

Whether or not you like stained glass—as in windows, sun catchers, jewelry boxes, and lamps—you're sure to know someone who does, so you just might want to schedule a half-hour or a day visiting **Louis DiCarlo's Stained Glass Gallery.** The home was constructed in 1885 but the pink and blue exterior will shock those Victorian thoughts right out of your mind. DiCarlo (an award-winning designer and stained-glass master craftsman) has an estimated 2,000 pieces on the walls, hanging from the ceilings, and taking up floor space. If it's an Irish or Jewish theme or dogs or angels that you want, he has it. Or, you tell him what you want and he'll create it. Oh, he has lots of typical items on his Web site, without prices. He doesn't "do" computers and doesn't want to fool around changing pictures or writing notes. Hey, he's a stained-glass maker.

DiCarlo tends to be in his shop most days, from 9 a.m. to 6 p.m., but you'll do well to call before you stop by. 214 I St (corner of Rte 135 and I, although you really can't miss that paint scheme); (301) 334-8222, www.stainedglass gallery.net.

It's glass of a different kind when you stop by the **Simon Pearce** factory and store. I bought my first piece of Simon Pearce glass from his original workshop in Quechee, Vermont, perhaps three decades ago. So, it was a real thrill when I learned he'd opened a workshop and store in Maryland in January 1999, occupying 190,000 square feet of space in the old Bausch & Lomb factory. His style is pretty enough to put in a museum and comfortable enough to use. Hold a goblet in your hand and you may think it was made just for you. You may find glassware, pottery, flatware, candles, desk accessories, lampshades, table linens, and wooden serving pieces.

About twenty glassblowers work in teams of two, and you can watch them perform their magic daily from 9 a.m. to 5 p.m., although after 3 p.m. there's usually only one or two teams. They may be working on anything from Stratton stemware to lamps. Should you just want to buy some of his beautiful pieces, you can find them at Sunnyfields, Jones Lighting Specialist, and Radcliffe in Baltimore; Albert Smyth Co. Inc., in Timonium; Red Orchard in Bethesda and Rockville; and Avoca Handweavers in Annapolis. Simon Pearce, 265 Glass Dr., Mt. Lake Park; (301) 334-5277; www.simonpearce.com.

Solomon Sterner opened the **Casselman Inn,** Main St., Grantsville, in 1824 to take in travelers from the National Pike. As is usual with restaurants, inns, and hotels along the pike, this one is on the north side, or the side that westbound travelers would be on. The two-story Federal-style brick house (with

MAJOR MARYLAND NEWSPAPERS

The Capital, 2000 Capital Dr., Annapolis 21401; (410) 268-5000 (editorial), (410) 268-4800 (circulation), (301) 261-2200 (Washington, D.C.); www.capitalonline.com.

Washington Post, 1150 Fifteenth St., Washington, D.C. 20071; (202) 334-6000 (editorial), (202) 334-6100 (circulation); www.washingtonpost.com.

Baltimore Sun, 501 North Calvert St., Baltimore 21278; (410) 332-6000; www.baltimoresun.com.

The Star Democrat, 29088 Airpark Dr., Easton 21601; (410) 820-6505; www.stardem.com.

bricks made on the property) has nine guest rooms, each individually decorated with antiques. A newer forty-room motel has handcrafted furniture created by members of the community. Stop by for dinner or visit the bakery downstairs where you can savor the smells while you watch breads, cakes, and pies being made. The restaurant is open Mon through Sat from 7 a.m. to 8 p.m. (or until 10 p.m. during the summer) at 113 East Main St.; call (301) 895-5055 or visit www .thecasselman.com.The phone number for the restaurant is (301) 895-5266.

Across the street from the inn is the **Ventures** with a quilt shop, print shop, and thrift shop in the old Grantsville elementary school building, with the original part constructed in the 1890s. The building also has apartments and offices. Call (301) 895-5737 for more information.

When the nearby **Casselman Bridge** on Alternate Rte 40 East in **Casselman River Bridge State Park** was built in 1813, it was the largest single-span stone-arch bridge in America. Gracefully curving 50 feet above the river, it was constructed so that the Chesapeake and Ohio Canal could travel beneath its span. The canal never came this far, but the bridge carried traffic for 125 years. It is now closed to motorized traffic, but the Casselman River Bridge State Park, Rte 40 East, Grantsville, has a picnic area and a scenic spot to enjoy for a few minutes or a few hours. Yes, it is on the National Register of Historic Places. For information, call (301) 895-5453 or visit www.dnr.state.md.us/publiclands/ western/casselman.html.

Just east of Casselman Bridge is **Penn Alps,** home to numerous crafters who work in log cabins that have been brought here from the surrounding countryside. The **Spruce Forest Artisan Village** features a number of artisans in log cabins and rustic structures set among towering spruce trees. You may find a village blacksmith, a weaver, a basket maker, a stained-glass worker, a teddy bear artist, or a potter. They make items you don't usually see in your average souvenir stand. The shops in the village are open May through Oct, Mon through Sat 10 a.m. to 5 p.m. Four artisans are on the premises by chance and by appointment from Nov through Apr. The village is at 177 Casselman Rd., Grantsville; call (301) 895-3332 or visit www.spruceforest.org.

Allegany County

Outdoor enthusiasts enjoy Allegany County and Cumberland, the county seat. Within the county borders are Rocky Gap and Dan's Mountain State Parks, Green Ridge State Forest, and the C&O Canal National Historical Park, where people can hunt, boat, fish, camp, bike, hike, and explore history.

The outdoor types celebrated the opening of the **Great Allegheny Passage,** a 150-mile trail system that runs from the historic C&O Canal towpath

Bicycling Information

The Maryland Department of Transportation has a 16-minute video of tips and information for cyclists riding in traffic on public roads. You can watch it online at http://onelesscar.org or by writing to Michael Jackson at mjackson3@mdot.state.md.us.

Bicyclists are prohibited from riding bicycles on Maryland Transportation Authority toll facilities, including bridges, tunnels, and approach roads. Understanding that this can be an oops in your travel plans, the Authority offers the following services as a courtesy to bikers:

Authority personnel will transport bikes and bikers across the Thomas J. Hatem (U.S. Hwy. 40, Susquehanna River) and Harry W. Nice (US 301, Potomac River) Bridges for the normal toll fee when time, personnel, and equipment permit. Call (410) 575-6650 for the Hatem Bridge, and (301) 259-4444 for the Nice Bridge, Mon through Fri 8 a.m. to 4:30 p.m. Try to give them at least an hour's notice.

at Cumberland through Frostburg, the Laurel Highlands and ends outside of Pittsburgh. It was twenty years in the planning means you can hike and bike through the countryside beyond the towpath with lots of lodging and dining options. Other Pennsylvania towns connected by the trail are Meyersdale, Rockwood, Confluence, Ohiopyle, Connellsville, and West Newton. It's part of a longer, 320-mile trail that goes to Washington, D.C.

To research the area prior to visiting, with suggested itineraries and more information, check the Web site, www.gaptrail.com or call (888) ATA-BIKE.

Culture lovers delight that there's another side to the county and to Cumberland—an artistic one. AmericanStyle magazine has named Cumberland the twenty-first best small city for art lovers. They cite "this former railroad center is a textbook example of arts revitalization." An Arts and Entertainment district, so designated as one of twelve in Maryland, and coordinated locally by the Allegany Arts Council, has attracted numerous artists to the area, which in turn attract other businesses to the area. The magazine says the **Savilla Gallery** (9 North Centre St., just off the Baltimore St. pedestrian mall; 301-777-2787) is a "don't miss" site," showing the work of national, regional, and local artists." Look for a free self-guided "Saturday Arts Walk" through the Arts and Entertainment District, rotating exhibits of local artwork at the Rocky Gap Lodge and Resort, and the annual Mountain Maryland Artists' Studio Tour.

The **Allegany Arts Council** has dozens of organizations actively involved in choral singing, theater, cinema, photography, crafts, instrumental music, and visual arts. A gallery exhibits works that are for sale and is open Mon through Fri from 9 a.m. to 5 p.m., Sat from 11 a.m. to 4 p.m., and Sun from 11 a.m. to 4 p.m. (seasonally, from mid-May through mid-Nov). Located at 9 North Centre, call (301) 777-2787 or visit www.alleganyartscouncil.org.

As previously mentioned, transportation has played and continues to play an important part of mountain life. To see the significance, drop by the **Queen City Transportation Museum** that opened in the fall of 2007 as an extension of the **Thrasher Carriage Museum** in Frostburg. It has carriages, carts, wagons, Model Ts, and so much more. Almost as interesting is the building that houses the museum, a 1925 castle design armory. The hours vary seasonally, so check to make sure it will be open when you want to visit. Located at 210 South Centre St. inCumberland, call (301) 777-1776.

Become famous and maybe in 250 years you'll be honored and recognized. And the newest statue honors one of the oldest visitors. As an aide to General Braddock, Lt. Colonel George Washington arrived in Fort Cumberland in 1755. A bronze statue of Washington, standing 8.5 feet tall, was installed in front of the courthouse (where Fort Cumberland was located) to commemorate the time the Father of Our Country spent in the area. Susan Luery, known for her Babe Ruth statue outside of Baltimore's Camden Yards, created the Washington statue.

LaVale, just west of Cumberland, was a significant stop along the National Road as it cut through the Narrows, a 1,000-foot breach between Will's and Haystack mountains. A seven-side Toll Gate House was built in 1836 by the state after it took over this section of the road in 1835. It now is the only remaining tollhouse in Maryland.

The **LaVale Toll Gate House** shows life as it was when the National Road (Rte 40) came this way. There's a neat sign showing the tolls for various animals, pedestrians, and wagons. This is the only remaining tollgate on the National Road in Maryland. The furnishings are fascinating as well; be sure to ask about the "courting candle." The house, which has been under the guidance of the LaVale Century Club, is changing hands as of this writing and the Historical Society is supposed to be taking control. Generally the house has been open on weekends from 1:30 to 4:30 p.m. from May through Oct and by appointment. It's located at 14302 National Hwy. Call (301) 777-5132 or (301) 777-8678 for more information.

The romance of early twentieth-century steam railroading is in the air on the **Western Maryland Scenic Railroad,** where passengers take a 16-mile ride combining mountaintop scenery and rich transportation history. The Western Maryland features a Consolidation 2-8-0 locomotive built in 1916 by the Baldwin Locomotive Works. As the train steams its way up the 2.8 percent grade on the westward trip from Cumberland to Frostburg, it travels along old Western Maryland Railway and Cumberland and Pennsylvania Railway rights-of-way. You can see the famous Cumberland Narrows (a natural 1,000-foot breach in Will's Mountain known as the "Gateway to the West"), an iron truss bridge, Bone Cave, and Helmstetter's Horseshoe Curve.

At the Frostburg terminus you can get a close-up view of the engineer and fireman in blue-and-white overalls and the locomotive turntable where the engine is turned around to go the other direction. Remember, firemen stock fires, firefighters extinguish them. Stop in the *Old Depot Center* complex, which now features a restaurant and the Thrasher Carriage Collection. This collection offers more than fifty examples of early nineteenth- and twentieth-century horse-drawn vehicles. The museum is open Tues through Sun from11 a.m. to 3 p.m. May through Sept, daily during Oct, and weekends only in Nov and Dec. Call (301) 689-3380.

The rail trip takes about three hours, including a ninety-minute layover in Frostburg. It runs on a seasonal schedule, so call for dates and times. There's

MARYLAND WELCOME CENTERS

Please remember that Maryland still loves you, even though budgetary cuts forced the state to close all but six welcome stations. Those that are open are closed in observation of Thanksgiving, Christmas, New Year's Day, and Easter. The following centers are eager to welcome you and provide travel, local traffic conditions (construction), and tourism information:

Interstate 70 West Welcome Center, I-70 West, mile marker 39 (just east of the Washington County–Frederick County line), General Delivery, Myersville 21773; (301) 293-4161. This center was torn down and rebuilt to achieve more energy efficient facilities. As of this writing, it's due to reopen July 1, 2010.

Interstate 70 East Welcome Center, I-70 East, mile marker 39 (just east of the Washington County–Frederick County line), P.O. Box 419, Myersville 21773; (301) 293-2526. This center was torn down and rebuilt to achieve more energy efficient facilities. As of this writing, it's due to reopen July 1, 2010.

Interstate 95 South Welcome Center, I-95 South, mile marker 37 (just south of State Rte 32), P.O. Box 288, Savage 20763; (301) 490-2444.

Interstate 95 North Welcome Center, I-95 North, mile marker 37 (just south of State Rte 32), P.O. Box 1058, Savage 20763; (301) 490-1333.

Chesapeake House Welcome Center, I-95 North/South, mile marker 97. The Welcome Center is closed. The food services and restrooms continue to operate. P.O. Box 785, Perryville 21903; (410) 287-2313.

Crain Memorial Welcome Center, U.S. Hwy. 301 North, 12480 Crain Hwy. (just north of the Governor Nice Memorial Bridge), Newburg 20664; (301) 259-2500. This center is open daily from 6 a.m. to 6 p.m.

U.S. Hwy. 13 Welcome Center, US 13 North, 144 Ocean Hwy. (just north of the Virginia state line), Pocomoke City 21851; (410) 957-2484. This center is open daily from 7 a.m. to 7 p.m.

an expanded schedule in Oct for fall foliage viewing. Ticket prices for the year 2009 started at $29 for adults, $27 for seniors age 60 and older, and $15 for children age 12 and younger.

Charter trips and special events such as dinner trips or trips featuring murder mysteries, dinner theater, or dancing are scheduled periodically. Private parties for weddings, birthdays, business meetings, school outings, and other events also may be booked. Write to Western Maryland Scenic Railroad, Western Maryland Station, 13 Canal St., Cumberland 21502, or call (800) TRAIN-50, (301) 759-4400; www.wmsr.com.

Whatever outdoor diversion you prefer, you're almost certain to find it in and around the 3,000-plus acres of Rocky Gap State Park. You'll find rugged mountains, the 243-acre Lake Habeen (fed by Rocky Gap Run after it tears through a mile-long gorge lined with steep cliffs), camping (30 of the 278 sites have electric hookups), boating (no gas-powered boats), and fishing (panfish, catfish, brown and rainbow trout, large and smallmouth bass—but you need a valid Maryland anglers license if you're sixteen or older). There's also hiking (you can see the gorge from the overlook on the quarter-mile-long Canyon Overlook Trail). For the serious hiker, try the five-mile Evitts Homesite Trail that has a 1,000-foot climb in 2.5 miles, a nature center (including an on-site aviary), and so much more.

You can take your choice of accommodations, from your own tent or camper to a cabin or chalet or you can stay at the gorgeous *Rocky Gap Lodge and Golf Resort*. The eighteen-hole course features a Jack Nicklaus–signature design carved out of the mountain. But don't despair, only the front nine has challenging elevation changes; the back nine has expansive, gently rolling fairways. (Well, maybe you should worry; even Nicklaus hasn't broken par on this course. Hmm.) Each golf cart has a ProLink GPS (Global Positioning System) that's supposed to make the rounds faster and lower the scores.

The lakeside lodge has 220 rooms, meeting space, dining, a sandy beach by the lake, spa services, and a fire pit for roasting those s'mores under the stars—what more could a person want?

Rocky Gap State Park, 12500 Pleasant Valley Rd., Flintstone; (301) 722-1480 (park headquarters), (888) 432-2267 (camper contact, seasonal phone line Memorial Day–Labor Day); www.dnr.state.md.us/publiclands/western/rockygap.html for reservations.

Backtracking a bit, head south off I-68 outside of Frostburg and head toward Lonaconing. The *Lonaconing Iron Furnace* was erected about 1836 by the George's Creek Coal and Iron Company and produced iron for the next twenty years. When the furnace was constructed, it was unique in several respects. It was 50 feet high and 50 feet square at the base—a daring departure from contemporary furnaces, which were 30 feet high and 30 feet square. Moreover, it was the first furnace built in this country that successfully used coke fuel at a time when all furnaces were using the less-efficient charcoal.

The furnace was built against a hillside because it was fed from the top. The site was chosen because the necessary iron ore, coal, wood, clay, limestone, sandstone, and water were readily available, although transportation to the marketplace was not convenient. Castings made here included stoves, farming implements, and dowels for the C&O Canal lock walls.

Today the furnace is the backdrop for a pleasant town park in Lonaconing, where you can stop to lunch at the picnic tables or enjoy the play equipment. A sign notes the location of the former Central School, and a bronze plaque honors Robert Moses "Lefty" Grove, a native son who was elected into the Baseball Hall of Fame in 1947. Lauded as the greatest left-handed pitcher of all time, he played for the Philadelphia Athletics from 1925 to 1933 and the Boston Braves from 1934 to 1941.

The furnace is located on Rte 36, 35 East Main St., Lonaconing; (301) 463-2289. The park is open daily from sunrise to sunset.

Washington County

Washington County—the first county to be named after George Washington—was founded on September 6, 1776, just months after our country itself was born. In a Civil War battle fought at Sharpsburg, along Antietam Creek, more than 23,000 casualties were suffered.

Antietam was one of the National Park Service projects that received funding from the American Recovery and Reinvestment Act funds in 2009. The nine miles of tour roads and walkways throughout the park were overlaid, and should be a benefit to the 300,000 visitors who visit the park each year.

That doesn't solve all the budget problems, and the National Park Service has reduced preservation and rehabilitation funding for Antietam and other parks. With more than three hundred War Department plaques, ninety-six monuments, and five hundred cannons on the battlefield, the price of upkeep is steep. The nonprofit Western Maryland Interpretive Association operates the Antietam Partner Program with several ways for individuals and groups to donate funds to the battlefield, including Adopt-A-Monument, Build-A-Fence, and Plant-A-Tree. Funds donated to these programs go directly to Antietam, unlike the entry fee to the park. Visit www.Antietampartner.com for more information.

Since 1989, an annual remembrance of the Battle of Antietam has been held the first Saturday in December. It is signified by 23,110 luminarias, one every 15 feet along a five-mile route, throughout the fields, and around monuments. Nearly one thousand volunteers systematically set up the luminarias throughout the day and candles are lit starting at 3 p.m. About 2,500 cars drive through the illumination each year, from 6 p.m. until midnight. The event, in cooperation with the American Business Women's Association, is free, but donations are appreciated. Cars should enter from Maryland Rte 34.

the arch

The *War Correspondents Arch,* Gathland State Park, South Mountain, built in 1886 by George Alfred Townsend, famous Civil War author and war correspondent, was the first monument in the world erected to the memory of war correspondents. The park is open from 8 a.m. to sunset. Call (301) 791-4767.

The idea for the candles came from the Rest Haven Cemetery, which had previously placed a luminaria at every grave site. Borrowing the idea, Hagerstown residents lit luminarias every night for the two weeks prior to Christmas. One night it was the north side of town, another it was the south side, and so it continued throughout the area. Band members of the high schools sold 81,000 lights in the neighborhoods.

The *Antietam National Battlefield* at Sharpsburg is open daily from 8:30 a.m. to 5 p.m. except on major holidays, with extended summer hours. The tour road is open sunrise to sunset. For more information, write P. O. Box 158, Sharpsburg 21782; or call (301) 432-5124 (visitor center), (301) 432-7648 (park headquarters); or visit www.nps.gov/anti.

Northeast of Sharpsburg is where you'll find *Turn the Page* bookstore, owned by novelist Nora Roberts (go Montgomery Blair HS Blazers!) and her husband Bruce Wilder. You'll find lots of Nora Roberts books (I should hope so), mysteries, science fiction, romance, and books about the Civil War. Check the Web site for special events, including book talks and signings, story hour, and a book club. As they say, Turn the Page is "a good place to buy books and coffee." Open Mon through Sat from 10 a.m. to 6 p.m. (open until 7 p.m. on Fri). (301) 432-4588; www.ttpbooks.com.

cantaloupe capital

People in the know head to Boonsboro in August and September when the Boonsboro cantaloupes ripen. You can buy them from a roadside stand, particularly on Saturday and Sunday, and you might be able to find a patch where you can pick your own. Then you'll really enjoy the thin-skinned "Heart of Gold" variety with all its natural sweetness.

In 2007 they bought *Inn Boonsboro.* Even though the hotel burst into flames in 2008 they persevered. The hotel has opened offering rooms named after fictional couples (think Elizabeth and Darcy or Jane and Rochester or Nick and Nora) and decorated in appropriate styles and bath amenities to match each room. Today is not forgotten and there is a 32" flatscreen TV in each room, private bath (with heated tile floors and towel racks) and, of course, an ample library. The inn has six rooms and two suites and rates start at $220 including breakfast for two. Marguerite and Percy, the ground floor room, is ADA compliant with a wheelchair-accessible shower, continuous grab bar, and body jets. The couple has purchased other buildings, one of which will be a restaurant operated by their son. Located at 1 North Main St., call (301) 432-4588 or visit www.innboonsboro.com.

Washington County parks rate with the best and include the C&O Canal National Historical Park, the Appalachian Trail (40 miles), Fort Frederick State Park, Washington Monument State Park, Pen Mar County Park, at least eight other county parks, and Hagerstown City Park; Hagerstown, as the county seat, has a lot of attractions and activities where you can spend hours or days.

The **Washington County Museum of Fine Arts,** which celebrated its seventy-fifth anniversary in 2006, in Hagerstown, is an outstanding museum overlooking the fifty-acre City Park Lake (home to numerous waterfowl). It was the idea and gift of Mr. and Mrs. William Henry Singer Jr., who had collected many possessions during their European travels and were looking for a beautiful place to house them. The cornerstone was laid on July 15, 1930, by Mrs. Singer's grandniece, Anna Spencer Brugh.

The museum was built of homewood brick with Indiana limestone trim. Two wings were added in 1949: the Memorial Gallery, in honor of Mr. Singer, who died in 1943, and the Concert Gallery, in honor of Mrs. Singer's love of music. Mrs. Singer was eighty-six when she died in 1962.

Among the museum's collection are the works of Mr. Singer, who was a Postimpressionist painter of note. Many of his landscapes show the fishing villages, fjords, and snow-covered mountains of Norway. Also in the collection are old masters, twentieth-century sculpture and painting, and a variety of decorative arts from around the world. The emphasis, though, is on American art.

georgedidn't sleephere

Four miles east of Boonsboro is the **Washington Monument,** in the state park of the same name; it was the first monument built and finished honoring George Washington (as opposed to the first architectural monument dedicated in Washington's memory—that's in Baltimore). Built of local stone by the citizens of Boonsboro in 1827, it offers a great view of the valley below after a short climb. The Appalachian Trail runs through the park. Call (301) 791-4767 or visit www.dnr.state.md.us/publiclands/western/washington.html.

In addition to tours, the museum offers art classes (weaving, clay, acrylics, quilting, and more), lectures, films, and music recitals. A bimonthly calendar is available.

If you love art, you can "adopt" a painting by contributing funds toward a conservator's fee to clean or restore a particular painting in the museum's collection. Frederick Childe Hassam's "White House, Gloucester" (1895) was the first adopted painting in the program that started in October 2004. The house had become yellow and it took Baltimore conservator Sian Jones thirteen hours to restore the work. Tax-deductible adoptions range from a few hundred dollars to $8,000, depending on the piece. You will receive recognition for your part in the work's conservation in the museum's newsletter and on a special object label near the adopted painting.

The museum, located on City Park Lake, is open Tues through Fri from 9 a.m. to 5 p.m., Sat from 9 a.m. to 4 p.m.; and Sun from 1 to 5 p.m. There is no admission fee, but a donation is requested. Call (301) 739-5727, (301) 739-5764 (TDD), or visit www.wcmfa.org.

Hagerstown's **Discovery Station** is located in the historic Nicodemus Bank building, across from the county courthouse. The original bank housed the Federal Depository during the Civil War, and the main vault with leaded glass was installed in 1913.

The three floors cover science, technology, and history. The first floor south area houses the 2,000-square-foot *Hagerstown Aviation Museum* (included in the admission price) that depicts the aviation heritage of the area. For 70 years, Hagerstown was one of the nation's leading centers of aircraft manufacturing. Also, catch the railroad exhibits that cover the important role Hagerstown played in transportation history.

Museum personnel say you should allow at least ninety minutes. And, perhaps best of all, the Treasure Gift Shoppe has gifts, toys, aircraft models, astronaut ice cream (Neapolitan is my favorite), games, books, greeting cards, and so much more, so you can take reminders of the interactive attractions home with you. You can stop by the gift shop without paying museum admission. There is also an Explorer Cafe.

The Discovery Station is open Tues through Sat from 10 a.m. to 4 p.m., and on Sun from 2 to 5 p.m. (Dec through May). It is closed on Monday, Thanksgiving, Christmas, New Year's Day, Easter, and on Mother's, Father's, and Independence Days. It is also closed on Sundays from June through Nov. Admission is $7 for adults, $6 for children ages 3 through 17, and $5 for seniors (55 and over) and military. The Discovery Station at Hagerstown is at 101 West Washington St.; call (301) 790-0076 or visit www.discovery station.org.

Hagerstown is the home of the *Hagers-Town Town and Country Almanack*, which has been printed since 1797. The weather forecasts generate the most interest, and people swear by them. In fact, a folk tale has it that the book called for snow on July 4, 1874, and that it did snow on that date. Research indicates that the almanac did not predict snow, and the minimum temperature for that day was said to have been in the high sixties—not too conducive to snow.

For lodgings with a real twist, you'll want to visit the **Tree House Camp** at Maple Tree Campground near Gathland State Park. The unusual feature of this campground is that you sleep in a tree house. Did you always want one when you were a kid, but you lived in the city or the only adults around had sixteen thumbs? This is not quite as rustic as you might remember, but it is as close as most of us will ever get. Your tree house—on stilts about seven feet off the ground—has a couple of bunks (bring a sleeping bag), a woodstove, a table with benches, and a filled wood bin. A communal bathhouse is nearby, you have acres of woods to roam through and explore, and you're not far from the Appalachian Trail.

When Phyllis Soroko started this campground after retirement, she dreaded the idea of tearing up the land and trees for campsites and dumpsites and was thrilled with this compromise. She has retired a second time (although she still visits the camp periodically), and now her daughter Louise operates the camp. She has added additional tree cottages and the new ones have lofts and ladders. You also have the option of tree cottages and tent sites. Louise suggests you bring padding and a lantern for the tree houses and bedding and a lantern for the cottages. She also had the bath house remodeled, with new tiles and toilets. Pets, on leash at all times, are welcome. Calvin keeps the firewood chopped, the repairs fixed, and takes care of the nightly quiet time restrictions. You don't want to upset him by breaking any of the rules. Reservations are recommended. There are nine tree houses and four tree cottages. The charge is $40 a night for the first four people in a tree house, $56 a night for the first four people in the older tree cottages, and $66 a night for the new ones. Each additional person is $10. Field tent sites are $8 per person per night (minimum of $22 per night), and wooden tent sites are $10 a night with a minimum of $25 per night. There is a two-night minimum on weekends. They offer a discount on Wednesdays, when it's 30 percent off everything. You are not allowed to bring your own firewood. The campground is located at 20716 Townsend Rd., Gapland (although the mailing address is Rohrersville because the Gapland post office is closed). Call (301) 432-5585 or visit www.thetreehousecamp.com.

As mentioned in the introduction, **Yogi Bear's Jellystone Camp** received a national "Plan-It-Green" award from the National Association of RV Parks and Campgrounds. In addition to camping spaces, they have a water zone with

400' water slides, a game room, ranger station (souvenirs), mini-golf, a den for TV and games, playgrounds, a koi pond, arts and crafts pavilion, horseshoe pits, four air-conditioned and heated bath houses, a Laundromat, and much more. Located at 16519 Lappans Rd., Williamsport; call (301) 223-7117 or (800) 421-7116 or visit www.jellystonemaryland.com.

Airplane and airport food don't exactly enjoy stellar reputations, but you're sure to change your mind when you stop at **Nick's Airport Inn** on U.S. Hwy. 11 at the Hagerstown Regional Airport. In fact, many people fly their private planes here just to enjoy the tasty offerings from the Giannaris family. Fresh seafood is brought in from Baltimore and the prices are more than reasonable. Even the crab cakes are worthwhile. Nick's is open Mon through Fri from 11 a.m. to 2 p.m., Mon through Thurs from 5 to 10 p.m., and Fri and Sat from 5 to 10:30 p.m. They're closed on Sun. Located at 14548 Pennsylvania Ave.; call (301) 733-8560 or visit www.nicksairportinn.com.

The **Wilson Country Store** is a classic country store with a post office, loose "penny" candy, yard goods, and much more. You'll also see a one-room schoolhouse (open by appointment only). The store is on Old Rte 40, and it is open Mon through Sat from 7:30 a.m. to 2 p.m. and Sun from 9 a.m. to 5 p.m. The general store is at 14921 Rufus-Wilson Rd., Clear Spring; call (301) 582-4718 or (888) 348-2012.

On your way to Wilson Village from Hagerstown, you may stop by the **Historic Wilson Bridge Picnic Area.** It's located along Rte 40 West, adjacent to five-arch **Historic Wilson Bridge,** which is the oldest (1819), longest (215 feet), and most graceful of the twenty-three stone-arch bridges in the county. Pennsylvanian Silas Harry erected the structure at a cost of $9,100. Its style represented a triumph for the justices of the Levy Court (until 1829, the body similar to a Board of County Commissioners), who insisted on an all-stone structure in the face of army engineers' arguments that a wooden bridge laid over stone piers would suffice.

Hagerstown Suns

Of interest to sports fans is the Hagerstown Suns baseball team of the South Atlantic League, an affiliate of the Washington Nationals. This Class-A team draws about 150,000 fans a year. In previous years, loyalists have seen the likes of Jeff Ballard, Jim Palmer, Bill Ripken, and Craig Worthington, all of whom have gone on to be well known in the baseball world. Palmer was elected to the Baseball Hall of Fame in 1989, his first year of eligibility. For information call the Municipal Stadium at (301) 791-6266 or visit www.hagerstownsuns.com.

Although a "new" concrete arch bridge was built in 1937, the "old" bridge was still being used until it was damaged by Hurricane Agnes in June 1972. The bridge is located about 200 feet north of the west end of the "new" bridge that crosses Conococheague Creek, 5 miles west of Hagerstown on Rte 40. This one-acre site offers picnic tables, parking, and canoe access to the Conococheague. Visit http://nationalpike.blogspot.com/2008/01/wilson-bridge.html for more information.

The *Hepburn Orchards Fruit Market* in Hancock is one of those places that draws you off the Interstate with sweet aromas of fresh-made fruit pies (sugar-free, too). Then, you look around a little bit and taste some of the fresh produce that's just be harvested. And then you see the preserves and apple butter (some of them without sugar, too), Burnt Cabin stone ground flours, candies and fudge, honey, country ham, slab bacon, and so much more. A traveling salesman once said he "had to stop by here to buy pies before I traveled into Washington or my clients wouldn't see me." They also carry Longaberger baskets (retired, collectible), souvenirs, crafts, and novelties. Located at 557 East Main St., Hancock; call (800) 227-7087 or visit www.hepburns.com.

close, but no cigar

On October 14, 1790, Col. Elie Williams and Gen. George Washington met at the springhouse in Williamsport (in Washington County) to discuss the possibility of the town being the new capital of the United States. The idea was dismissed because the Potomac River was not navigable by large ships.

Seven miles west of Hancock, near the border between Allegany and Washington Counties, is *Sideling Hill.* Interstate 68 bypasses traffic off a steep, tricky road that twists to a roundhouse curve at the top of Sideling Hill. The four-and-a-half-mile section of the road took twenty-eight months to complete and cost about $21 million. Workers blasted an incredible, breathtaking 360-foot-deep cut in the mountain, which revealed millions of years of geological history. As I'm not a geologist, the most curious thing about the cut is that the rock layers are in a syncline, so the newer sedimentary layers are on top. This is one of the best rock exposures in the northeast.

Places to Eat in Western Maryland

ACCIDENT

Annie's Kitchen
414 South Main St.
(301) 746-8578

Bumble Q's
145 Bumble Bee Rd.
(301) 387-21520

BOONESBORO

Old South Mountain Inn
6132 Old National Pike
(301) 432-6155
(301) 371-5400
www.oldsouthmountaininn
.com

CUMBERLAND

The Inn at Walnut Bottom
120 Greene St.
(301) 777-0003
(800) 286-9718
www.iwbinfo.com

Puccini
12901 Ali Ghan Shrine Rd.,
Exit 46
(301) 777-7822
www.puccinirestaurant
.com

FROSTBURG

Acropolis Restaurant
45 East Main St.
(301) 689-8277

Au Petit Paris
86 East Main St.
(301) 689-8946
www.aupetitparis.com

Frostburg Freeze
Rte 40 West
(301) 689-3020

GRANTSVILLE

Penn Alps Restaurant
125 Casselman Rd.
(301) 895-5985
www.pennalps.com

HAGERSTOWN

Michelle's Restaurant
10 East Washington St.
(301) 733-6608
www.michellesof
hagerstown.com

Schmankerl Stube
58 South Potomac St.
(301) 797-3354
www.schmankerlstube
.com

HANCOCK

**Weaver's Restaurant
& Bakery**
77 West Main St.
(301) 678-6346
www.weaversrestaurant
.com

OAKLAND

Brenda's Pizzeria
21311 Garrett Hwy.
(301) 387-1007

**Cornish Manor
Restaurant &
French Bakery**
830 Memorial Dr.
(301) 334-6499

Four Seasons
20160 Garrett Hwy.
(301) 387-5503
(888) 590-7283
www.willothewisp.com

Places to Stay in Western Maryland

ACCIDENT

**Bear Creek Crossing Bed
and Breakfast**
29380 Garrett Hwy.
(301) 746-8623
www.bearcreekbb.net

CASCADE

**Cascade Inn Historic Bed
& Breakfast**
14700 Eyler Ave.
(301) 241-4161
(800) 362-9526
www.thecascadeinn.com

CUMBERLAND

Inn at Walnut Bottom
120 Greene St.
(301) 777-0003
(800) 286-9718
www.iwbinfo.com

FROSTBURG

Frostburg Inn
147 East Main St.
(301) 689-3831
www.frostburginn.com

GRANTSVILLE

**Casselman Valley Farm
Bed and Breakfast**
215 Maple Grove Rd.
(301) 895-3419
www.bbonline.com/md/
casselman

HAGERSTOWN

Clarion Hotel and Conference Center at Antietam Creek
901 Dual Hwy.
(301) 733-5100
www.clarionantietam.com

Country Inn & Suites
17612 Valley Mall Rd.
(301) 582-5003
(800) 596-2375
www.countryinns.com/hagerstownmd

Hampton Inn
1716 Dual Hwy.
(301) 739-6100
www.hamptoninn.com

Holiday Inn Express & Suites
241 Railway Lane
(301) 745-5644
(800) 356-3584
www.hagerstownexpress.com

Inn on Potomac
400 North Potomac St.
(301) 739-5679
(800) 761-8313
www.innonpotomac.com

OTHER ATTRACTIONS WORTH SEEING IN WESTERN MARYLAND

African-American Heritage Society
Cumberland
(301) 777-7785
www.mountaindiscoveries.com/stories/ss2002/africansociety_plain.html

Doleman Black History Museum
Hagerstown
(301) 739-8185
www.marylandmemories.org/african_american.html

Fort Frederick State Park
Big Pool
(301) 842-2155
www.dnr.state.md.us/publiclands/western/fortfrederick.html

Frostburg State University Planetarium
Frostburg
(301) 687-4270
www.frostburg.edu/planetarium

Hagerstown Roundhouse Museum
Hagerstown
(301) 739-4665
www.roundhouse.org

Jonathan Hager House and Museum
Hagerstown
(302) 739-8393
www.hagerhouse.org

Kennedy Farm House (John Brown Headquarters)
Sharpsburg
(301) 977-3599
www.johnbrown.org

Muddy Creek Falls Swallow Falls State Park
Oakland
(301) 334-9180
www.dnr.state.md.us/publiclands/western/swallowfalls.html

Washington County Rural Heritage Museum
Sharpsburg
(240) 420-1714
(240) 420-1713 (weekends)
www.ruralheritagemuseum.org

Wisp Ski and Golf Resort
McHenry
(301) 387-4911
(800) 462-9477
www.wispresort.com

MCHENRY

Lake Pointe Inn Bed & Breakfast
174 Lake Pointe Dr.
(301) 387-0111
www.deepcreekinns.com

Wisp Mountain Resort
290 Marsh Hill Rd.
(301) 387-5581
(800) 462-9477
www.wisp-resort.com

OAKLAND

Haley Farm Bed & Breakfast & Retreat Center
16766 Garrett Hwy.
(301) 387-9050
www.haleyfarm.com

SAVAGE

Commodore Joshua Barney House
7912 Savage Guilford Rd.
(301) 362-1900
(800) 475-7912
www.joshuabarneyhouse.com

SHARPSBURG

Antietam Guest House
111 West Chapline St.
(301) 992-9017
www.antietamguesthouse.com

Historic Jacob Rohrbach Inn
138 West Main St.
(301) 432-5079
(877) 839-4242
www.jacob-rohrbach-inn.com

Inn at Antietam
220 East Main St.
(301) 432-6601
(877) 835-6011
www.innatantietam.com

Mary Hill House
211 East Main St.
(301) 432-7984
(240) 329-1969
www.maryhillhouse.com

CENTRAL MARYLAND →

There probably is more geographical, occupational, and socio-logical diversity than in the area referred to as central Maryland than anywhere else in the state. In the rolling foothills and picturesque landscapes of this region are horse farms and vineyards, the commercial center of Baltimore City, huge stone farmhouses and old mills, busy waterways surrounding the Chesapeake Bay and its tributaries, some of the oldest towns in the country, and modern, vibrant cities. This core of five counties and two major cities encompasses it all.

If we're lucky we learn something every day. Unfortu-nately, sometimes we learn after it's almost too late. One thing we've learned is that river dams and "fish ladders" to help spawning fish, particularly the shad and herring, navi-gate back up the Patapsco River was not a good idea. Many of the dams were built in the early 1900s to help power the numerous, but now defunct, mills along the river. Removing the dams was considered about two decades ago and thought to be too expensive so the ladders were installed. According to the Department of Natural Resources, "the destruction of the dams help renew and restore the stream flow and water conditions."

CENTRAL MARYLAND

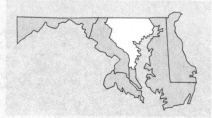

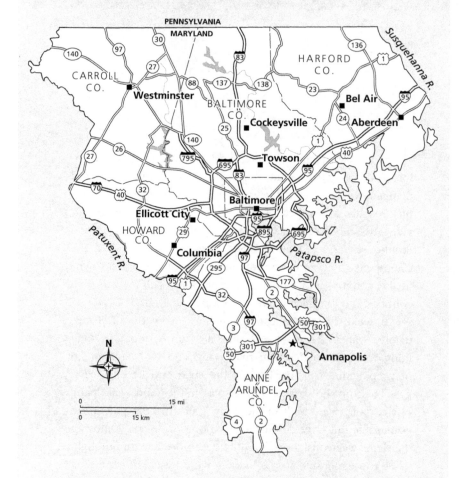

Sixteen million vehicles use the **William Preston Lane Jr. Bridge** (Chesapeake Bay Bridge) every year. Only 50,000 people walk across it, though, on Chesapeake Bay Bridge Walk Day. Once, Maryland was a leading contender in the number of vehicular "kissing" or covered bridges; now we have only six and one of them is here.

Countless people stop by **Annapolis** to see its waterfront, **Ego Alley** (where the expensive boats parade), and the **United States Naval Academy.** They watch the sailboats in the harbor—even in the winter, when there is a Frostbite series of sailboat races—or the Naval Academy's noon meal formation, when the brigade of midshipmen assembles in front of Bancroft Hall for inspection.

Picking a starting point is tough, for several interstate highways lead into and out of this area of five counties and Baltimore City, including Interstate 95 going north to Philadelphia and New York and south to Washington, D.C.; Interstate 83 going north into Pennsylvania; Interstate 70 going into the western part of the state; and Interstate 97 heading south and then east into Annapolis.

Anne Arundel County

Perhaps the best place to start is at **Baltimore-Washington International Thurgood Marshall Airport** (a.k.a. BWI Marshall Airport), where millions of people pass through either going to or coming home from someplace or picking up a passenger before exploring the wonderful options available in this area.

It may be a scandalous thought, but you might actually want to arrive early or even stay a few minutes, for BWI has become a destination in itself. There's a beautiful observation gallery with information about flying and pieces of airplanes on display. The $6.4 million gallery has cutaway airplane sections (great to view if you or someone in your party has never flown or seen the workings of a plane), an interactive weather station (so you can see what a cold front is and how it affects weather, or check for the temperature in your destination city), and a 147-foot-wide observation window to watch airplanes refueling, taxiing, taking off, and landing. Plunk yourself in front of a computer screen, punch in your flight number, and the screen displays just where the plane is, how high and how fast it's flying, and when it's expected to land. Should you be an aviation history buff, then the story of Maryland aviation should satisfy your curiosity. A children's play area is in the lower of the two levels and is open twenty-four hours a day. The upper level with the gift shop, cafe, and interactive displays is open from 9 a.m. to 9 p.m. There is no admission charge.

BWI is home to the largest USO facility, for as many as a quarter-million military personnel and family members can use the facility annually. Why so many? Because 99 percent of the U.S. military personnel being sent to Europe or the Middle East travel through BWI. The $1.1 million, 5,000-square-foot USO International Gateway Center has a nursery, television lounge, sleeping room, computer room, and free coffee. Lower level, near baggage claim number fourteen, and it's open daily from 6 a.m. to 10 p.m. Call (410) 859-4425 for more information.

While wandering around the airport you may spot a large stained-glass crab sculpture. Named *Calinectes douglassi*, this 400-pound crab was created in 1986 by Jackie and John Douglass of Shady Side. It was stored for a while and then returned to the airport in Dec 2001 and situated between Concourses C and D. It's gorgeous and almost delectable enough to eat. It certainly makes one want to go out and steam up a bushel of those savory crustaceans. For various reasons it was displayed; it wasn't; it was; etc. The crab is made of white glass from West Germany and multicolored Blenko glass from West Virginia—about 5,000 pieces of glass in all. It's five feet high, 10 feet wide, and seven feet deep.

Pet Airways, the airline just for pets, began service at BWI Marshall in 2009, with service for dogs and cats. The transportation of birds, reptiles, pigs, and other creatures will be considered. Visit www.petairways.com for more information.

A shuttle bus connects the airport to the nearby Amtrak station, and limousine (van and bus) service provides door-to-door transportation to and from the airport. The airport has seen a lot of construction in the past few years. New parking structures, terminal expansion, etc., and, of course, increased security means you can't sit in your car in the driveway while awaiting inbound passengers. There is a cell phone area where you can wait until your passenger calls. However, I get around potential auto inspections, backups, and other problems by dropping my car off at **Park 'N Fly** airport parking (790 Camp Meade Rd., Linthicum; (410) 850-5300; www.pnf.com/baltimore/default.htm). I catch the shuttle to the airport, then return on it when passenger and luggage

AUTHOR'S FAVORITES CENTRAL MARYLAND

Elioak Farm	Oriole Park at Camden Yards tour
Fort McHenry National Monument and Historic Shrine	U.S. Naval Academy
Havre de Grace Decoy Museum	

are ready to leave. They either won't take any money or just charge a dollar or two. I park there regularly because they'll start a dead battery, change a flat tire, and pick me up and drop me off at my car instead of at a possibly very distant bus stop. A discount parking coupon is available on their Web site.

G & M restaurant, about three miles from the airport, is an incredible restaurant, one that receives my vote for the best crab cake in the entire state of Maryland! (Of course, that means in the entire world because the best crab cakes are made in Maryland; other people must agree because the G & M goes through about 500 pounds of crab meat a day!) These crab cakes contain about eight ounces of backfin crab meat with almost no filler. That's large enough to take home half of it for another meal, yet you can order a crab cake platter, which has just about everything from soup to nuts, including two crab cakes. I've even taken a cooler full of them to Los Angeles to satisfy those ex–East Coast pats living on the Left Coast. G & M is open daily from 11 a.m. to 11 p.m. and the carry-out is open from 10 a.m. to 11 p.m. You can order crab balls and other goodies from their Web site. Located at 804 North Hammonds Ferry Rd., Linthicum; call (410) 636-1777 or (877) 554-3723; or visit www.gandmrestaurant.com.

millingaround

Just two miles from the BWI runway, off the Baltimore-Washington Parkway at Rte 100, is Arundel Mills, home to about 200 outlet, off-price, and retail stores, movie theaters, restaurants, and more. Dozens of other "parasite" stores, restaurants, and hotels have been built around the mall. Located at 7000 Arundel Mills Circle, Hanover; call (410) 540-5100 or visit www.arundelmillsmall.com.

When construction started on May 4, 1947, the airport site was known as Friendship, and many old homes and farms on the 3,200-acre tract were demolished. Only Rezin Howard Hammond's home was left standing, where it remains today at the edge of the airport. Originally known as Cedar Farm because of the cedar trees on the property, it was built in 1820 from bricks made of clay dug on the farm. It is now the ***Benson-Hammond House*** and is used by the Anne Arundel County Historical Society. Their purpose is to encourage appreciation among the general public of "the smaller centers of culture where so much of our heritage lies hidden." Within the house are a collection of dolls, a display of tokens known as "picker checks" (made of aluminum, fiberboard, and brass stamped into various shapes and used as currency by farmers, each of whom had his own set of checks with his initials), and a miniature replica of Angel's Store in Pasadena. The museum is open for tours on special occasions and Thurs through Sat from 11 a.m. to 3 p.m. from spring through Dec. The suggested donation is $2 a person. The Browse and

Buy Shoppe is also located at the house at 7101 Aviation Blvd; call (410) 768-9518 or visit www.aachs.org. A second Browse and Buy shop is open Tues through Sat from 10:30 a.m. to 3 p.m. at the Old WB&A Railroad Power Station on Jones Station Rd.

Should you be wandering this way on a Sunday afternoon and you'd like to wander about as far off the beaten path as you're likely to get in Anne Arundel County, head east on State Rte 100 to **Hancock's Resolution** near the end of Bayside Beach Rd. and the community of Bayside Beach. Formerly a farm that encompassed more than 400 acres, this circa 1785 farmhouse and outbuildings have been restored to their nineteenth-century appearance. Because the house never had indoor plumbing or electricity, restoration was a fairly simple matter and the work was completed within a year. John Henry "Harry" Hancock was the last Hancock to live in the house and was almost ninety when he died in 1962. His main concession to his advancing years was an oil heater when he could no longer chop wood for the fireplace. There's no definitive answer regarding the meaning of "Resolution," but the assumption is there had been some family disagreements about the property ownership and when it was finally resolved, the name was given.

inmemoriam

Across the Severn River from the Naval Academy in Annapolis is a memorial to Marylanders who served in World War II. Dedicated on July 23, 1998, the $2.7 million memorial is off State Rte 450, just below the Gov. Ritchie Overlook, with a commanding view of the Severn River, the Naval Academy, and Annapolis. A four-sided, open-air amphitheater is surrounded by a 100-foot-diameter ring of forty-eight 9-foot-tall gray granite slabs etched with the names of the 6,454 Marylanders killed during the war.

Included in the $250,000 restoration of the farmhouse and property are plantings of typical crops from those days, including heirloom yellow cucumbers (little round vegetables), heirloom beans, Thomas Jefferson's red hibiscus, yellow tomatoes, flax, hops, the coralberry, strawberries, and the Anne Arundel County melon. Hancock's Resolution is open on Sun from 1 to 4 p.m. Apr through Oct. Located at 2795 Bayside Beach Rd., Pasadena; call (410) 255-4048 or visit www.historichancocksresolution.org.

Annapolis

Take Rte 100 west to I-97 south, tool into historic Annapolis, and prepare yourself for a treat. Lots of them. Annapolis is full of authentic Colonial architecture and the city is called a "museum without walls" because of the dozens of eighteenth-century buildings, but Annapolitans are quick to point out that it is a living museum, not an artificial one. Annapolis is Old World charm, the United States Naval Academy, sailboats and powerboats by the hundreds, antiques shops, taverns, and, most of all, narrow, winding, hilly, and brick-paved streets that invite walking and exploring.

Whether you boat or drive into town, you can avoid the automobile hassles of parking and finding your way around town by "renting" a bike for a few hours or a day. The *Free Wheelin' Bike Program* runs from June through Oct 1. The half-dozen bikes were used 700 times in 2009. Yes, they're looking for bike donations if you have one you aren't using anymore. The bikes are available at the Harbor Master's office at City Dock from 9 a.m. to 8 p.m. You must be 18, have a photo ID and credit card, and sign a waiver. Unless you've made other arrangements or have a serious problem, the bike must be returned by 8 p.m. Should you bike off more than you can pedal, you can take the Annapolis Transit bus for free and stow the bike on the bus rack. Call (410) 263-7964 ext 6003 or visit www.annapolis.gov for more information.

Working with materials old and new are the artisans represented at *ARTFX,* a shop I consider the most "dangerous" place (for my living space and wallet) in Annapolis, but an essential shopping spot whenever I'm looking for a beautiful, hand-crafted gift. About seventy noted and upcoming artists are featured, most of whom are local to the Annapolis, Baltimore, and Washington, D.C. area, covering a variety of media and prices that range from a few to many dollars. It's the only place in Annapolis that carries wheel-thrown crab pottery. You will see pottery, jewelry, glass, sculpture, soy and beeswax candles, wood-turnings, etched leaves, jewelry boxes, photography, paintings,

Distinctively Annapolis

Since 2000, the National Trust for Historic Preservation has designated a dozen distinctive communities through the country that offer authentic experiences. If you ever feel you could be in any town in any state, then head for one of the distinctive places. Look for interesting architecture, a sense of place and character, a dynamic downtown area, and a strong commitment to historic preservation and revitalization.

Annapolis personifies that description and then some. It was selected as a distinctive destination in 2005 because of the fifteen hundred restored historic buildings that provide the largest concentration of eighteenth-century architecture in the county. The Trust noted its water-based historical existence, the U.S. Naval Academy, and its year-round emphasis on arts and entertainment, and the fact that it is active and alive and more than a museum. It was selected from eighty nominations from forty-four states.

and wheel-thrown crab pottery. "First Sunday Arts" features a different artist each month, with music, wine, and a new art exhibit from 3 to 6 p.m. ARTFX is open Tues through Sat from 11 a.m. to 5 p.m., and Sun from 1 to 5 p.m., closed Mon. Located at 3 Church Circle; call (410) 990-4540 or (877) 857-4540, or visit www.artfxgallery.org.

The *Banneker-Douglass Museum* is installed in a handsome Victorian-Gothic structure that was the Mount Moriah African Methodist Episcopal Church, the first African Methodist Episcopal Church of Annapolis, serving the community from 1874 until 1971. A storm damaged the building in 1897, so it was rebuilt with its present Gothic-Revival facade, including the splendid stained-glass rose window. The building is listed with the National Register of Historic Places, as a National Historic District, and in the National Register of Historic Districts.

The museum is named for Benjamin Banneker (mathematician, scientist, astronomer, and surveyor) and Frederick Douglass (writer, journalist, civil libertarian, abolitionist, and U.S. minister and consul general to Haiti), both of whom were born and lived in Maryland. Banneker was appointed to serve on a commission that surveyed and laid out the capital. He had such a phenomenal memory that he produced, in detail, Pierre L'Enfant's plans for the District of Columbia when L'Enfant left—with the plans—before the job was finished.

Rotating displays are staged in the Hall of National Greatness, the Gallery of Black Maritime History, the Herbert M. Frisby Hall (Frisby was a Baltimore science educator, war correspondent for African-American newspapers, and explorer who made twenty-one trips to the Arctic region and was the second black explorer to reach the North Pole), and the reference library. A permanent exhibit, "Deep Roots, Rising Waters," explores the history of African-Americans in Maryland from the 1630s to the Civil Rights Movement.

signonthe dottedline

Each of these four signers of the Declaration of Independence—Charles Carroll, Samuel Chase, William Paca, and Thomas Stone—had homes in Annapolis. Three of the homes are still open to the public. William Paca's house and gardens is on the National Historic Landmark list and is a huge Georgian mansion at 186 Prince George St.; (410) 990-4538 or (800) 603-2040. Charles Carroll, the only Catholic to sign the Declaration, was one of the wealthiest men in Colonial America. His home, with eighteenth-century terraced gardens, is a restoration in progress, and overlooks Spa Creek; 107 Duke of Gloucester; (410) 269-1737; http://charlescarroll house.com. Samuel Chase built the Chase Lloyd House in 1769 at 22 Maryland Ave.; (410) 263-2723.

The Banneker-Douglass Museum is open Tues through Sat from 10 a.m. to 4 p.m. There is no admission charge. Located at 84 Franklin St., Annapolis; call (410) 216-6180 or visit www.bdmuseum.com.

You can spend at least a day seeing all the interesting things to see at the *U.S. Naval Academy.* Start with a visit to the *Armel-Leftwich Visitor Center* (just inside and to the right of Gate 1 off King George St.), where you can see a 12-minute movie—*To Lead and To Serve*—and displays about life as a midshipman. You can then explore on your own or take a seventy-five minute guided tour. Tour prices are $9 for adults, $8 for seniors (62 plus), and $7 for students (1st through 12th grades). The hours of operation vary according to the day and the season, but the noon tour departs at 11:45 to see the Noon Meal Formation, weather permitting. The center is open from 9 a.m. to 5 p.m.

thankyoutourists

Thanks to the $65.9 million in tourism tax revenue, Anne Arundel County taxpayers pay about $335 less in additional taxes, according to a study released in November 2006. Expressed another way, the county school system receives nearly $300 per student. Tourism accounts for 12 percent of the county's employment.

Mar through Nov, and 9 a.m. to 4 p.m. the rest of the year. It is closed Thanksgiving, Christmas, and New Year's Day. Call (410) 293-8587; or visit www.usna.edu/NAFPRODV/VC/tours.html for more information. NOTE: Unless you have Department of Defense identification, you must park off the Academy grounds (handicapped tags excepted). All visitors sixteen and older must have a photo ID. Check the security requirements at www.usNA.edu.

Dem Bones, Dem Bones

In July 1989 some fifteen small, brittle bones, carefully wrapped in yellowed paper, were gently placed in a golden urn and laid to rest in a shady cemetery plot near St. Mary's Church in Annapolis. In mid-1987 the Reverend John Murray of St. Mary's had found these remains of St. Justin, who was beheaded at the age of twenty-six in the second century AD. According to Murray, it is not unusual for churches in Europe to have special tombs containing the relics of saints or martyrs, but few churches in the United States can claim such items because the country is so young. St. Justin's remains arrived in Baltimore in 1873 so the Reverend Joseph Wissel could protect them while Italy was in the middle of a political upheaval. The Reverend Wissel and those who followed him displayed them prominently, but during the 1960s the church was renovated and the remains were placed in a box in a church safe. Call (410) 263-2396 for additional information.

JANUARY

Bridal Extravaganza
Turf Valley Resort
Ellicott City
(410) 465-1500
www.turfvalley.com

Maryland State Police Polar Bear Plunge
Sandy Point State Park
(410) 789-6677
www.somd.org

FEBRUARY

American Craft Council Show
Baltimore
(212) 274-0630
www.craftcouncil.org/baltimore

Annapolis Restaurant Week
Annapolis
(443) 482-9277
www.annapolisrestaurantweek.com

Irish Evening of Music and Poetry
Columbia
(410) 772-4568
www.hocopolitso.org

MARCH

Antique Bottle Show and Sale
Essex Campus
Community College of Baltimore County
(410) 265-5745
www.baltimorebottleclub.org

Maple Sugarin' Festival
Westminster
(410) 848-9040

Maryland Day
Annapolis
(410) 990-4539
www.annapolis.org

APRIL

Annapolis Nautical Flea Market
Annapolis
(410) 268-8828
www.usboat.com/anfm_home.php#Anchor-49575

Decoy, Wildlife Art, and Sportsman Festival
Havre de Grace
(410) 939-3739
www.decoymuseum.com

My Lady's Manor Steeplechase Races
Monkton
(410) 557-9570 ext 11
www.marylandsteeplechasing.com/main/mlm/datetime.htm

Patuxent Cleanup
Various towns
(301) 249-8200, ext. 6
www.cleanpatuxent.org

Skipjack Martha Lewis Bull and Oyster Roast
Havre de Grace
(410) 939-4078
www.skipjackmarthalewis.org

MAY

Baltimore City's Rite of Spring
Baltimore
(410) 323-0022
www.flowermart.org

Columbia Triathlon
Ellicott City
(410) 964-1246
www.tricolumbia.org

Decoy and Wildlife Art Festival
Havre de Grace
(410) 939-3739
www.decoymuseum.com

Flower and Jazz Festival
Westminster
(410) 848-9393
http://community.carr.org

Lithuanian Festival
Catonsville
(410) 646-0261

Preakness Race
Baltimore
(410) 542-9400
www.preakness.com

JUNE

Charles Village Garden Walk
Baltimore
(410) 243-5033
www.charlesvillage.net

Columbia Festival of the Arts
Columbia
(410) 715-3044
www.columbiafestival.com

HonFest
Hampden
(410) 243-1230
http://honfest.net

Latinofest
Patterson Park, Baltimore
(410) 563-3160
www.latinofest.org

Strawberry Festival
Sykesville
(410) 549-5150
http://ccgov.carr.org/farm

JULY

Artscape
Baltimore
(410) 752-8632
(877) 225-8466
www.artscape.org

Baltimore Pow Wow
Timonium State Fair Grounds
(410) 675-3535
www.baic.org

Carroll County 4-H and FFA Fair
Westminster
(410) 848-3247
www.carrollcountyfair.com

Catonsville's July Fourth Celebration
Catonsville
(410) 744-9655
http://catonsvillecelebrations.org

Cecil County Fair
Fair Hill
(410) 392-3440
www.cecilcountyfair.org

Harford County Fair
Bel Air
(410) 838-8663
www.farmfair.org

AUGUST

Annapolis Art Walk
Annapolis
(410) 267-7077
(301) 261-2124
www.artinannapolis.com

Havre de Grace Seafood Festival
Havre de Grace
(410) 939-1525
www.hdgseafoodfestival.org

Howard County Fair
West Friendship
(410) 442-1022
www.howardcountyfair.org

Iron Girl Columbia Women's Triathlon
Columbia
(410) 964-1246
www.tricolumbia.org

Maryland Renaissance Festival
Crownsville
(410) 266-7304
(800) 296-7304
www.rennfest.com

Maryland State Fair
Timonium
(410) 252-0200
www.marylandstatefair.com

SEPTEMBER

Anne Arundel County Fair
Crownsville
(410) 923-3400
www.aacountyfair.org

Baltimore Book Festival
Mount Vernon Place, Baltimore
(410) 752-8632
www.baltimorebookfestival.com

Catonsville Arts and Crafts Festival
Catonsville
(410) 719-9609
www.catonsville.org/events/artsfest.html

Legacy Chase at Shawan Downs
Lutherville-Timonium
(410) 666-3676
www.shawandowns.org

Maryland Seafood Festival
Sandy Point State Park
Annapolis
(410) 266-3113
www.mdseafoodfestival.com

Maryland Wine Festival
Westminster
(410) 386-3880
http://ccgov.carr.org/farm

OCTOBER

Great Chesapeake Bay Schooner Race
Baltimore to Portsmouth, Virginia
(757) 480-4402
www.schoonerrace.org

United States Powerboat Show
Annapolis
(410) 268-8828
www.usboat.com/us_powerboat_show.php

United States Sailboat Show
Annapolis
(410) 268-8828
www.usboat.com/us_sailboat_show.php

NOVEMBER

Lights on the Bay
(through Dec)
Sandy Point State Park
(443) 481-3161
www.dnr.state.md.us

Miracle on 34th St.
(continues through Dec)
Hampden
www.christmasstreet.com

DECEMBER

Eastport Yacht Club Lights Parade
Annapolis
(410) 267-9549
www.eastportyc.org

First Night Annapolis
Annapolis
(410) 263-2574
www.newyearsannapolis.org

A short walk from the visitor center, along the seawall, is the foremast of the USS *Maine,* still misshapen from the mysterious explosion in Havana Harbor on February 15, 1898. The mast was recovered on October 6, 1910, and erected along the Academy Seawall at Trident Point on May 5, 1913.

At the site of the Noon Meal Formation is the Tecumseh Statue (in front of Bancroft Hall), a bronze replica of the wooden figurehead that graced the USS *Delaware*. It is frequently decorated by midshipmen as a symbol of victory and passed exams. Bancroft Hall Dormitory, at 52 King George St, houses the entire 4,000-member brigade and (depending on who you consult) is either the largest dormitory in the world, or only one of the largest. Take a peek around the building, check out one of the model rooms, and delight in the murals and artworks that decorate the public areas.

One of the most fascinating exhibits in Annapolis is the display of model ships at the **U.S. Naval Academy Museum** on the ground floor of Preble Hall. My mind is totally boggled every time I visit this exhibit. In the collection are ship models from about the time the pilgrims landed in America to just after the War of 1812. Although some of these models may have been created after the ship was built, many of them were built prior to blueprints so shipbuilders could use the models to build the ships, only real-life size. The big (100-gun) ships took one person from four to six years to build, plus another year for the rigging. With likely more than one person doing all the work, there would have been a master model maker supervising a crew of workers or apprentices, thus speeding up the process. You'll also want to see Bone Ships, which were crafted by prisoners of war on frigates from meat bones. They are intricate and accurate portrayals of the fighting ships of the times. Other exhibits include Academy class rings, silverware from naval vessels, flags, uniforms, medals, weapons, navigational instruments, documents, and the stories of several naval heroes, including John Paul Jones. The museum is open Mon through Sat from 9 a.m. to 5 p.m. and Sun from 11 a.m. to 5 p.m. Located at 118 Maryland Ave., call (410) 293-2108 or visit www.usna.edu/Museum/visitor.htm.

The basement of the Naval Academy chapel is one of those "gee, I didn't know that" spots that I love to take visitors to, because that's where the crypt of Revolutionary War hero John Paul Jones is located. A little history and some personal effects complete this final resting place.

A new oak organ console, a gift of the Naval Academy graduating class of 1951, now rings out in the chapel. With five manual keyboards, a pedal board, 520 draw knots, fifty-three coupler tabs, 171 thumb pistons, and forty-seven foot controls, it took the R.A. Colby Inc. Company of Johnson City more than one thousand hours to build. It's said to be the largest organ of its type and unique because of its detail. Oh, and the price tag ran between $700,000 and $800,000.

Upstairs the chapel is pretty awesome as well, with Tiffany studio-designed stained-glass windows behind the altar and elsewhere. A $2.3 million renovation project was completed in 2009 that included restoration of the wooden floors and pews, repairing the plaster trip, replacing pew cushions and carpeting, returning the building to its original color scheme, and sprucing up the chapel's majestic dome. Built on the highest point of ground at the academy (or "in the Yard"), the chapel cornerstone was laid in 1904 by Admiral Dewey. When you see television coverage of newly married couples leaving a chapel under raised swords, this is the chapel they're exiting. Call (410) 263-6933 or visit www.usna.edu/chaplains for more information.

threecoinsin thefountain

No, it's not the famed Roman Trevi Fountain, just a decorative three-tiered bronze item on the Government House lawn. Hilda May Snoops, a longtime companion of former governor William Donald Schaefer, commissioned it in 1990. Showing crabs, oysters, corn, terrapins, and tobacco leaves, the fountain was turned off by Parris Glendening (Schaefer's successor) as a water-conservation effort even though it's a recirculating operation. Once Glendening was out of office, the fountain was turned on again.

For almost two years St. Anne's church (the third on this site) was invaded by plumbers, woodworkers, and other crafters working on a multimillion-dollar renovation. Expansion wasn't possible because of its historic background and a number of unmarked graves on the property. Among the treasures in the church is a Tiffany window (south wall) depicting Anne instructing Mary at her knee. Located at 199 Duke of Gloucester St.; call (410) 267-9333or visit www .stannes-annapolis.org.

Annapolis is called America's Sailing Capital for a reason—people are always sailing. Yes, even during the winter. The **Frostbite Sailing Series** is for those who don't mind donning tons of cold-weather gear as long as the wind can fill a sail. About seventy sailboats gather at the mouth of the Severn River near the Naval Academy seawall every Sunday (there is a break for the holidays). Regulations require a minimum number of sailors and no spinnakers. If you'd like to participate, stop by the Annapolis Yacht Club, 2 Compromise St., about noon, to join the fun; call (410) 263-9279 or (410) 269-0779, or visit www.annapolisyc.com.

The **National Sailing Hall of Fame and Museum** opened during the 2006 Volvo Ocean Race and resides in a temporary setting at the pier end of

City Dock. Dedicated to preserving the history of sport sailing and its impact on our culture, it honors those who have made outstanding contributions to the sport and hopes to inspire and encourage junior sailing development. The exhibit is open daily from 10 a.m. to 5 p.m. Located at 67-69 Prince George St.; call (410) 295-3022 or (877) 295-3022; or visit www.nshof.org.

While at Annapolis Dock, stop by to see the Alex Haley statue, dedicated in December 1999. The life-size statue stands near the spot where the author's ancestor Kunta Kinte was brought ashore from a slave ship. Ed Dwight, a former astronaut, was the sculptor. In addition, a 100-foot story wall and an 18-foot Compass Rose have been added to the park area, all commemorating the 1767 arrival of Kunta Kinte on the slave ship, *Lord Ligonier.* Haley recaptured this moment and others in his Pulitzer Prize–winning book, *Roots,* which was then made into the Emmy Award–winning television series of the same name. The Story Wall has text from Haley's book. Call (410) 841-6920 or visit www.kunta kinte.com.

thegovernoras headofthechurch

Yeah, forget about this separation of church and state thing. According to old Maryland law, the governor is the head of the Episcopal Church in Maryland. This was also true when Marvin Mandel, of Jewish background, was elected to the state's highest position (1969–1979). Mandel says he received a letter from St. Anne's (the church at Church Circle) very early in his gubernatorial days asking for a contribution—as head of the church, of course. He agreed, with the request that he be allowed to present the sermon at an upcoming church service. The church agreed. The last time I talked to Mandel, he no longer remembered how much he donated or what the topic of his sermon was.

Another statue, this one of former Maryland state comptroller Louis L. Goldstein, was installed between the Goldstein Treasury Building and the Income Tax Building in Annapolis in mid-2000. Goldstein died in 1998 at the age of eighty-five after six decades of public service and was well-known for his "God bless y'all real good." Sculptor Jay Hall Carpenter, chosen from nearly two dozen artists who submitted proposals, is best known for his twenty-two years at the Washington National Cathedral. Carpenter never met Goldstein, but he studied photographs and videos to capture the comptroller's movements, expressions, and gestures.

Fallen firefighters and emergency workers and the families they left behind are honored by the bronze statue Rodney Carroll sculpted. The Baltimore artist included a wall inscribed, now, with the names of the 376 people who have died in the line of duty. Dedicated on June 11, 2006, it stands at the corner of

FAST FACTS ABOUT THE CHESAPEAKE BAY

At 200 miles long by 25 miles wide at some points, covering about 4,400 square miles, the Chesapeake Bay is five times as large as the state of Maryland. It is the largest estuary in the United States.

The bay holds about 19 trillion gallons of water.

The average depth of the bay is just 21 feet, but at Bloody Point, near Kent Island on the upper Eastern shore, the water is 174 feet deep.

More than 3,000 species of plants and animals, including 295 types of fish, live in the bay. It is the biggest producer of blue crabs in the country.

Forty-eight rivers and one hundred small tributaries flow into the bay, with the Susquehanna River contributing about 50 percent of the bay's fresh water.

The population of the Chesapeake Bay watershed, which stretches over six states, is 15.5 million.

Historians debate whether Viking explorer Thorfinn Karlsfennias (in the eleventh century), Italian sailor Giovanni da Verrazano (in 1524), or Spanish explorer Pedro Menendez de Aviles (in 1566) was the first European in the bay.

The name Chesapeake is derived from the Native American word Tschiswapeki. Earlier names included "Great Waters," "Mother of Waters," and "Great Shellfish Bay."

The biggest problem endangering the bay is pollution, in the form of nitrogen and phosphorus.

Thomas Point Shoal Lighthouse, built in 1875, is the most photographed lighthouse on the Chesapeake.

Rowe Blvd and Bladen and Calvert streets; visit www.mdfirerescuehero.org for additional information.

The ***Annapolis Maritime Museum*** in Eastport is housed in the historic McNasby Oyster Company building and operates as a community center for waterfront education. The house was the last oyster packing plant in the area. Damaged in 2003 by Hurricane Isabel, repairs, renovations, and improvements to the plant and the Barge House have been made by staff and volunteers. The museum will be delighted if you think of them when you clean out your boat "stuff" and they'll say "Planks for the Memories" when you become a plank owner at the museum. One of the more interesting things to do is the three-hour trip and tour to the Thomas Point Shoal Lighthouse. Located at 723 Second St.; call (410) 295-0104 or visit www.amaritime.org/index.html.

Whether by land or sea, when you're near Annapolis you may as well take a drive or sea cruise over to ***Cantler's,*** noted for Jimmie Cantler, hospitality, crabs all year, and delicious food since the 1970s. The crab-cake and soft-shell crab sandwiches are superb. Located at 458 Forest Beach Rd., Annapolis; call (410) 757-1311 or visit www.cantlers.com.

An unofficial declaration of spring's arrival is the annual ***Chesapeake Bay Bridge Walk Day,*** held on the first Sunday in May. Unfortunately, the bridge has been under renovation, reconstruction, or call-it-what-you-will, and the walk hasn't taken place for a few years (see page 149). The walk was first held in 1975 after a Towson, Maryland, scout leader noticed that one span was closed for construction. He suggested one span should be closed for a daylong walk.

An estimated 50,000 pedestrians, as well as people in wheelchairs and on crutches, cross the eastbound lanes of the bridge, and the only automobiles and trucks permitted are official vehicles and media trucks. Jogging, running, skateboarding, biking, and pets (except service dogs) are prohibited; an early morning race has been established for those who want to speed across the bridge instead of spending about ninety minutes walking and investigating various expansion joints, girder construction, architectural design, and engineering and assembly facets.

Pedestrians normally are not allowed on the four-and-one-third-mile structure connecting the Annapolis area to the large spit of land known as the Eastern Shore. Blue waters lap innocuously about 185 feet below the twin spans of the bridge, also known as the William Preston Lane Jr. Memorial Bridge. Parking lots in Annapolis, at Anne Arundel Community College, and also on the Eastern Shore start filling up at 8 a.m. Buses start taking walkers to the east side at 9 a.m. There is no charge for parking, but there is a $1 charge for the bus. Call (410) 228-8405 or (877) BAYSPAN, or visit www.bay bridge.com.

Capt. Salem Avery was a waterman of the 1860s, and to the delight of the members of the Shady Side Rural Heritage Society, his home on the banks of the West River became available to them to use as a museum. The

Aris T. Allen

As you drive around Annapolis, you may notice Aris T. Allen (1910–1991) Blvd (State Rte 665). Allen was president of his class at Howard University while in medical school there, becoming a physician and flight surgeon during the Korean conflict in the early 1950s. He served in the Maryland House of Delegates and then the state Senate, and was the first African-American chair of the state Republican party. As a delegate to the Republican National Convention he served as the secretary of the convention, the person who calls the roll of states for voting. He also ran for lieutenant governor with former U.S. Senator J. Glenn Beall Jr. You can find a statue of Allen near the intersection of Forest Dr., Chinquapin Round Rd., and Aris T. Allen Blvd in Annapolis.

Maritime Republic of Eastport

Across Spa Creek from downtown Annapolis is Eastport, originally home to the close-knit community of construction workers who built the Naval Academy. It has become much more gentrified, but as of a singular moment on Super Bowl Sunday, January 1998, the cohesion became palpable again. For that's when the Annapolis town fathers closed the Spa Creek bridge for three weeks for much needed repairs. That didn't totally isolate the residents of Eastport; they could get back and forth through a slightly more circuitous route, but they were concerned that "outsiders" would not take the effort to frequent the local businesses. A group of Eastporters decided it was time to promote their town, so they staged a mock secession from Annapolis and renamed their community the Maritime Republic of Eastport (aka MRE). They created T-shirts and sponsored a half-mile race and other festivities to make sure people remembered to find their way over there. Imagine their pleasure when business actually increased during the three-week period! Since then, they've been celebrating and reaffirming the anniversary of their secession, continuing the half-mile race (started by a cannon and rifle shots), a parade, a dog show, and more. They also sponsor other events and donate a lot of money to charities while having an appropriate amount of fun. Call (443) 994-7619 or (410) 267-8796; or visit http://themre.org.

Captain Salem Avery House opened its doors in 1989 as a museum to "protect, document, and illustrate the history and traditions" of Shady Side. The society members are particularly pleased that they were able to obtain some of the original Avery furniture from the owners of the house. They're also pleased as punch (or should that be grog?) that the museum was named to the National Register of Historic Places in Dec 2005. Another proud moment came when Mavis Daly, member of the board of trustees and publicity chair, received the Four Rivers Heritage Award for her years of tireless effort and unceasing enthusiasm to and for the museum. The house is open on Sun from 1 to 4 p.m., Mar through Dec and by appointment. The library is available on Mon from noon to 3 p.m. The grounds are open daily from dawn to dusk. There is no admission fee. Located at 1418 East West Shady Side Rd., Shady Side; call (410) 867-4486 or visit www.averyhouse.org.

Check out the **Smithsonian Environmental Research Center** in Edgewater for a slew of family-oriented activities, from toddlers to 50 uppers and 60 uppers and beyond. An outreach program started in 2006 offers hands-on experiments, projects for home-schoolers, a lunchtime speakers' series, and more at the 3,000-acre science center. Programs range from how paper is made and recycled to a winter waterfowl walk. A popular event, the guided canoe tours of the Rhode River and its tributaries came to a screeching halt in the summer of 2008 when a summer storm destroyed all but two of their canoes and the canoe shed. Fortunately, the community responded with ample donations. The center provides trail maps and brochures if you'd like to bring your own canoe or kayak and explore the 14 miles of undeveloped shoreline yourself. Some events are free while others have a fee. They request that you not bring your four-footed friends. SERC is open Mon through Sat from 9 a.m. to 4:30 p.m.; it's located at 647 Contees Wharf Rd., Edgewater. Call (440) 482-2200 or visit www.serc.si.edu/public_programs.

The multimillion-dollar ***Historic London Town and Gardens Visitor Center*** in Edgewater opened in spring 2006. It's an orientation center, an educational facility for interpreting on-site archaeological finds, and a museum. The center, a large part of which is underground, is an excellent example of a re-adaptive use of an old wastewater treatment plant. In the historic area is the circa 1760 William Brown House that's part of the archaeological search for the "lost town" of London. Eight acres of woodland garden with native plants and exotic special are arranged along a one-mile trail that just invites you to enjoy a leisurely stroll. The center is open from Wed through Sat from 10 a.m. to 4 p.m. and Sun from noon to 4 p.m. from Mar through Dec. Located at 839 Londontown Rd., Edgewater; call (410) 222-1919 or visit www .historiclondontown.org.

For those who love to spoil a good walk by playing golf—and if you'd love to try some of those killer holes where the championship tourneys are played—then stop at ***Renditions Golf Course*** in Davidsonville. This is a course with hole designs taken from other courses. So, holes 6, 7, and 8 are modeled after Augusta National holes 11, 12, and 13. Hole 13 is the number 17 from TPC at Sawgrass. And number 16 is number 16 from Shinnecock Hills. When you're finished (or before you start), there's a 10,000-square-foot clubhouse, restaurant and bar, and golf shop. Find it at 1380 West Central Ave. (State Rte 214), Davidsonville; call (888) 451-4144 or (410) 798-9798; or visit www.renditionsgolf.com.

Baltimore City

Now, zip on back to I-97 and head north to Baltimore. It's a slight left zig (off a right-hand ramp) to the beltway (Interstate 695) to the west, and then a hop north onto the Baltimore–Washington Parkway (which becomes Russell St.), and there you are.

As you enter, on your left you'll see the ***Lee Electrical*** building, at 600 West Hamburg St., near Camden Yards, and on it a Wyland whale painting, which former mayor Kurt L. Schmoke dedicated in 1993. The mural is of extinct Atlantic gray whales, and it's 260 feet long by 20 feet high. Wyland was born in 1956 in Detroit, and it's said he created his first painting, of dinosaurs, at the age of four. He first saw a whale a decade later, and began painting whales and dolphins in 1972. Wyland painted his first whale mural in 1981 in Laguna Beach, California.

Almost across the street is the *M&T Bank Stadium,* home of the Ravens football team, and not far away is *Oriole Park* at Camden Yards, where the Baltimore Orioles baseball team nests for home games. The O's management has tried to solve the problem of scalped tickets by having a scalp-free zone where people who have tickets to sell meet with people who want to buy tickets, with the stipulation that the sellers can't charge more than face value. The scalp-free zone is wonderful, and other teams should adopt this practice.

Take the approximately ninety-minute walking tour of the stadium. As you walk around, you'll hear that the warehouse, which houses the Orioles offices, souvenir shop, reception areas, and Camden Club, is the longest brick building east of the Mississippi (it's 1,016 feet long by 51 feet wide). The tour guide may also tell you that the warehouse is longer than the Empire State Building is tall. The validity of that statement depends on whether you count antennas. At the very least, this is a long building. Should your guide not tell you, ask about the unbreakable windows and how many home-run balls have hit the building on the fly (to give you a clue, none in regulation play). As you walk around the stadium, you'll see the townhomes or row houses across the street that were part of an urban revitalization project. They sold for $1 a piece and were overpriced. The stipulation, of course, was the buyer had to renovate and was obligated to a residency requirement. The tour takes you to a party room, a sky suite, the press room, some of the 25 miles (length depending on your tour guide) of beer pipe for draft brews (so they don't have to schlep kegs around the stadium, clean up, have refrigeration for the kegs at each refreshment stand, and so on). During the season, tours are given Mon through Sat at 11 a.m., noon, 1 and 2 p.m. (varies for day games), and Sun at 12:30, 1, 2, and 3 p.m. (the latter when the team is away). Private group tours can be scheduled. The tour, as of 2009, costs $9

awe-inspiring

The Basilica of the Assumption in Baltimore was the first Roman Catholic cathedral built in the United States. It was founded in 1821, and Mass is still celebrated there daily. Located at 409 Cathedral St.; call (410) 539-5741 or visit www.baltimorebasilica.org.

for adults, $7 for children (14 and under) and seniors (55 and over) and is well worth it. There's no charge for children 3 and under, although taking them on this tour probably is not a good idea. Located at 333 Camden St., Baltimore; call (410) 547-6234; or visit http://baltimore.orioles.mlb.com/bal/ballpark/tours.jsp.

For years the old **Camden Yard** train station (north of the warehouse) stood as a silent reminder of Baltimore's railroad history. Now it's open and welcomes you. On the ground floor you'll find the **Sports Legends at Camden Yards.** More than 10,000 artifacts covering the Orioles, the Baltimore Colts and Johnny Unitas, the Negro Leagues in Baltimore, Maryland college sports, the Baltimore Ravens, and the Maryland

lights!camera! raven?

The Ravens stadium, home to the NFL Baltimore Ravens, made its "theatrical" debut in 2000 as Nextel Stadium, the home field of the Washington Sentinels, in the movie The Replacements. Those who've seen the film are sure to recognize the distinctive purple seating.

Athletic Hall of Fame are in the vast collection. The museum is open Tues through Sun from 10 a.m. to 5 p.m. The admission fee is $8 for adults, $6 for seniors, and $4 for children (3 to 12). A combination ticket to the Sports Legends and Babe Ruth Birthplace is $12 for adults, $8 for seniors, and $5 for children. Located at 301 West Camden St.; call (410) 727-1539 or visit www.baberuthmuseum.com.

Upstairs in the old station is **Geppi's Entertainment Museum.** Dedicated to the art of illustration, comic books, and Americana, it is sure to be one of those places that make you think (or say), "I had one of those." Or, maybe bring back memories of "It's Howdy Doody Time." Now, singing this ditty at home might bring looks of disbelief, but at GEM, you can show those scoffers what or who Howdy Doody was, and throw in Betty Boop, Captain America, Captain Video, and other relics that have contributed so much to our pop culture. Steve Geppi, born in the Little Italy section of Baltimore, became the world's largest distributor of English-language comic books, all from his love of comic books as a child. He turned another childhood love, baseball, into reality when he became part of the local ownership of the Baltimore Orioles in 1993. Geppi's is on the second floor of the Camden Station, above Sports Legends at Camden Yards. GEM is open Tues through Sun from 10 a.m. to 6 p.m. Admission is $10 for adults, $9 for seniors (55 plus), and $7 for students with lots of discounts on Tues and Thurs, game days, and if you traveled by public transportation. Located at 301 West Camden St.; call (410) 625-7060 or visit www.geppismuseum.com.

According to *AmericanStyle* magazine Baltimore is the eleventh-best big city art spot, citing the Baltimore Museum of Art, American Visionary Art Museum (www.avam.org), Walters Art Museum (www.thewalters.com), Contemporary Museum (www.contemporary.org), Craig Flinner Gallery, and the C. Grimaldis Gallery (www.cgrimaldisgallery.com).

child'splay

Port Discovery, which opened in Baltimore in December 1998, is one of the largest children's museums in the country. Aimed toward six- to twelve-year-olds, there's plenty to keep the young-at-heart occupied. Call (410) 727-8120 for more information.

Besides the delectable art attractions at BMA, there's a 200-seat theater, and Gertrude's, with cuisine by noted cookbook author and TV show host John Shields. Along with outdoor dining, you can dine on $10 and $12 entrees on Tuesday evenings. Check the children's menu and remember: BMA members receive a 10 percent discount off a minimum $5 purchase. The museum is closed Mon and Tues; it's located at 10 Art Museum Dr. Call (410) 573-1700 or visit www.artbma.org.

A spectacular way to start your Baltimore visit is at the ***Top of the World*** observation deck and museum. On a clear day you will see an eye-opening, five-sided panoramic view of the city, its harbor, and beyond from the twenty-seventh floor of the tallest pentagonal building west of Houston, designed by I. M. Pei. Exhibits, films, and audiovisual material will familiarize you with Baltimore's past, present, and future. The observation deck visiting hours change seasonally so check the Web site to see if it will be

Fifteen Minutes of Warhol

The Baltimore Museum of Art has a huge Warhol collection on display in the $10 million modern wing that opened in 1994. Included in the display are several pieces that had never been on permanent public exhibit, including *Brillo Box, Del Monte Box*, and gold *Jackie*. The New Wing for Modern Art has an unusual design allowing the display of the large Warhol works. Instead of doors in the middle of each exhibit room wall, the "doors" are placed at the corners, normally dead areas in an exhibit space. This also allows visitors a chance to look into the other three connecting galleries. An energy-saving cooling system creates big sheets of ice overnight when energy costs are low, which then are dropped into an underground pool during the day to sustain the seventy-degree temperature desired in the building. Located at 10 Art Museum Dr.; call (443) 573-1700; or visit www.artbma.org. *Note:* As of October 2006 the BMA no longer charges an admission fee.

Charming, Just Charming

Foodies who can't get enough of Duff Goldman, cake baker extraordinaire, owner of **Charm City Cakes**, host of *Ace of Cakes* on the Food Network, and food contest competitor, can bow to the King as they drive by his place. This is not a walk-in storefront bakery, but a place that takes special orders as much as a year in advance. An unexpected drop-in is not welcome, although you might try calling to see if you can stop by to watch Duff and his genius team at work. He might even welcome your scout troop or other group of visitors. Located at 123 West 27th St.; call (410) 235-9229 or visit www.charmcitycakes.com.

open when you want to visit. Admission is $5 for adults, $4 for seniors (60 plus) and military (with ID), and $3 for children ages 3 through 12. It's located at 401 East Pratt St., 27th Floor; call (410) 837-8439 or visit www .viewbaltimore.org.

Much of Baltimore revolves around the ***Inner Harbor,*** where the World Trade Center is. Here you'll find a carousel, the festival marketplace with its eateries and boutiques, paddle or pedal boats, the Maryland Science Center, the aquarium, and a submarine, the USS *Torsk.* The 311-foot black submarine (with a shark's-tooth grin at one end) sits by the aquarium. Under the command of Bafford E. Lewellen, the sub sank two small Japanese ships on August 14, 1945. The Japanese surrendered the next day, so the *Torsk* sank the last ships of World War II. Admission is $10 adult, $8 for seniors, $5 for youth and free for active duty military and stowaways (children 5 and under). The ship is part of the Baltimore Maritime Museums (*Constellation, Torsk, Lightship Chesapeake,* and the USCG Cutter *Taney*) and a package ticket is available if you will be visiting two to four ships. The ship is open Mar through Dec daily from 10 a.m. to 5 p.m. with extended summer hours, and in Jan and Feb Fri through Sun from 10 a.m. to 5 p.m. Pier 3, East Pratt St., Baltimore. Call (410) 396-3453 or visit www.usstorsk.org. Admission is $10 for adults, $8 for seniors, and $5 for children 6 to 14 years of age. The sub is only open Fri through Sun in the winter.

don't look so crabby

Faidley's Seafood in Baltimore's Lexington Market reportedly shipped 2,800 orders of its famous crab cakes, each handmade by Nancy Faidley Devine, during Christmas week of 2003. Started in 1886 by John W. Faidley Sr. and now operated by descendants Bill and Nancy Devine, it's located at 203 North Paca; call (410) 727-4898 or visit http://faidleyscrab cakes.com.

In July 1999 the USS *Constellation* returned to Baltimore's Inner Harbor. When last in the harbor, her timbers were so rotten that the mast had to be removed, lest it fall through the bottom of the ship to the bottom of the harbor.

it'sgreektome

Among the many fascinating exhibits at the Baltimore Aquarium is a Giant Pacific Octopus (the largest of them all). As of this writing, there's only one octopus, but it may have company by early 2010. Once there's more than one, then the plural is octopodes. The standard English plural of octopus is octopuses. However, the word octopus comes from Greek, and the Greek plural form is octopodes. Modern usage of octopodes is so infrequent that many people mistakenly create the erroneous plural form octopi, formed according to rules for Latin plurals.

Originally thought to have been built in 1797 and the sister ship of Boston's USS *Constitution,* after three years of restoration, she's known to be a sloop of war built in 1854, the last Navy ship powered solely by sail. A thirty-six-gun frigate bearing the name *Constellation* was dismantled in 1853. A second ship was built a year later (but in Norfolk, not in Baltimore as the first ship had been). Nearly 12 feet longer than the first, the second *Constellation* is the one that's in the harbor now. It served in the Mediterranean in the mid-eighteenth century, as an antislavery patrol ship, as a supply ship for famine-stricken Ireland, and for a dozen years as a training ship for the U.S. Naval Academy. The Navy still honors the name, with its USS *Constellation* aircraft carrier. If you saw the ship before its restoration, you may notice that the second gun deck, added at some point to make it look more like the older frigate, has been removed, and her stern is rounded now, instead of squared off.

The *Constellation* is open for tours daily from 10 a.m. to 6 p.m. May through Oct and from 10 a.m. to 4 p.m. the rest of the year. It's closed on major holidays. Admission to the ship is $7.50 for adults, $6 for seniors sixty and older, and $3.50 for children 6 through 14. It's located on Pier 1, Inner Harbor, 301 Pratt St., Baltimore; call (410) 539-1797 or (888) 225-8466; or visit www.constellation.org.

The eponymously named **Roy's Restaurant,** one of Roy Yamaguchi's Hawaiian fusion eateries, is a few blocks from the active Inner Harbor and definitely worth wending your way to Aliceanna Street for. The miso butterfish is spectacular, and the chocolate soufflé is every chocoholic's wish fulfilled. Located at 720 B Aliceanna St.; call (410) 659-0099 or visit www.roys restaurants.com.

On May 28, 1989, the **Maryland Vietnam Veterans Memorial,** a circular-shaped version of the national Vietnam memorial, was dedicated to the memory of 1,046 Marylanders who were killed or became missing in action in the Vietnam conflict. The names and inscriptions are readable whether one is standing, in a wheelchair, or at a child's-eye level. The veterans' names are etched into granite, along with this inscription:

MARYLANDERS, WHILE IN THIS PLACE, PAUSE TO RECALL OUR NATION'S IDEALS, ITS PROMISE, ITS ABUNDANCE, AND OUR CONTINU-ING RESPONSIBILITIES TOWARD THE SHARED FULFILLMENT OF OUR ASPIRATIONS. REMEMBER, TOO, THOSE WHOSE EXERTIONS AND SACRIFICES UNDERLIE THESE BLESSINGS. REMEMBER, INDEED, THE LIVING AND THE DEAD.

Funds were raised by Maryland veterans who called themselves "The Last Patrol." They marched across the state during sweltering August heat in 1986, from Oakland in western Maryland to Ocean City in the east, and another 200 miles from Point Lookout to Baltimore the next year. Architect Paul Spreiregan designed the monument that stands in Middle Branch Park at 2825 South Hanover St.; call (410) 354-3550 or visit www.msa.md.gov.

globalharbor

Much of the credit for the revitalization of the Inner Harbor goes to Marty Millspaugh, who helped form Charles Center-Inner Harbor Management, Inc. and who, with other visionaries, saw the potential in taking the wide open inner harbor park area and filling it with a festival marketplace for locals and tourists. This concept was so successful that officials from more than 100 cities have visited and taken home ideas they could implement. Look at the waterfront area of Barcelona and Melbourne and you see the influence. A PBS television documentary, Global Harbors, was created in 2008 and is available on DVD from www .globalharbors.org.

Architectural Monument with a View

The Washington Monument and Museum in Baltimore, a 178-foot column, was the nation's first architectural monument (distinguishing it from the monument honoring George Washington that's in Boonsboro in western Maryland). Robert Mills, architect of the Washington Monument in Washington, D.C., designed it. You reach the top via a 228-step spiral stairway, where you can get a four-window panoramic view of the city. (I'm not sure what the difference is in that definition of "architectural monument" compared to the one in Washington State Park, for they both claim they were the first). The marble, a white, crystalline metalimestone, is Cockeysville marble, from a quarry near Texas, about one and a half miles north of Baltimore. This stone was also used for the first 152 feet of the Washington Monument in Washington, D.C. It's open Tues through Sun from 10 a.m. to 4 p.m. Admission is $1. Call (410) 396-0929 for more information.

The Book Thing of Baltimore never sells a single book. It gives them away. Russell Wattenberg is the owner of this store that "puts unwanted books into the hands of those who want them." So, if you've been boating along the Intracoastal Waterway or driving around and you've finished the book you brought with you, stop by the Book Thing and drop off your reading material, then pick up something you haven't read yet. The store is open weekends from 9 a.m. to 6 p.m. As Wattenberg says, "Buses and hovercraft welcome." So are donations, from money and volunteers, to plastic grocery bags and gift certificates to Home Depot, Staples, gas stations, etc. Located at 3001 Vineyard Lane; call (410) 662-5631 or visit www .bookthing.org.

lettherebe
entertainment!

After a massive $26.8 million renovation, the Peabody Institute of the Johns Hopkins University (the nation's oldest music conservatory) has reopened. Set in Baltimore's Mount Vernon Cultural District, the Peabody is host to more than 800 musical and dance performances a year. Its newly refurbished concert space now rivals those of other major American cities. Located at 1 East Mount Vernon Place, Baltimore; call (410) 659-8100; or visit www.peabody.jhu.edu.

Old Baltimore has long been known for its blocks and blocks of row houses, with their brightly scrubbed white-marble steps. Almost as historic, but not nearly as well known, are the painted screens for windows and doors that decorate the houses lining the streets of East Baltimore. It is said that William Oktavec painted the first screen on a hot summer day in 1913. Oktavec was a green grocer whose fresh produce was wilting in the heat, so he took it inside and painted groceries on the screens to show his customers what he had available.

When you understand that this area is all cement and brick, with very little greenery, no front yards, and few gardens or trees, you can appreciate the thoughts some had about providing a little colorful decoration. Another advantage of the painted screens is that windows and doors can be left open for the breezes, because the paint allows those who are inside to look out, but outsiders cannot see in.

People started painting on the screens pictures of red-roofed bungalows and ponds with ducks or swans swimming around in them. Rainbows and religious scenes were popular topics, with most of the artwork reflecting the memories of the inhabitants' home countries in Europe and scenes of a new life in America. The scenes depicted the single-family, country-cottage homes of the sort everyone dreamed of owning.

For the best screen viewing, start at the former ***Haussner's Restaurant*** at 3242 Eastern Ave., and travel along both sides of Eastern Ave. The ***Hatton***

Senior Center, at the corner of Fait and South Linwood Ave, has screens in each of its twenty windows. This generally is a seasonal display, with the screens in place between May and Oct. Six or seven screen painters remain, but they are in their fifties or older. They still work away at it, saying, "Practice makes perfect, and perfect practice makes art."

norainon thisparade

The first umbrella factory in the United States was established in Baltimore in 1828. The umbrellas carried a very Madison Avenue–type slogan: born in Baltimore—raised everywhere.

You can have a screen painted even if you do not live in or visit Baltimore. Write the Painted Screen Society of Baltimore, Box 12122, Baltimore 21281; or phone them at (410) 744-0703. Or you can check out the work of Dee Herget at www.screenpainter.com; (410) 391-1750. Select the subject you want, send her the screening, and she'll create your keepsake.

Baltimore has a number of "wow!" looking places, and the ***Reginald F. Lewis Museum of Maryland African American History & Culture*** certainly is among them. Opened in June 2005, the $33 million facility features in-depth collections of artifacts, rare objects, and interactive exhibits covering more than 350 years of African-American history and culture. Lewis was an entrepreneur and philanthropist, and the International Law Center building at Harvard Law School is named after him. Other attractions in the

Lights, Camera, Action!

The NBC television series *Homicide: Life on the Street* was shot primarily in the Fell's Point area of Baltimore, one of the stops on the water-taxi route. You can catch glimpses of buildings used in the series, from the police headquarters to the bar across the street. Barry Levinson, the show's producer, is a Baltimore native who attended Forest Park High School, and he has set many of his movies, including *Diner, Tin Man,* and *Liberty Heights,* in town and in the suburbs of his younger days.

John Waters is also a product of the area and has shot a lot of his films here. *Hairspray* was set here. Divine, the female impersonator who starred in *Pink Flamingos, Mondo Trasho,* and *Polyester* and died on March 7, 1988, grew up at 1824 Edgewood Rd. in Loch Raven (no, his parents aren't living there anymore). Divine is buried in Prospect Hill Cemetery, York Rd, Towson.

Another series, HBO's *The Wire,* was also shot in Baltimore. It was written by David Simon (who wrote the book on which *Homicide* was based). Look for familiar settings around Port Discovery and other locales in the area.

82,000-square-foot facility include a resource center, a theater, classrooms, a recording/listening oral history studio, museum shop, cafe, and a distance-learning lab. It is the largest museum dedicated to African-American history on the East Coast. With its outside terrace and reception areas, it's also a great place to hold a function. The museum is open Tues through Sat from 10 a.m. to 5 p.m. and Sun from noon to 5 p.m. Admission is $8 for adults, $6 for seniors and college students (with ID), and free to museum members and children six and under. The museum is located at 830 East Pratt St.; call (443) 263-1800 or visit www.africanamericanculture.org for more information.

Public transportation around Baltimore City is becoming pretty convenient in the last few years. It doesn't go everywhere you want, but it's a good start. The subway system is fine. There's also Ed Kane's **Water Taxi,** which makes seventeen stops around the harbor, going to almost every popular waterfront attraction, including Harborplace, the Maryland Science Center, the National Aquarium in Baltimore, the Baltimore Museum of Industry, Fell's Point, Little Italy, and Canton. Thus, you can park for the day and take the water taxi around to various spots you want to visit, not having to worry about finding parking places, having correct change, or fighting traffic. The blue-and-white water taxis, or water buses, run about every eight to eighteen minutes Apr through Oct and about every forty-five minutes the rest of the year. Operating hours vary by the season. All-day unlimited ticket price is $9 for adults and $4 for children 10 and under. Call (410) 563-3901 or (800) 658-8947; or visit www.the watertaxi.com.

A new free Charm City Circulator bus system was scheduled to incrementally start service as of January 11, 2010. The first route, the east-west Orange Rte, goes between the B&O Railroad Museum to the Inner Harbor, Harbor East, and Fells Point. A second route connects Cross Street Market with Penn Station, and a third rides between the Johns Hopkins Hospital, Fells Point and Harbor East.

Another transportation option is the light-rail system, taking you from

brainfreeze

A snocone is a summer Baltimore delicacy that dates back to at least the turn of the previous century. Sometimes it's a snowcone and sometimes it's a snowball. Whatever it's called, it is shaved ice, not crushed ice. It's topped with whatever flavors you want, but the hands-down quintessential topping is marshmallow. Chocolate is always on the top-ten list, but there's still marshmallow on top. You can buy a snowball at numerous places, and one of the favorites, with more than fifty flavors, is the **Old Fashioned Ice Cream Shoppe** at 9150-17 Baltimore National Pike, Ellicott City; (410) 480-2856; www.oldfashioned icecreamshoppe.com.

the suburbs to Oriole Park at Camden Yards and back again for less expense and aggravation than driving into the city and parking. It runs from Glen Burnie to Hunt Valley Mall, with stops in downtown Baltimore, including Camden Yards, with spurs to BWI Airport and Penn Station. It operates about every fifteen minutes from 6 a.m. to 11 p.m. Mon through Sat, and every thirty minutes from 11 a.m. to 7 p.m. on Sun. Hours are extended or modified during the baseball season. Free parking is available at designated light-rail stops, and all light-rail trains are wheelchair accessible. The cost is $1.60 per trip, $3.50 for an all-day pass that's good on the subway, the bus system, and the light-rail. Call (410) 539-5000 or visit www.mtamaryland.com for more information.

The biggest change in a transportation mode is the ***Port of Baltimore passenger cruise terminal and service.*** Thanks to Carnival Cruise Lines, the 2,124-passenger 88,500-ton *Pride* began year-round 7-day cruise service out of Baltimore. The ship has two itineraries (as of this writing) including an Eastern Caribbean departure (Grand Turk, Turks & Caicos, private Bahamian island of Half Moon Cay), and Freeport, the Bahamas. The second itinerary visits Port Canaveral, Florida, Nassau, and Freeport. Carnival says it expects that more than 115,000 guests will depart from Baltimore because, according to Governor Martin O'Malley, 40 million people live within a six-hour drive of the city. For those who fly in, it's a lot more convenient than more northern ports. Call (800) CARNIVAL or visit www.carnival.com for more information. In Nov 2009, Celebrity Cruises started offering two itineraries out of Baltimore aboard the Mercury. Continuing through February, the voyages included a nine-night Bahamas cruise with port calls at CocoCay, Nassau, and Charleston and Key West in the U.S. A second, 12-night itinerary stopped at five Caribbean islands. Contact Celebrity Cruises at (800) 647-2251; 2001 East

forwhomthe belltolls

Whenever you hear a church bell ring, think of the McShane Bell Foundry in Glen Burnie because the odds are good that they made it. They've been in business since 1856, producing church bells, ring peal, and chimes and carillons, and are the lone surviving maker of large church bells in the country. They have produced more than 300,000 bells that can be heard in cathedrals, churches, municipal buildings, and universities all over the world. Among their credits is a bell for Western Maryland College in Westminster, a 43" diameter bell for the Belair Fire Department in Belair, and last, but not least, they were an instrumental part of the bell remembrance program in honor of those who died in the attacks of September 2001. Visit them on the Web at www.mcshanebell.com.

McComas St.; or on the Web at www.celebritycruises.com. Royal Caribbean is scheduled to start year-round service in 2010.

Other ships planning Baltimore departures are *American Spirit, American Glory, Independence,* and *Enchantment of the Seas,* for a total of 81 sailings. Parking at the Port is in a fenced-in-lot and costs $15 a night. Call (866) 427-8963 or visit www.cruisemaryland.com.

Toby's Dinner Theatre of Columbia helped put Columbia on the map. A lot of talented performers came through its doors, including Ed Norton. Now there's a second Toby's venue, this one in Canton. Among the shows set for the 2007 season are *The Full Monty, Grease, Fiddler on the Roof, Dreamgirls,* and *Holiday Hot Nostalgia.* A huge buffet comes before the show; 5625 O'Donnell St.; (410) 649-1660 or (866) 649-1669; www.tobysdinner theatre.com.

Should you cross the ***Francis Scott Key Bridge*** (instead of taking the tunnels or driving around the west loop of the Baltimore Beltway), look for a large, dark, hexagonal bulk sitting in the water at the southwest end of the bridge. It's ***Fort Carroll,*** sitting on a three-acre constructed island of brick and stone, a structure built under the supervision of engineer Robert E. Lee before he became superintendent of the United States Military Academy. Although not completed, the fort was officially named for Charles Carroll (1737–1832), the last surviving signer of the Declaration of Independence. A lighthouse was added in 1853.

After years of neglect, the fort was once again staffed at the approach of the Spanish–American War in 1898 and new construction began; but that wasn't completed either until 1900 and the Spanish–American War was history. The lighthouse was automated in 1920, and in 1921 the Army removed what remained of the military equipment, taking it to Fort Howard. The island has been purchased, leased, and used as a private picnic area over the years, but time and Mother Nature have pretty well destroyed it. Today it's a crumbling structure overrun with trees and vines and is said to be the home to the most diverse colony of bird species within 100 miles. Its future is uncertain. If you'd like to see the fort, rather than trying to see what's happening as you're speeding over the bridge, you can check out photos at www.geocities.com/baltforts/Fort_Carroll.

Baltimore County

Baltimore City is surrounded on the east, north, and northwest by Baltimore County, and the easiest way out of the city (barring rush-hour accidents) is to the north along I-83.

The **Glenn L. Martin Aviation Museum** is on a much smaller and intimate scale than the huge aviation museum in the Smithsonian Institution complex in Washington, D.C. This collection honors and promotes the contributions to aviation of Martin and his company. Look for industrial models of aircraft and rockets, wind tunnel models, restored and partially restored aircraft, and photos documenting the growth of the company. People of a "certain" age are sure to find wonderful childhood memories among the exhibits. There is no admission charge, but contributions are always welcome. The museum is open Wed through Sat from 11 a.m. to 3 p.m. (except holidays). Located at 701 Wilson Point Rd., Hangar 5, Lower Level, Suite 531, Martin State Airport, Middle River; call (410) 682-6122 or visit www.maryland aviationmuseum.org.

At Towson University, in the Fine Arts Center, is the **Asian Arts and Cultural Center** at the Roberts Gallery. The gallery is named in honor of Frank Roberts, who donated a large number of Asian artifacts and artworks to start this collection. Changing and permanent displays of Asian, African, and pre-Columbian works are featured. Concerts, films, lectures, and workshops are sponsored throughout the school year. The Asian Arts Center in the Fine Arts Building is open Mon through Fri from 11 a.m. to 4 p.m. and Sat from 1 p.m. to 4 p.m. when exhibits are on display. No admission is charged. Groups are welcome by appointment. Call (410) 704-2807 or visit www.towson.edu/asianarts.

Supposedly, duckpin bowling (played with smaller balls and pins) was invented in Baltimore in 1900. **Stoneleigh Lanes** opened in 1946 when it had 17 lanes. The Sherman pinsetters (made at the Bethlehem Steel Plane in Sparrows Point) were installed in the late 50s or early 60s at which point the lane count was reduced to 16. They still have the original wood lanes. With smaller balls for smaller hands and no liquor license, it's been a great place to introduce little ones to the game, particularly with a birthday party (they have about 600 a year). Owner Ken Staub says people come from all over the world to bowl here and it's not unusual to see a movie or TV shoot taking place.

o!saycanyousee

The lyrics to the "The Star-Spangled Banner," as penned by Francis Scott Key in 1814 after watching the Battle of Baltimore, are on display at the Maryland Historical Society in Baltimore. Call (410) 685-3750 or visit www.mdhs.org.

Stoneleigh is open Mon and Wed from noon to 10 p.m.; Tues and Thurs from 3 to 10 p.m., Fri from 3 p.m. to 1 a.m., Sat from 11 to 1 a.m., and Sun from 11 a.m. to 6 p.m. Located at 6703 York Rd., Towson; call (410) 377-8115 or visit www.stoneleighlanes.com.

If you saw Clint Eastwood's film Absolute Power then your visit to **Maryvale** will be a déjà vu moment for you: the castle at Maryvale Preparatory School was the setting where the dastardly deed was done. The stone manor, set on 150 acres, was constructed in 1917 and modeled after Warwick Castle in England. Its Gothic arched windows, a great hall with European oak-paneled walls, diamond-paneled beveled-glass doors opening onto the terrace, boxwood gardens, stone towers, and incredible staircase are available for rent for your special event. As the school says, it fulfills "every girl's fantasy of the perfect storybook wedding." Maryvale, open by appointment only, is at 11300 Falls Rd., Brooklandville (just north of the I-695 and I-83 intersection); call (410) 252-3528 or visit www.maryvale.com. (See an additional note about the film in the Cecil County section.)

One of the remaining covered bridges in Maryland connects Harford and Baltimore Counties and crosses over Gunpowder Falls. The **Jericho Covered Bridge** was constructed in 1864 and measures 88 feet, with a 14⅔-foot roadway. Steel beams, steel stringers, steel crosstie rods, and bottom chord were installed later for reinforcement, and today it remains in good condition. To reach the bridge, take State Rte 152 from exit 74 off I-95, turn left onto Jerusalem Rd., and proceed to Jericho Rd.; call (410) 638-3509.

Ashland Furnace is one of the six relatively easy-to-reach furnaces in Maryland (the others are Catoctin Furnace, Lonaconing Iron Furnace, Antietam, Principio, Nassawango. Said to have been named for the Kentucky home of Henry Clay, Ashland's three furnaces, engine room, and casting house were kept functioning from around 1844 to 1893. Originally there were also large storage buildings for raw materials and a village with a school, church, store, and about five dozen houses.

West of Ashland Furnace is the **Oregon Ridge Park and Nature Center,** a great place to take a break after hours of driving and seeing regular tourist attractions. Within its 836 acres are a number of marked trails of varying length and difficulty, downhill and cross-country skiing areas, a greenhouse, an archaeological research site, an outdoor stage, and a launching site for hang gliders. Starting in the nature center, you can see how a honeybee hive works, look at local flowers and plants in the greenhouse, or check on such live animals as fish, frogs, mice, salamanders, snakes, and Stubby, the pet opossum, all native to the park.

A huge tree exhibit reveals the various parts of the forest ecosystem, from the worms and moles living among the roots and underbrush to the owls and hawks perching in its highest limbs. The area's history is depicted by artifacts retrieved from archaeological digs in the park. The nature trails crisscross the park, so a hiker sees the natural interactions of birds, fields, ponds, streams, swamps, wildlife, and woods.

For those who like nature on the cultured side, summer concerts are presented here by the Baltimore Symphony. The Center is open Tues through Sun from 9 a.m. to 5 p.m. The grounds are open daily from dawn to dusk. Located at 13555 Beaver Dam Rd., Cockeysville; call (410) 887-1815 or visit www.oregonridge.org.

Hampton National Historic Site, 535 Hampton Lane, Towson, was the largest private home in the country when it was built in 1790 and is known for having produced iron instead of cotton. Perhaps more notable is the Ridgely family freeing about 340 slaves in one of the largest emancipations in the state's history. A National Park Service property, the formal gardens—home to 30 plus flowering plant species of which some are native and some exotic— were reopened in 2009 after going through a restoration period. The mansion is opened daily from 9 a.m. to 4 p.m. and 45-minute guided tours are offered daily at 10 and 11 a.m. and 1, 2, 3, and 4 p.m. Although most of the site is handicap accessible, some parts of the site have limited or no accessibility. The second floor of the manor is not wheelchair accessible. Other tours in other parts of the property are offered. Check the Web site (www.nps.gov/hamp) or call (410) 823-1309 or (410) 962-4290 ext. 224for the schedule. There is no admission fee.

You may have noticed that Maryland wineries are growing in number. The new *Piedmont Wine Trail* now has eight wineries. As you follow it, you'll find you're going through rolling hills and historic towns, and by thorough- bred horse farms. The oldest of the wineries is Boordy Vineyards, founded in 1945. Degon Vineyard, opening this past fall (2009) is the newest. Others include Woodhall Wine Cellars, Basignani Winery (all in Baltimore County), Fiore Winery and Distillery, Harford Vineyard and Winery (also new), Legend Vineyard, and Mount Felix Estate Vineyard & Winery (all in Harford County). Thirty-eight wineries are located in Maryland and a total of four wine trails. Visit www.marylandwine.com for more information.

Carroll County

West of Baltimore County, out State Rte 30 or 140, you're getting into horse country with some beautiful scenery to go along with your history. The county was named for Charles Carroll, an American Revolutionary War leader and Maryland signer of the Declaration of Independence.

Near Westminster, the county seat, is the *Carroll County Farm Museum.* This complex has a general store that's reminiscent of the 1800s and sells items handcrafted by Farm Museum artisans, souvenirs, nickel candies, and much more. Among the activities scheduled on the grounds are a Civil War

Final Resting Place

In 1992 Frederick Hubbard Gwynne and his wife, Deborah, moved to a farm in rural Maryland. You may remember him as Fred Gwynne, the tall (6'5") and lanky actor who portrayed Herman Munster in TV's *The Munsters* and as Gunther Toody in *Car 54, Where Are You?* He also played the part of Big Daddy in the 1974 Broadway revival of *Cat on a Hot Tin Roof,* among many other distinguished parts. His last films were *Fatal Attraction, Pet Sematary,* and *My Cousin Vinny.* He also wrote several children's books, including *A Little Pigeon Toad, A Chocolate Moose for Dinner, The King Who Rained,* and *Pondlarker.* Gwynne died of pancreatic cancer on July 2, 1993, just days short of his sixty-seventh birthday. He is buried at Sandymount Methodist Church off Old Westminster Pike.

encampment (19th Georgia Regiment), Fall Harvest Days, a fiddlers' convention, a day devoted to antique farm machinery, and a day to celebrate Maryland wines.

General admission is $5 for adults, $3 for children 7 to 18, and 60 and over, and free for those under age 7. Group tours and rates are available. The museum is open weekends from noon to 5 p.m. and also Tues through Fri in July and Aug from 10 a.m. to 4 p.m. Located at 500 South Center St., Westminster; call (410) 386-3880 or visit www.carrollcountyfarmmuseum.org.

Carroll County's streams, valleys, farms, woodlands, and villages provide an ideal backdrop for exploring off the highway, and the best way to do that is by bicycle. Each route is on a separate map with its own description of the tour. Brochures are available at the visitor center in Westminster.

For example, the Taneytown route, northwest of Westminster, is nearly 14 miles long, beginning at Taneytown Memorial Park. The moderately hilly ride takes you through rustic areas filled with deer and pheasants. The New Windsor tour, west of Westminster, travels for eight miles through the rolling hills of Wakefield Valley. Attractions include **Robert Strawbridge's Home** (the birthplace of American Methodism, 2650 Strawbridge Lane, New Windsor) and *A Greater Gift Shop* at the New Windsor Service Center (500 Main St., New Windsor).

According to local legend, you and I are not the only visitors to Carroll County. Several apparitions also frequent the countryside, and you may even meet a friendly one. The first of the ghosts of Carroll County is at the **Shellman House** on East Main St. in Westminster. A little girl in white, they say, delights at having visitors stop by the visitor center, the Historical Society of Carroll County, at 210 East Main St., Westminster; call (410) 848-6494 or visit www.hscc.carr.org.

Spirits, in addition to the liquid kind, are said to reside at **Cockey's Tavern,** 216 East Main St.; since the early 1800s this tavern has been the site of political rallies for Andrew Jackson, antitax meetings, fancy balls, and all-night debauchery. At Main and Court Sts., the ghosts of slaves supposedly return to the Carroll County auction block, where slave trading was done in pre–Revolutionary War times. Other specters have been reported at Ascension churchyard, the courthouse, the old Westminster jail, McDaniel College (Levine Hall has a musical ghost), and Avondale—the home of Legh Master, the most celebrated of Carroll's ghosts—on Stone Chapel Rd. in Wakefield Valley. It is said that Master was a tyrant, a miser, a lecher, and a cad.

Two Confederate ghosts reportedly visit the last remaining building of Irving College on Grafton St., and during a full moon, an Indian walks along a ridge in the tiny town of Lineboro. For those of you who choose to pursue these nocturnal visitors, talk with the Historical Society.

Harford County

Head northeast of Baltimore City and east of Baltimore County, and you're probably taking I-95 to or from the Northeast corridor. Take a few minutes off that interstate, known as the Gateway to the Chesapeake Bay, and you'll find that Harford County goes from covered bridge to the Concord Point Light.

Havre de Grace is the home of the **Concord Point Light.** Constructed in 1827, it is the oldest operating lighthouse on the East Coast. Following its decommissioning in 1975, it was vandalized and then, thank goodness, restored, and it is now in tip-top shape. You can climb the twenty-eight steps plus six steps on a ladder and see an impressive view of the Susquehanna River and Chesapeake Bay from the top of the 39-foot lighthouse. The lighthouse is open on Sat and Sun from 1 to 5 p.m. May to Oct, or by appointment. Located on Lafayette St. Havre de Grace, call (410) 939-9040 for more information.

The town (and its residents and visitors) are enjoying the boomlet that's happening here. From the lighthouse you can walk a half mile via a promenade (boardwalk) along the shore of the Chesapeake Bay to Tydings Park at Lafayette and Concord Sts.

Another interesting attraction is the **Susquehanna Museum of Havre de Grace,** where you can learn just about everything you need to know about the southern terminus of the Susquehanna and Tidewater Canal. There's a restored lockhouse and a pivot bridge. Admission is free, although donations are accepted. The museum is open from 1 to 5 p.m. Fri through Sun May through Oct. The museum is located at the Lock House, 817 Conesto St., Havre de Grace; call (410) 939-5780 or (866) 939-5780 or visit www.hdgtourism.com/do_museums.html.

A self-guided historic walking-tour brochure is available from the **Havre de Grace Visitor Center** on Pennington Ave. It highlights a sample of the 800 structures that contribute to the Havre de Grace Historic District. The buildings range in period from the 1780s through the Canal era (1830–1850) and the Victorian era (1880–1910) to the contemporary.

Havre de Grace is the self-proclaimed duck decoy capital of the world, and the **Havre de Grace Decoy Museum** has complete collections of decoys by Madison Mitchell and Paul Gibson among the 1,200 decoys and decorative carvings. An annual Decoy Festival is held about the first weekend of May at the museum and at the Havre de Grace Middle and High Schools. The Decoy Museum is open Mon through Sat from 10:30 a.m. to 4:30 p.m. and Sun from noon to 4 p.m., except major holidays. Admission is $6 for adults, $5 for those age 65 and older, and $2 for children ages 9 to 18. Located at 215 Giles St., Havre de Grace; call (410) 939-3739 or visit www.decoymuseum.com.

actingdebut

Edwin Booth's first theatrical performance was in the original Harford County Courthouse.

Crossing the Susquehanna River north of Havre de Grace via U.S. Hwy 40 is the **Thomas J. Hatem Memorial Bridge,** between Harford and Cecil Counties (nice to know about when the bridge on I-95 is backed up). It opened in 1940 as the Susquehanna River Bridge and was renamed in 1986 to honor Hatem, a prominent Harford County resident who devoted his life to public and civic service. The bridge is one-and-a-half miles long and rises 89 feet above the river, connecting the communities of Havre de Grace and Perryville. More than nine million vehicles use the bridge each year. The toll is $4 (eastbound only) for passenger cars.

South of Havre de Grace is Aberdeen, once known primarily for its military base, the Aberdeen Proving Grounds. On the grounds of the base is the **U.S. Army Ordnance Museum,** with a comprehensive collection of small arms and just about everything else military you'd want to see that would be too small to fit in a parade or would not be suitable for exterior display. After being closed for a while due to security issues, the museum is once again accessible. Enter through the Maryland Ave. gate and request a one-day museum pass.

The museum is open daily from 9 a.m. to 4:45 p.m.; it is closed on major holidays except Memorial Day, Fourth of July, and Veterans Day/Armed Forces Day. There is no admission charge. Call (410) 279-3602 or visit www.ordmusfound.org.

The other big gun from Aberdeen is Cal Ripken Jr., the Iron Man, the one who broke Lou Gehrig's record of 2,130 consecutive baseball games played. West of I-95 is the **Ripken Baseball Stadium,** which opened in June 2002. The minor league baseball team, the Aberdeen Ironbirds, plays thirty-six home games in this new stadium. Special events are almost always scheduled, including a number of theme nights when they give away such promotional items as baseballs, caps, and

luckoftheirish

The town of Dublin, in Harford County, is named after Dublin, Ireland. In the eighteenth century it was a Scots-Irish settlement.

T-shirts. Some of the items from Ripken's career can be seen at the club level of Stadium. Fireworks displays are a frequent item on the calendar. Plans for the complex include several youth-size stadiums modeled after famous ballparks and a baseball academy that will house up to 200 youngsters and coaches for weeklong camps, clinics, and tournaments, and, eventually, the Cal Ripken World Series. The stadium is located at 923 Gilbert Rd., Aberdeen; call (410) 297-9292 or visit www.ironbirdsbaseball.com.

Northwest of Aberdeen is Bel Air, the Harford county seat, and there you can enjoy the pleasures of **Liriodendron,** a Palladian-style mansion with Greek columns, French doors, marble walls in the kitchen and bathroom, and thirteen fireplaces. Built as a palatial summer home in 1898 for Dr. Howard A. Kelly, one of the "big four" founders of Baltimore's Johns Hopkins Hospital and Medical School, the Kelly Mansion is now on the National Register of Historic Places. This historic house museum features changing exhibits and art displays as well as a permanent exhibit of memorabilia from the Kelly Collection.

nodirtyoperation

Johns Hopkins Hospital in Baltimore was the site of the first use of silk sutures and the first use of rubber gloves to reduce the risk of surgical infection.

It also serves as a cultural center for Harford County, with superb facilities for exhibitions, lectures, and concerts. The museum is open for tours from 1 to 4 p.m. on Sun from Mar through Dec. A donation is suggested. Located at 502 West Gordon St., Bel Air; call (410) 838-3942 or visit www.liriodendron.org.

Howard County

South and west of Baltimore City, out I-70 or down I-95, is Howard County, a place offering tremendous contrasts in lifestyles, from Ellicott City, a former mill town, with its original stone buildings, antiques and specialty shops, historic sites, and Ellicott City B&O (Baltimore and Ohio) Railroad Station Museum, to Columbia, the planned community, with its huge mall, and almost a dozen "neighborhoods."

Although you can find any number of really good places to enjoy some hardshell crabs—places where they do the cooking and the cleaning—once in a while you want to do it yourself. *Frank's Seafood* is a no-frills market in Jessup that carries culls (one-clawed lobsters), crabs, shrimp, whole fish, fillets, oysters, clams, mussels, and more. Check the Web site or sign up for e-mail for coupons, tips, recipes, and weekly specials. Located at 7901 Oceano Ave., Suite B, Jessup; call (410) 799-5960 or visit www.franksseafood.com.

Drive a little into the Patapsco Valley State Park, just off U.S. Hwy. 1, and you can spot a bridge of note that is for trains rather than cars, known as the *Thomas Viaduct* (1833). Crossing the Patapsco River, eight elliptical arches support a 60-foot-high granite block structure, which allowed tall ships to pass under. Just as the Ellicott City Railroad Station has endured as a landmark to the growth of railroading in Maryland, so does the viaduct. When B&O Railroad officials began looking to expand the railroad south to Washington, D.C., they faced a monumental problem: how to cross the Patapsco River. They solved it with a monumental structure, the Thomas Viaduct. Named for the first president of the B&O Railroad, Philip Thomas, it was designed by Baltimorean Benjamin Latrobe, and it was the first curved, stone-arched bridge in America. Construction began July 4, 1832, and it was completed exactly three years later at a cost of a little more than $142,000. It still carries passenger and freight trains and is the country's oldest main line railroad span. The viaduct is off Levering Ave. at 6086 Old Lawyers Hill Rd., Elkridge, in the Patapsco Valley State Park which charges a small admission fee. Tell the guard if you're just going to look at the bridge and they probably won't charge you. Picnic areas and other recreational activities are available in the park, which is open from sunrise to sunset; located at 8020 Baltimore National Pike, Ellicott City. Call (410) 461-5005 or visit www.dnr.state.md.us/publiclands/central/patapscovalley.html.

itwasagrind

Ellicott Mills, in Howard County, was started in 1772 by three Ellicott brothers from Bucks County, Pennsylvania. By 1774 it was said to be the greatest gristmill in colonial America, with seven mills in operation at its peak. Besides producing animal feed, flour, iron nails, oil, lumber, paper, wagons, and wool, the first commercial electricity in the county was produced in 1891 in a mill on Tiber Alley.

Another bridge of interest, at Savage, is the Bollman Truss Bridge

(1869). The red cast-iron, open railroad bridge is the only one of its type in the world. It is said to be the first bridge constructed of iron, as opposed to wood or stone. Restoration of the bridge took place in 1974, near Savage Mill (which is now filled with antiques shops and artists' studios), and there is a nice little park and hiking trails around the bridge. The bridge is off US 1, at Savage, near Savage Mill. Call(410) 792-2820 or (800) 788-MILL for more information.

Should you decide you'd like to make your own wine, talk with the people at *Tin Lizzie Wineworks* in Clarksville. Located on 157 acres of pristine farmland, head winemaker David Zuchero and others will provide everything you need from professional equipment to a wide selection of wine grapes to a highly trained winemaking staff. Among the options is a premium package with your choice of local and California grapes through the process with a custom personalized label on your bottles for about $10 a bottle. The ultra premium package has a few more bells and whistles (not literally) and runs about $20 a bottle. A full barrel produces about 21 cases while a quarter barrel produces about five cases. Or, you can join the wine-maker's club and make as little as a single case of wine. If you're the kind of person who likes to watch paint dry or grass grow, check the Winecam set up on the Web site and you can watch wine age inside the barrels. Located at 13240 Greenberry Lane; call (301) 318-9954 or (410) 212-3018 or visit www .tinlizziewineworks.com.

Howard County is home to a few farms that are open for pick-your-own fruits and vegetables and lots of family fun. Thousands of children ventured through the *Enchanted Forest* between 1955 and the late 1980s. It was a magical world that delighted (and enchanted) the imagination. Although there were several attempts to revive the Forest, there was no way to compete with today's theme parks or rising real estate values. Fortunately Mary Clark at *Elioak Farm* obtained the very large orange Cinderella pumpkin coach from the Enchanted Forest and displayed it on her farm so a younger generation could be enchanted, as well. That led to an agreement with Kimco Realty, the Enchanted Forest Shopping Center owners, who said Elioak could remove other items, too. In 2005 they moved Mother Goose and her gosling, the black duck, the six mice that pulled Cinderella's pumpkin coach, papa bear, the giant mushrooms, the bell-shaped flowers, two giant lollipops, a number of gingerbread men, a large candy cane, the little red schoolhouse, the crooked house and the crooked man, and more. Additional items were displayed in 2006. The farm staff and volunteers have spent hours and more than a few dollars restoring these treasured items. There's also a petting farm ($4), hayrides ($2), pony rides ($2), and

Jousting in Maryland

The state sport is *jousting,* the oldest equestrian sport in the world, with men and women competing. Like other sports and competitions, jousting originated as a test of a man's occupational skills. In Maryland, the challenge in jousting is not to toss a man off his horse, but to spear a series of metal rings while riding on a horse.

The 80-yard course has three arches from which rings are suspended; in each round, the size of the rings decreases. These are not huge rings to begin with: The largest ring is 1¾ inches in diameter and the smallest is ¼ inch.

Numerous jousting tournaments are scheduled throughout the year (see pages 38–40). The schedule usually starts in April and continues through to the Maryland State Championship and the Nationals in October. Events may take place in Hagerstown, Frederick, St. Mary's City, Annapolis, Denton, Trappe, Port Republic, Lily Pons, Clear Spring, Chestertown, and Havre de Grace. Each tournament has its pageantry and fun, its food, and its partying. Usually there is an admission charge, which often is used to benefit a charitable organization. Call (410) 795-5067 or visit http://marylandjousting.com for further information.

a Halloween pumpkin patch on the 540-acre farm that's been in operation since 1797. Located at 10500 Clarksville Pike, Ellicott City; call (410) 730-4049 or visit www.clarklandfarm.com.

Larriland Farms has a pick-your-own season starting in late May through the first Sunday in November. The market is in a 128-year-old post-and-beam barn. Larriland Farms, owned and operated by the Moore family, also offers hayrides, evening campfires, and other programs that let city folk enjoy the pleasures of rural life. Farm operating hours vary by season, so call or check the Web site for details. Located at 2415 Woodbine Rd., Woodbine; call (410) 442-2605 or visit www.pickyourown.com.

Toby's Dinner Theatre of Columbia celebrates the creative genius of Toby Orenstein and her dedication to fine theatrical productions. All the time she is working to entertain you, she is working to teach her "kids" the hows and whys of show business so they can go on to professional careers in entertainment if they wish. The productions may be an outstanding Broadway show from years gone by, such as *Funny Girl* or *Singin' in the Rain,* or an entirely new attraction, such as a musical version of *It's a Wonderful Life,* which was created at Toby's and offered during the 1989 holiday season. Other selections have included *The Pirates of Penzance, Sunday in the Park with George,* and *Ain't Misbehavin'.* In other words, it's good family entertainment. The most interesting aspect of Toby's is the theater, which has performances in the round. You are never far from the action.

Dinner at Toby's is an all-you-can-eat buffet that features prime roast beef, steamed shrimp, fresh salad and vegetables, and a dessert table. It's located at 5900 Symphony Woods Rd. in Columbia; call (410) 730-8311, (301) 596-6161, or (800) 88-TOBYS; or visit them on the Web at www.tobysdinnertheatre.com.

Places to Eat in Central Maryland

ABERDEEN

New Ideal Diner
104 South Philadelphia Blvd.
(410) 272-1880

ANNAPOLIS

Carpaccio Tuscan Kitchen
1 Park Place, Suite 10
(410) 268-6569
www.carpacciotuscan
kitchen.com

Chop House Restaurant
1915 Towne Centre Blvd.
Suite 250
(410) 224-4344
www.thechophouse
restaurant.com

Chick and Ruth's
165 Main St.
(410) 269-6737
www.chickandruths.com

49 West
49 West St.
(410) 626-9796
www.49westcoffeehouse
.com

Hell Point Seafood
12 Dock St.
(410) 990-9888

Ports of Call
210 Holiday Court
(410) 573-1350
www.portsofcallannapolis
.com

Stoney River Legendary Steaks
2190 Annapolis Mall
(410) 224-8312
www.stoneyriver.com

BALTIMORE

B&O American Brasserie
2 North Charles St.
(443) 692-6172
www.bandorestaurant.com

Brewer's Art
1106 North Charles St.
(410) 547-6925
www.thebrewersart.com

Cafe Hon
1002 West 36th St.
(Hampden)
(410) 243-1230
www.cafehon.com

Corks
1026 South Charles St.
(410) 752-3810
www.corksrestaurant.com

Hampton's Restaurant
Harbor Court Hotel
550 Light St.
(410) 234-0550
www.harborcourt.com

Henninger's Tavern
1812 Bank St.
(410) 342-2172
www.henningerstavern
.com

Obrycki's Crab House
1727 East Pratt St.
(410) 732-6399
www.obryckis.com

Royal Kosher Restaurant
7002 Reisterstown Rd.
(410) 484-3544
www.royalkosherrestaurant
.com

Roy's Restaurant
720 B Aliceanna St.
(410) 659-0099
www.roysrestaurants.com

Ruth's Chris Steak House
600 Water St.
(410) 783-0033
www.ruthschris.com

Sabatino's
901 Fawn St.
(410) 727-9414
www.sabatinos.com

Velleggia's Italian Seafood Restaurant
110 Water St.
(410) 986-4445
www.velleggiasitalian
seafood.com

BEL AIR

Manny's Family Restaurant
1433 Rock Spring Shopping Center
(410) 879-6976
www.mannysrestaurant.com

COLUMBIA

Kings Contrivance
10150 Shaker Dr.
(410) 995-0500
http://greatfoodmd.com

Strapazza
8775 Centre Park Dr.
(410) 997-6144
www.strapazza.com

EDGEWOOD

Giovanni's Restaurant
2101 Pulaski Hwy.
(410) 676-8100
www.giovannis-rest.com

ELLICOTT CITY

Crab Shanty
3410 Plum Tree Dr.
(410) 465-9660
www.crabshanty.com

Kelsey's
8480 Baltimore National Pike
(410) 418-9076
www.kelseysrestaurant.com

Tersiguel's French Country Restaurant
8293 Main St.
(410) 465-4004
www.tersiguels.com

ESSEX

Mr. Bill's Terrace Inn
200 Eastern Blvd.
(410) 687-5994

HAMPSTEAD

Greenmount Station Restaurant & Lounge
1631 North Main St.
(410) 239-0063
www.greenmountstation.com

HANOVER

Golden Corral
7047 Arundel Mills Blvd.
(other locations)
(410) 799-0959
www.goldencorral.com

Remomo
Inside Arundel Mills Mall
(410) 579-6666
http://remomo.com

Timbuktu
1726 Dorsey Rd.
(410) 796-0733
www.timbukturestaurant.com

HAVRE DE GRACE

Aquatica
601 Concord St.
(410) 939-7686

MacGregor's
331 St. John St.
(410) 939-3003
www.macgregorsrestaurant.com

Price's
654 Water St.
(410) 939-2782
www.pricesseafood.com

Tidewater Grille
300 Franklin St.
(410) 575-7045
www.thetidewatergrille.com

ODENTON

Bangkok Kitchen
1696 Annapolis Rd.
(410) 674-6812
www.bkkitchen.com

PERRY HALL

DeSantis Gourmet Pizza Grill & Bar
9638 Belair Rd.
(410) 256-2770

SPARKS

The Milton Inn
14833 York Rd.
(410) 771-4366
www.miltoninn.com

TOWSON

Stoney River Legendary Steaks
Towson Town Center, Suite 1157
(410) 583-5250
www.stoneyriver.com

Strapazza
12 West Alleghany Ave.
(410) 296-5577
www.strapazza.com

WESTMINSTER

Hoffman's Ice Cream & Deli
934 Washington Rd.
(410) 857-0824
www.hoffmansicecream.com

Maggie's
310 East Green St.
(410) 848-1441
(877) 816-1900
www.maggieswestminster
.com

Places to Stay in Central Maryland

ANNAPOLIS

Doubletree
210 Holiday Court
(410) 224-3150
www.doubletree.com

Inn at 30 Maryland Bed and Breakfast
30 Maryland Ave.
(410) 263-9797
www.30maryland.com

Loews Annapolis Hotel
126 West St.
(410) 263-7777
(800) 526-2593
www.loewsannapolis.com

BALTIMORE

Admiral Fell Inn
888 South Broadway
(410) 522-7380
(800) 344-8404
www.admiralfell.com

Baltimore Monaco
2 North Charles St.
(443) 692-6170
(888) 752-2636
www.monaco-baltimore
.com

Brookshire Suites
120 East Lombard St.
(410) 625-1300
800-344-8404
www.harbormagic.com

Celie's Waterfront B&B
1714 Thames St.
(410) 522-2323
(800) 432-0184
www.celieswaterfront.com

Harbor Court Hotel
550 Light St.
(410) 234-0550
(800) 824-0076
www.harborcourt.com

Marriott Inner Harbor
110 South Eutaw St.
(410) 962-0202
www.marriott.com

Pier 5 Hotel
711 Eastern Ave.
(410) 539-2000
(800) 344-8404
www.harbormagic.com

Radisson Plaza Lord Baltimore
20 West Baltimore St.
(410) 539-8400
(800) 395-7046
www.radisson.com/
lordbaltimore

Tremont Grand Hotel
222 Saint Paul St.
(800) TREMONT
www.tremontgrand.com

ELLICOTT CITY

Turf Valley Resort
2700 Turf Valley Rd.
(410) 465-1500
www.turfvalley.com

HANOVER

Hilton Garden Inn
7491-A New Ridge Rd.
(410) 878-7200
www.hilton.com

LINTHICUM

Sheraton BWI Airport Hotel
1010 Old Elkridge Landing Rd.
(443) 577-2100
www.sheraton.com

Westin Baltimore Washington Airport
1012 Old Elkridge Landing Rd.
(443) 577-2300
www.westin.com

SYKESVILLE

Inn at Norwood
7514 Norwood
(410) 549-7868
www.innatnorwood.com

TANEYTOWN

Antrim 1844 Country Inn
30 Trevanion Rd.
(410) 756-6812
(800) 858-1844
www.antrim1844.com

WOODBINE

Ramblin' Pines RV Park & Campground
801 Hoods Mill Rd.
(410) 785-5161
(800) 550-8733
www.ramblinpines.com

African Art Museum of Maryland
Columbia
(410) 730-7106
www.africanartmuseum.org

American Visionary Art Museum
Baltimore
(410) 244-1900
www.avam.org

B&O Railroad Museum
Baltimore
(410) 727-2490
www.borail.org

Babe Ruth Birthplace and Orioles Museum
Baltimore
(410) 777-1539
www.baberuthmuseum.com

Baltimore Museum of Art
Baltimore
(410) 396-7100
www.artbma.org

Berger Cookies
Baltimore
(800) 398-2236
www.bergercookies.com

Boordy Vineyards
Hydes
(410) 592-5015
www.boordy.com

Cab Calloway Jazz Institute Museum
Coppin State College, Baltimore
(410) 951-3000
www.coppin.edu

Carroll Mansion
Baltimore
(410) 605-2964
www.carrollmansion.info

Centerstage
Baltimore
(410) 332-0033
www.centerstage.org

Dominic "Mimi" DiPietro Family Skating Center
Patterson Park, Baltimore
(410) 396-9392
www.pattersonpark.com/skating/skating.html

Ellicott City B&O Railroad
Station Museum
Ellicott City
(410) 461-1944
www.ecborail.org

Enoch Pratt Free Library
Baltimore
(410) 396-5430
www.epfl.net

Eubie Blake National Jazz Institute and Cultural Center
Baltimore
(410) 225-3130
www.eubieblake.org

Cylburn Arboretum
Baltimore
(410) 267-2217
www.cylburnassociation.org

Edgar Allan Poe House and Museum
Baltimore
(410) 396-7932
www.eapoe.org

Evergreen House
Baltimore
(410) 516-0341
www.jhu.edu/historichouses

Flag House and Star-Spangled Banner Museum
Baltimore
(410) 837-1793
www.flaghouse.org

Fort McHenry National Monument and Historic Shrine
2400 East Fort Ave.
(410) 962-4290
www.nps.gov/fomc

Frederick Douglass Museum and Cultural Center "Twin Oaks"
3200 Wayman Ave.
Highland Beach
(410) 267-6960
http://highlandbeachmd.org

Hammond-Harwood House
Annapolis
(410) 263-4683
www.hammondharwoodhouse.org

Irish Shrine & Railroad Museum
Baltimore
(410) 669-8154
www.irishshrine.org

Joseph Myerhoff Symphony Hall
Baltimore
(410) 783-8000
(800) 442-1198
www.baltimoresymphony.org

Jug Bay Wetlands Sanctuary
Lothian
(410) 741-9330
www.baygateways.net

Lacrosse Museum/National Hall of Fame
Baltimore
(410) 235-6882
www.lacrosse.org

Ladew Topiary Gardens
Monkton
(410) 557-9466
www.ladewgardens.com

Lexington Market
Baltimore
(410) 685-6169
www.lexingtonmarket.com

M&T Bank Stadium
Baltimore
(410) 547-8100
www.baltimoreravens.com

Maryland Science Center
Baltimore
(410) 586-5225
www.mdsci.org

Maryland State House
Annapolis
(410) 974-3400
(800) 235-4045
www.msa.md.gov/msa/mdstatehouse/
html/home.html

Maryland Zoo in Baltimore
Baltimore
(410) 396-7102
www.baltimorezoo.org

Morris Meadows Historical Museum
Freeland
(800) 643-7056
www.morrismeadows.us/museum.htm

National Aquarium
Baltimore
(410) 576-3800
www.aqua.org

(continued on next page)

OTHER ATTRACTIONS WORTH SEEING IN CENTRAL MARYLAND (CONT.)

National Cryptologic Museum
Fort Meade
(301) 688-5849
www.nsa.gov

National Great Blacks in Wax Museum
Baltimore
(410) 563-3404
www.greatblacksinwax.org

National Museum of Dentistry
Baltimore
(410) 706-0600
www.dentalmuseum.org

Peabody Conservatory of Music
Baltimore
(410) 659-8100
www.peabody.jhu.edu

Port Discovery
Baltimore
(410) 727-8120
www.portdiscovery.org

Pride of Baltimore II
Baltimore
(410) 539-1151
www.pride2.org

Sherwood Gardens
Baltimore
(410) 786-0444
www.guilfordnews.com/sherwood

Steppingstone Museum
Havre de Grace
(888) 419-1762
www.steppingstonemuseum.org

Storyville
Rosedale Library, Baltimore
(410) 887-0512, ext. 149
www.bcplstoryville.org

Sykesville Gate House Museum of History
Sykesville
(410) 549-5150
www.sykesville.net/gatehouse.html

Thurgood Marshall Memorial
Lawyer's Mall, Annapolis
(410) 585-0070
www.mdarchives.state.md.us

Ukazoo Books
Towson
(410) 832-BOOK
www.ukazoo.com

Union Mills Homestead and Grist Mill
Westminster
(410) 848-2288
www.unionmills.org

Urology Museum
Linthicum
(410) 689-3785
www.urologichistory.museum

Walters Art Museum
Baltimore
(410) 547-9000, ext. 337
www.thewalters.org

Wheels Skating Center
Odenton
(410) 674-9661
www.wheelsrsc.com

William Paca House and Garden
Annapolis
(410) 267-7619
www.annapolis.org

CAPITAL REGION

→

Prince George's, Montgomery, and Frederick Counties make up the Greater Washington area. Washington, D.C. is at the center of a huge suburban megalopolis formed by the blending of these three counties and northern Virginia. Although some areas are densely populated with seemingly miles upon miles of row or town houses, you can also find miles and miles of parkland, green spaces, and farm lands. Because so many people who live here come from other places, such as places where it never snows, traffic seems to get jammed as soon as the TV and radio weather forecasters think about snow. Forget about what happens when it actually does snow. If you should be here when it snows, tune in to a radio or TV station, and go for public transportation. Or find a nice fireplace and cuddle up with a good book.

As a native of this area, I have enjoyed visitors from all over the world who want to tour Washington. I take them to the subway station, and the Metro Rail takes them downtown to the many Smithsonian buildings, galleries, the zoo, or anything else they want to see. The Washington Metro is as clean and safe as any subway system around and at last count was the second busiest subway in the country.

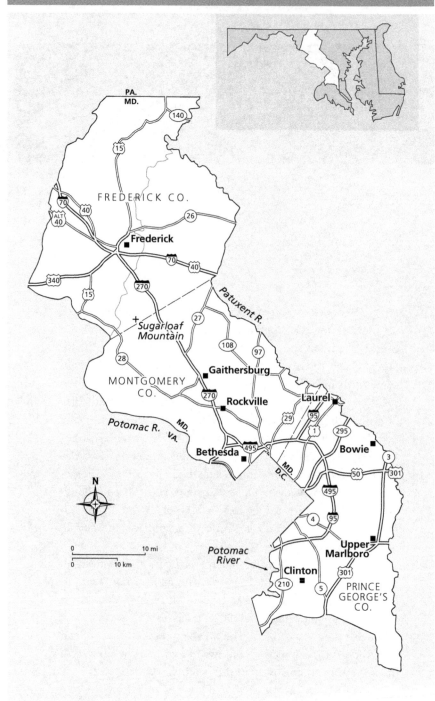

Metro lines are designated by color and by final destination. So, the Orange line has one terminus at New Carrollton, in Maryland, and Vienna/Fairfax-GMU is the other terminus, in Virginia. Check the map at www.wmata.com/rail/maps/map.cfm. If you catch an Orange line train at New Carrollton or some other station between there and your destination (say, Smithsonian), then you want to look for an Orange line train with a New Carrollton destination when you return. Complicating that a little bit is the fact that the Orange and Blue lines both stop at some stations. If you're boarding at Stadium-Armory to go to Capital South, you can ride either the Blue or Orange line train.

trackthe
escaperoute

In the spring and the fall, the Mary Surratt Society sponsors a "Booth's Trail" tour that follows the path of John Wilkes Booth from Ford's Theatre in Washington, D.C., to Dr. Mudd's home, to the Garrett Farm in northern Virginia. These fascinating tours fill up quickly, and reservations are essential. Call (301) 868-1121 for tour dates and information.

Three lines run in Prince George's County: the Green, the Orange, and the Blue. Green line stations are at Greenbelt, College Park, Prince George's Plaza, West Hyattsville, Branch Ave., Suitland, and Naylor Rd.; Orange line stations are at New Carrollton, Landover, and Cheverly; and Blue line stations are at Addison Rd., Capitol Heights, Morgan Blvd, and Largo Town Center.

In Montgomery County, the Red line runs somewhat parallel to itself, with one terminus at Glenmont and the other one at Shady Grove. The middle of the Red line is Metro Center. The Shady Grove line has stations at Shady Grove, Rockville, Twinbrook, White Flint, Grosvenor, Medical Center, Bethesda, and Friendship Heights going in toward Washington. The Glenmont line has stations at Takoma Park, Silver Spring, Forest Glen, Wheaton, and Glenmont. In both the Prince George's and Montgomery station listings, those

AUTHOR'S FAVORITES CAPITAL REGION

College Park Aviation Museum

Mount Olivet Cemetery

Patuxent Research Refuge

Roddy Road Covered Bridge

U.S. Department of Agriculture Research Center

White's Ferry

are the stations within each county, not all of the stations on each line as they enter Washington, D.C.

Basically, trains run Mon through Thurs from 5 a.m. to midnight and until 3 a.m. on Fri night. On Sat and Sun, the stations open at 7 a.m. However, the last train may depart the station before it is officially closed. Operating hours are extended for such things as the fireworks on the Mall or the Marine Marathon. In other words, check the Web site, www.wmata.com for current schedules.

One more thought about taking Metro downtown for sightseeing. What appears to be the "best" station isn't always so. If you're going to the National Gallery of Art, you probably will do better going to the Archives-Navy Memorial-Penn Quarter station than going to the Smithsonian station. Additionally, some entrances are closed on weekends, so you want to know where you're going when you're going. Once you do this, Metro is a piece of cake. Just don't eat or drink while you're in the stations or on the trains.

Trains run about every five to fifteen minutes, depending on the time of day. Fares are based on time and distance, with rush hour costing more than off-peak times. The minimum fare is $1.65 and the maximum fare is $4.50 (except for seniors, disabled, etc.). Up to two children, four years and younger may ride free with each adult paying full fare. A one-day pass, good for unlimited rides from 9:30 a.m. (weekdays) or all day (weekends) until closing, is $7.80. For a bicycle permit, call (202) 962-1116. For general information about Metro Rail and Metro Bus (such as how to get from your door to your destination), call (202) 637-7000. This number is operational weekdays from 6 a.m. to 10:30 p.m. and weekends from 8 a.m. to 10:30 p.m. You must have a SmarTrip card to exit a Metro parking facility. Be sure to buy one before you exit the station. Visit www.wmata.com for additional information.

At the junction of the Beltway (Interstates 95 and 495) and John Hanson Hwy. (U.S. Hwy 50) is the New Carrollton Metro station, a MARC and AMTRAK railroad station, a first in intermodal transportation stops.

Public art can be found at many Metro stations thanks to the MetroArts program. In Montgomery County, stop at the Glenmont station to see Deirdre Saunder's glass mosaic frieze *Swallows and Stars* (2001) and the Wheaton station to see Marcia F. Billig's bronze sculpture *The Commute* (1994). Sally Calmer's *Penguins Rush Hour*, which should be on display at the Silver Spring station, is in storage during construction. See more details in the Silver Spring section. Prince George's County Metro stations include art by Heidi Lippman with Ben Van Dusen, who created the glass and stone mosaic frieze *Dawn and Dusk* (1999) at the New Carrollton station; Ray King, who made the stainless steel and glass sculpture *Largo Beacon* (2004) at the Largo Town Center

Station; Athena Tacha, who fashioned the sculpture *Stop & Go For Garrett A. Morgan* (2004) at the Morgan Blvd station; George Peters and Melanie Walker, who did the neon wall sculpture *Light Wheel* (2004); and Clark Weigman, whose painted metal and glass sculpture *Departure* (2004) is at the Branch Ave. station. Oh, by the way, Garrett Morgan is credited with inventing a type of traffic signal.

Prince George's County

People hear more about Prince George's County in the news than they realize. Marriages are performed on the old wooden roller coaster at the Six Flags theme park outside Kettering; space flight information is reported from the Goddard Space Flight Center (and Museum) in Greenbelt, the hub of all NASA tracking activities; the Washington Redskins football team plays at Fedex Field in Largo; and the president or a visiting dignitary arrives at Andrews Air Force Base, the home base for Air Force One.

The **Suitland Bog,** which technically is a fen, is home to some interesting and rare plants (twenty species are on Maryland's rare, threatened, or endangered list), and such carnivorous plants as the spatulate-leaved sundew and the Northern pitcher plant. The Suitland Bog is the last undisturbed Maryland coastal plain bog in Prince George's County. A short, winding wooden boardwalk cuts a shaded path through the area, and signs are placed by the rarer plants. Call the Clearwater Nature Center for a guided tour reservation from May to Sept. Located at 14955 Pennsylvania Ave., Upper Marlboro; call (301) 627-7755 or visit www.pgparks.com.

Upper Marlboro is the county seat for Prince George's. Understanding that Prince George's County was and still is an agrarian county, you will appreciate the work of W. Henry DuVall. A lifelong Prince Georgean, DuVall had the foresight to save tools from the nineteenth century, whether it was a scythe, can opener, carpenter's plane, or foot-operated dental drill. This was the beginning of the **DuVall Tool Museum.** There is even a white building

this party is out of this world

Yuri Gagarin, the first man in space, is honored each year around the world by more than 200 Yuri's Night parties. Started in 2000, the parties, generally held the first week of April, may have space cocktails, a space wedding, or a visit from a Lunar Rover. Starting in 2008, NASA Goddard was the location of the DC area party. To don your favorite space outfit or become your favorite space character and join others who do likewise, check http://dc.yurisnight.net.

livedanddied forthesky

Andrews Air Force Base was named Andrews Field (formerly Camp Springs Army Base) on March 31, 1945, in memory of Lt. Gen. Frank Maxwell Andrews. During the early stages of World War II, Andrews was the Commander of all Air Forces in Europe, serving with Gen. Dwight D. Eisenhower. An outspoken proponent of air power, Andrews was born on February 3, 1884, in Nashville, Tennessee. He was killed in an aircraft accident in Iceland on May 3, 1943, and buried in Section 3 of Arlington National Cemetery.

block that is blackened on one side, which apparently was obtained during a nineteenth-century architectural revision of the White House. The dark stains are said to be soot from the burning of the building during the War of 1812. DuVall's collection, which he started in the 1930s, had more than 1,200 items by the time he died in 1979.

The Maryland–National Capital Park and Planning Commission bought the agglomeration so that it would not be lost to the twentieth or twenty-first century. More tools are accepted, so if you have something tucked away in your attic or out in the garage—particularly if it is unique to southern Maryland history—donate it here instead of to the dump. You can return to yesteryear by visiting the museum, located in the Patuxent River Park, Sun from 1 to 4 p.m. and by appointment. It's located at 16000 Croom Airport Rd., Upper Marlboro; call (301) 627-6074 or visit www.pgparks.com/places/historic/duvall.

Just south of Upper Marlboro is the old-turned-to-new **Prince George's Equestrian Center and Show Place Arena** that was formerly Marlborough Race Course where thoroughbred races were held from Colonial days until the 1990s. Among the events scheduled here annually are the county fair, concerts,

crainhighway

State Rte 3, running between U.S. Hwy. 50 and the Potomac River, is also known as Crain Highway, named after Robert Crain, a Charles County farmer and lawyer who persuaded the state to fund a highway so farmers could transport their crops from southern Maryland to northern cities. The highway had its official opening ceremonies in October 1927, with 20,000 people in attendance.

and other special events. In a tribute to yesteryear, the water tower has a scene of thoroughbreds grazing in the countryside. Located at 14900 Pennsylvania Ave.; call (301) 952-7900 or visit www.showplacearena.com.

Northwest of Largo is Bladensburg and the **Dueling Creek Natural Area,** known in long-ago days as "The Dark and Bloody Grounds" because of the more than four dozen duels held there during the first half of the nineteenth century. Offended gentlemen and politicians faced each other at ten paces with pistols and muskets. As noted on the historical marker placed by the Maryland–National Capital Park and Planning Commission, one of the most famous was that between Commodores Stephen Decatur and James Barron, which was settled here on March 22, 1820. Commodore Decatur, who had gained fame as the conqueror of the Barbary pirates, was fatally wounded by his antagonist. Although Congress passed an antidueling law in 1839, duels continued here until just before the Civil War. Now the 60-acre park is home to water-based mammals, birds, amphibians, and, of course, human visitors. The staff at the *Mount Rainier Nature/Recreation Center* should be able to answer your questions, be they historical or nature-based. Located at 4701 31st Place, Mt. Rainier; call (301) 927-2163 or visit www .pgparks.com.

bunchofhotair

On June 17, 1784, the first documented unmanned balloon flight in the United States took place in a field near the town of Bladensburg. Peter Carnes, the balloon owner, sent the manned balloon aloft a week later in Baltimore.

Clements Pastry Shop, a Washington, D.C. institution since 1928, still lives. Really. That's sure to be a delight for dessert lovers far and wide. Started by Italian-born and classically trained pastry chef Clement Maggia and his brother Theo, Clements developed a steady and loyal following, including Presidents Eisenhower and Truman, Tony Curtis, and Kate Smith. Those customers followed the aromas from the original location to a storefront on 13th Street in 1957 and then again to G Street in 1965. It moved one more time, to this Hyattsville location, in 2000. Now operated by Richard, Matthew, and John Barrazotto, you can feast on the cakes, similar to the one made for Lynda Bird Johnson's wedding, or your fondest memory cake. There is no storefront through which you can amble, but you can call in your order (with two days' notice and a credit card), see the products online, or ask your bakery to order for you. And, if you remember an old-time favorite (ours is the mocha rum cake, not the Italian rum), you can ask if they'll make it for you. According to Mary Jo Barrazotto, mother of the three men mentioned above, the chocolate truffle or strawberry short cake (yellow cake with whipped cream and strawberries in the middle and whipped cream and strawberries on top) are tied for favorites. The shop is at 3355-B 52nd Ave., Hyattsville; call (301) 277-6300 or visit www.clementspastry.com.

Lake Artemesia, in Berwyn Heights, not far from Greenbelt, has a 2.2 mile loop birding trail dedicated to Luther Goldman, a county resident who was a wildlife biologist, avid birder, and the first official photographer for the U.S. Fish and Wildlife Service. The trail loops the 38-acre lake and connects with the Calvert Road Park and the College Park Airport and Aviation

TOP ANNUAL EVENTS IN THE CAPITAL REGION

JANUARY

Winter/Spring Display: Spring Has Sprung
Wheaton
(301) 949-8230

MARCH

Maple Syrup Demonstration and Mountain Heritage Festival
Thurmont
(301) 271-7574
www.dnr.state.md.us

APRIL

John Wilkes Booth Escape Route Tour
(also runs in Sept)
Clinton
(301) 868-1121
www.surratt.org

MAY

Andrews Air Force Base Open House
Camp Springs
(301) 568-5995

Colesville Strawberry Festival
Colesville
(301) 607-8770

Mayfest
Frederick
(301) 698-8188
www.downtownfrederick.org

JUNE

Montpelier Summer Concert Series
Laurel
(301) 776-2805

AUGUST

Dog Days of Summer
Frederick
(301) 698-8118
www.downtownfrederick.org

SEPTEMBER

Great Frederick Fair
Frederick
(301) 663-5895
www.thegreatfrederickfair.com

Museum. The park is open daily from sunrise to sunset. Located at 8200 55th Ave., Berwyn Heights; call (301) 927-2163 or visit www.pgparks.com/places/nature/artemesia.htm.

The city of Bowie has several museums that let you explore the history of the area, and even some more modern electronic history. The ***Belair Mansion,*** circa 1745, is a five-part Georgian plantation house that was home to Samuel Ogle, provincial governor of Maryland. For several years it belonged to William Woodward, a noted horseman, and it was after his death in 1955 that suburban developer William Levitt bought the property and started building his Maryland version of a "Levittown." Objects on view range from paintings by Philippe Mercier (1689–1760) to a bronze statue of 1932's Triple Crown winner Gallant Fox, who spent his yearling season at the Belair Stables. Open Wed

**John Wilkes Booth Escape
Route Tour**
(also runs in April)
Clinton
(301) 868-1121
www.surratt.org

OCTOBER

Butler's Orchard Pumpkin Festival
Germantown
(301) 972-3299

**F. Scott Fitzgerald Literary
Conference**
Rockville
(301) 309-9461
www.montgomerycollege.edu/
potomacreview/fscott

Taste of Bethesda
Bethesda
(301) 215-6660
www.bethesda.org

NOVEMBER

**Gaithersburg Railroad and
Transportation Show**
Gaithersburg
(703) 536-2954
www.gserr.com

Garden of Lights
Wheaton
(301) 962-1453
www.brooksidegardens.org

Veteran's Day Parade
Frederick
(301) 600-4023
www.fredericktourism.org

DECEMBER

**Candlelight Tour of Historic Houses
of Worship**
Frederick
(301) 600-4047
(800) 999-3613
www.fredericktourism.org/calendar/
index/2

through Sun from noon to 4 p.m. and for groups of ten or more by appointment. It's located at 12207 Tulip Grove Dr., Bowie; call (301) 809-3088 or visit www.cityofbowie.org/comserv/museums.htm.

Also spending their yearling seasons at the Belair Stables were Nashua, the Horse of the Year in 1955, and Omaha, Gallant Fox's son. It's said that the first thoroughbred horse, Selima, was stabled on the Belair Farm, making her the mother of all American Thoroughbred stock today. Until its closing in 1957, Belair was the oldest continually operating horse farm in the United States. Learn this and more at the **Belair Stables Museum,** open Wed through Sun noon to 4 p.m., 2835 Belair Dr., Bowie; (301) 809-3089; www.cityofbowie.org/museum.

Genealogists will want to stop by the **Prince George's Genealogical Library** with its 5,500 volumes, periodicals, surname files, family group

Reading Is Fun-damental

Special library collections abound in Prince George's County. As the Belair Estate in Bowie claimed to be the "Cradle of American Racing," it seems entirely appropriate that the Bowie Library has the Selima Room, with its extensive collection of horse-racing records and materials. Selima was one of the original mares who started the bloodline that flows in almost every racehorse in this country. Other special collections in the Prince George's County library system include the Tugwell Room in the Greenbelt Library, and the Sojourner Truth Room in the Oxon Hill branch.

sheets, Bible records, and microfilms. The library is open every Wed from 10 a.m. to 7 p.m., except the first Wed of the month when it's open only until 1 p.m. It's also open by appointment on the last Sat of the month. Located at 12219 Tulip Grove Dr.; call (301) 262-2063 or visit www.rootsweb.ancestry .com/~mdpgcgs/library/index.htm.

The ***Bowie Railroad Station and Huntington Museum*** in "Old" Bowie is housed in buildings constructed in the early 1900s. This is the place to learn about railroading in this area, and watch today's trains zoom past on their way to New York, Boston, Washington, and points south. Check out the old photographs and equipment from Bowie's bygone railroading days. The station is open Tues through Sun 10 a.m. to 4 p.m. at 8614 Chestnut Ave.; call (301) 809-3089 or visit www.cityofbowie.org.

There's no historical reason that the ***Radio and Television Museum*** is located in Bowie; it's just that the Radio History Society needed space, and Bowie had it in the form of a home originally built around 1906, then rebuilt in the mid-1980s after a fire. Inside the two-story structure are perhaps hundreds of pieces of radio and television history. Everyone of a certain age (there's no need to say what age that is) will recognize something in this collection, whether it's a crystal set (didn't every Boy Scout make one?) or a cathedral-shaped radio of the '30s and '40s. The collection also includes several examples of Nipper, the RCA mascot. If you were around the D.C. area in the 1960s and 1970s, you may remember

hoofbeats heard on the bridge

The shortest covered bridge in Maryland is in Bowie. There's nothing historic about this bridge, as far as its age goes, for it was built in 1988, but its use could be unique. It's located at the Bowie Race Course, which is now an equestrian center rather than a racetrack. The bridge is used to move horses from the stables to the track for their workouts, not for people or cars.

The Joy Boys of Radio on WRC. Ed Walker, one of the Joy Boys, has donated a number of items to this collection. Willard Scott, famed NBC Today Show weather man, was the other Joy Boy. The museum is open Fri from 10 a.m. to 5 p.m. and Sat and Sun from 1 to 5 p.m. at 2608 Mitchellville Rd.; call (301) 809-3089 or visit www.radiohistory.org.

None of these museums charges an admission fee, although contributions definitely are welcome.

Take US 50 west from the Bowie area, then head north around the Beltway, and you'll come to College Park, home of the University of Maryland and near there, the **College Park Airport.** This is where the first military training in a military-owned airplane took place in October 1909. The plane was designed by Orville and Wilbur Wright. College Park claims to be the "world's oldest continually operated airport," and today it is the only operating airport within the Capital Beltway. Pilots say they get a kick out of flying from the same airfield that the Wright brothers used almost a century ago.

Budding aviators are sure to enjoy the 26,000-square-foot **College Park Aviation Museum** that opened in 1998. Tours, movies, and special events are scheduled throughout the year, including an annual AirFair in Sept. The museum is open daily from 10 a.m. to 5 p.m. except major holidays. Admission is $4 for adults, $3 for seniors, and $2 for children. Located at 1985 Corporal Frank Scott Dr. (named for the first civilian killed in an air accident), in College Park. Call (301) 864-6029 or visit www .collegeparkaviationmuseum.com for more information.

Just minutes from College Park is a planned city whose history started in the 1930s. If you think planned cities are something new, then visit **Greenbelt.** From its inception, Greenbelt had a sense of history about it. It has been

firstfemaleflight

Mrs. Ralph H. Van Deman said, "Now I know why birds sing," after becoming the first woman in America to fly as a passenger in an airplane, when she went aloft with Wilbur Wright in College Park on October 27, 1909.

chronicled, cataloged, dissected, scrutinized, and studied many times over in thorough detail. Although the town is now surrounded by town house communities for Washington commuters, you still can see the core of the town, its art deco architecture, and its attempts to retain its identity. The town was built around an inner core, allowing residents to walk everywhere they had to go on pedestrian paths so that people on foot would not have to intermingle with cars. The town was superorganized and highly democratic, and residents met to discuss everything. (In fact, at one point they met to declare a moratorium on meetings.)

For a more thorough explanation and visual interpretation, stop by the **Greenbelt Museum** on Sun between 1 and 5 p.m. There's no admission charge. The museum is located at 15 Crescent Rd., Greenbelt; call (301) 474-1936 or visit www.greenbeltmuseum.org.

Head north up Baltimore-Washington Parkway (I-295) and you'll come to the outskirts of Laurel, the **Montpelier Cultural Arts Center,** and the Montpelier Mansion. The Arts Center is noted for its visual arts, serving as a home for eighteen professional resident artists. A rather full curriculum of classes is offered at 12826 Laurel-Bowie Rd., Laurel; call (301) 953-1993 or visit www.pgparks.com.

Next door is the **Montpelier Mansion,** built in 1783 by Maj. Thomas Snowden, a significant landowner in Prince George's County. At one point the Montpelier site was about 10,000 acres of gently rolling parkland. Among the famed guests who stopped here were George and Martha Washington and Abigail Adams. William Breckinridge Long, undersecretary of state in the Franklin Roosevelt administration and U.S. ambassador to Italy from 1933 to 1936, was the twentieth-century owner, and his guests also were notable, including Presidents Roosevelt and Wilson. Long's daughter, Christine Long Wilcox, donated the house in the late 1950s to the Maryland–National Capital Park and Planning Commission. The mansion and other buildings sit on about seventy-five acres of the original estate. Many original Snowden pieces are still in the mansion, and other furnishings are period antiques. You may take a self-guided tour through almost a dozen rooms of the historic mansion Mon through Thurs from 11 a.m. to 3 p.m. Guided tours are offered on Sun at noon, 1, 2, and 3 p.m. from Mar through Nov. From Dec through Feb, guided tours are offered on Sun at 1 and 2 p.m. Admission is $3 for adults, $2 for seniors age 55 and older, and $1 for children ages 5 to 15. Located at 9650 Muirkirk Rd.; call (301) 377-7817 or visit www.pgparks.com.

And, if you wish, enjoy a lovely afternoon tea at the mansion, with a choice of teas and some delicious nibbles (finger sandwiches, cakes and pastries, buttery scones, etc.). Check the Web site for dates and reservations are required. Tea is $25 per person.

A **Pennsylvania Dutch Country Farmers Market** has been located in Burtonsville (north of Silver Spring) for years. That shopping center was scheduled for demolition so in Sept 2009, the market moved to Laurel. The much-anticipated opening brought such crowds that traffic units were called to deal with the mob. You can find unimaginably delicious baked goods (even gluten-free items), homemade candies, hand-butchered meats, salads, poultry, produce, a small restaurant, and so much more. The market is open Thurs from 9 a.m. to 6 p.m., Fri from 9 a.m. to 8 p.m., and Sat from 8 a.m. to 3 p.m. Located at 9701 Fort Meade Rd., Laurel; call (301) 421-1454 or visit www.burtonsville dutchmarket.com.

Situated on 12,841 acres, the **National Patuxent Wildlife Research Center** specializes in research on endangered species, migratory birds, and environmental contaminants. Throughout the years, the center has been involved in history-making discoveries, including the detrimental effects of DDT. Rachel Carson did most of her research here for her book *Silent Spring*. It has successfully completed a program of repopulating America's proud symbol, the bald eagle. Half-hour tram tours are given, seasonally (and weather dependent), through forest, meadows, and wetlands, on weekends from mid-Mar through mid-Nov at 11:30 a.m., 1, 2, and 3 p.m. on a first-come, first-serve basis. In the summer, tours are given on weekdays at 11:30, and 1 and 2:30 p.m. The fee is $3 for adults, $2 for seniors (55 and over), and $1 for children (12 and under). The visitor center, with information about hiking trails, a gift shop, and more, is open daily from 9 a.m. to 4:30 p.m. The trails and grounds are open daily from 8 a.m. to 4:30 p.m. except on federal holidays. Cash Lake fishing requires a current Maryland non-tidal fishing license and a seasonal Refuge Fishing Permit (free). Located at 10901 Scarlet Tanager Loop, Laurel; call (301) 497-5580 or visit www.fws.gov/northeast/patuxent/index.htm.

A little south of Laurel is Beltsville and the home of the **U.S. Department of Agriculture Research Center**, with a visitor center in the Log Lodge. Built by the Civilian Conservation Corps during the 1930s, it contains a Hall of Fame of agriculture scientists.

Approximately half of the 125 pounds of potatoes you eat each year are found in processed foods, a lot of which are instant potato flakes, developed in 1954 to use up a surplus of potatoes. Approximately 400 million pounds of potato flakes are produced each year in the United States. John F. Sullivan is honored for that invention and other works.

He's one of forty-four scientists honored for their contributions to our agricultural well-being. Herbert J. Dutton is enshrined for pioneering research

turningpoint mural

The striking 500' "Turning Point" mural on the retaining wall at the intersection of Piney Branch Rd. and New Hampshire Ave. was created by the Two County Turning Point Mural Project, through the Arts on the Block program. It used to be a graffiti canvas. The project also helped provide life skills, leadership development training, job readiness, and stipends to more than a dozen at-risk and out-of-school youngsters from Langley Park, Long Branch, and surrounding communities. The mural features the sun, moon, comets, and other heavenly bodies. Call (240) 283-1526 or visit www.artsontheblock.com for more information.

leading to the establishment of soybean oil as the predominant edible vegetable oil in the world. And James H. Tumlinson III is celebrated for his research leading to the eradication of the boll weevil from the southeastern United States.

The visitor center, in Building 186 (East), is open weekdays from 8 a.m. to 4:30 p.m. Guided tours are available by appointment. Call (301) 504-9403. The mailing address is U.S. Department of Agriculture, National Agriculture Library, Second Floor, 10301 Baltimore-Washington Blvd, Beltsville 20705. The Web site is www.barc.usda.gov. There is no admission charge.

National Harbor, the 300-acre development at the Beltway and the Potomac River and Gaylord National Resort & Convention Center started welcoming people in early 2008. A multi-use project of some kind for this property has been discussed, designed, and defeated for at least two or three decades. Finally, the Peterson Companies put everything together and it's definitely been worth the wait.

The *Gaylord National Resort and Convention Center* with 2,000 guest rooms and 470,000 square feet of meeting and conference space is the cornerstone of the development. It's the largest non-gaming meeting facility on the East Coast. Just wandering through the lobby and around the property, seeing the 18-story glass atrium and enjoying a fine steak at the signature restaurant, Old Hickory, seafood from Moon Bay Coastal Cuisine, Italian selections from the stations in the Pienza Italian Market Place, or catching the game while you catch a bite to eat at the national Pastime Sports Bar and Grill is worth a visit all by itself or themselves. Okay, plan to spend enough time for a massage or a facial at the Relache spa, or stay overnight so you can enjoy the indoor pool. The Gaylord people know how to celebrate a special event and one of the biggest celebrations is the winter holiday season. Local choirs entertain. Snow falls inside the hotel every night. The incredible ICE sculpture that takes more than a month to construct will amaze you. The 60' suspended glass Christmas tree can remind you of your own Nutcracker experience. Look around and you're sure to find unusual places to shop and other "who else but Gaylord" activities. Located at 201 Waterfront St, National Harbor; call (301) 965-2000 or visit www.gaylordnational.com.

There are several other hotels and condos in the National Harbor complex, and a couple of dozen restaurants (including Ketchup and Grace's Mandarin) and shops, seasonal farmers market, three marinas with in-the-water boat shows, fireworks, and the home of the visiting Cirque du Soleil company.

This is where Seward Johnson's "The Awakening" statue was moved to from its long-time D.C. home at the end of Hain's Point. This is where the former **National Children's Museum** will open in 2013 although they have a storefront in the meantime from which they organize regular activities. The museum is located at 112 Waterfront St, National Harbor; call (301) 686-0225 or visit www.ncm.museum.

One store at National Harbor is a first-of-its-kind, **Peeps,** where those little marshmallow delectables (to some people, anyway) and paraphernalia are sold. *Just Born,* the "parent" company, opened the 3,500 square foot store in late 2009 and you can buy Peep pillows, pens, and Peeps dressed as the Village People. Just be careful of the glowing five-foot chick surrounded by cuddly, plush Peeps. You can make your own favorite blend of Mike and Ike candies. The store is open Mon through Sat from 10 a.m. to 9 p.m. and Sun from noon to 6 p.m. It's located at 150 National Plaza, National Harbor; call (301) 749-5791 for more information. You can also catch a water taxi to Alexandria, VA, Mount Vernon, and Georgetown. Check for times because they vary by season. A mile-long walking/jogging path along the Potomac connects to the pedestrian path across the new Woodrow Wilson Bridge and to the 17 miles of pedestrian path along the Virginia side of the Potomac. Contact the National Harbor Office, 137 National Plaza, Suite 300; or visit them on the Web at www.nationalharbor.com for more information.

With all the food options at National Harbor, you may not want to think about food, but you should. Bernard Brooks and Jermaine Smith are in charge of the sweet potato pie cooking at *Henry's Soul Café* (and two Henry's Deli places in the District). Come Thanksgiving week, they will sell about 6,000 pies. Usually, they sell about 50,000 pies a year. This tradition started in 1968 when Jermaine's father, Henry Smith, opened his shop on U Street, in Washington. His combination of spices and secret ingredients made people stand up and stand in line. You can also buy stuffing and potato salad, fried fish, fried chicken, BBQ, meatloaf, and lots of other items, all cooked to order. If your family thinks you're good enough to be on Top Chef but you know better, then buy the pie preparations, assemble, sprinkle a little flour on your hands and in your hair and voila! As long as they don't see the carry-out bag from Henry's, they'll never know. Located at 5431 Indian Head Hwy., Oxon Hill; call (301) 749-6856 or visit www.henryssoulcafe.com.

Fort Washington has protected the nation's capital for more than 180 years although, fortunately, it has never been attacked and has never had to defend. Only one gun stands silent guard. Fortunately, the fort is a great place to learn about history, view Washington and the Virginia shoreline, follow hiking/biking trails and visit a playground. Talk about something being off the beaten path and yet just minutes from massive civilization. Recent renovations and restorations have uncovered a cache of archeological wonder, including bottles, cans, oyster shells, shoes, and a handmade checkerboard from the attic of the Enlisted Men's Barracks dating from 1861–1869. One Sunday a month, from Apr to Oct the park has Civil War artillery demonstrations. From Apr through Oct, the buildings are open from 9 a.m. to 5 p.m. During the rest of the year, they close at 4:30 p.m. The park grounds are open from 8 a.m. to sunset; 13551 Fort Washington Rd., Fort Washington; (301) 763-4600; www .nps.gov/fowa.

Montgomery County

Northwest of Prince George's County and north and west of Washington, D.C., Montgomery County goes from really high-density suburbia at the south end to gorgeous open country with huge landed estates and farms in the middle and then into a mixture of town house developments set in the rolling countryside nearing the foothills of the Appalachian Mountains.

Start at the D.C./Maryland border, where the unincorporated area known as Silver Spring is seeing a long-promised redevelopment. (I remember when the first department store opened out there and when the bus cost 5 cents, but you could never stand at a bus stop long enough to catch a bus, because a neighbor would drive by and give you a ride into town.)

Just blocks from the D.C./Maryland line, just off Georgia Ave., is the *Silver Spring Acorn*—it ain't what it used to be. The first Silver Spring Discovery Communications building is next to it and the little grassy area around the acorn and spring are all that remains of the area where, in 1840, Francis Preston Blair and his daughter were horseback riding and discovered the spring. Five mural panels by Mame Cohalon are mounted on the building, facing the acorn.

Old timers will tell you the acorn is located near the old Canada Dry building which now houses condos. Heroic efforts were exerted by the Silver Spring Historic Preservation Society to preserve the familiar landmark once the bottling operation had ceased in 1999. The yellow-brick building with the two-story glass block rotunda was constructed in 1946 and was one of the first steps in Silver Spring becoming a full-fledge suburb. It was designed by architect Walter Monroe Cory, who, with his partner brother, were quoted as saying "factories can be beautiful." The agreement that allowed the building to be turned into 210 (now sold out and occupied) condominiums in the building now called the "Silverton" included restoring the front façade. Find it at 1201 East West Hwy., Silver Spring.

silverspring singular

Incidentally, the area, which is not incorporated, is called Silver Spring, not "springs" as in the Florida town.

MBHS Alums

The humongous building behind the noise-barrier walls along the outer loop of the Beltway (Interstate 495) between the Colesville Rd. and University Blvd exits is Montgomery Blair High School, home to approximately 2,500 students. It has all the bells and whistles one would like in a high school that saw its first students in September 1998. Its predecessor stands at Dale Dr. and Wayne Ave. near downtown Silver Spring, maybe a mile away as the crow flies. That school opened in 1935, and I was graduated from there a few years later. Among the other students attending Blair (go Blazers!) a few years before, after, and during my time were Goldie Hawn, Ben Stein, Carl Bernstein, Sylvester Stallone, Phyllis Mudrick Cohen, and former Baltimore Orioles pitcher Steve Barber.

You never know where a Blair student will wander. On a Web site listing the contents of a home owned by the late Ruby Robins, editor and publisher of the *Ozark County Times* in Gainesville, Missouri, were copies of Blair's Silverlogue yearbooks from 1942 and 1945.

Read a George Pelacanos book and you're almost certain to read about the 1945 ***Baltimore & Ohio Railroad Station,*** just west of Georgia Ave. He even mentions the conversion from train station to museum and now you can see the station, the only building in downtown Silver Spring to be on the National Register of Historic Places list. This is the station where I caught the train to go to college and years later my daughters disembarked after their first train ride from Washington, D.C.' s Union Station. The station has been restored, after an automobile crashed into its front door in 1997 and then its owner, CSX, wanted to demolish the building. Montgomery Preservation accepted the station from CSX in 1998, complete with leaking roof, falling plaster, filthy floors and tile, and graffiti. Restoration was complete in late 2002 with advice from Robert B. Davis, the former stationmaster. A plaque is on the trackside bench commemorating his forty-two years of service. ***Class Acts Arts, Inc.,*** a Silver Spring performing arts organization (301-588-7525; www.classactsarts.org), now occupies the former baggage area and the agent/operators office. The passenger waiting room is available for rentals and will serve as a visitor center and museum as part of the planned Metropolitan Branch Hiker/Biker trail.

An open house is held at the station the first Sat of each month, from Apr through Dec. Located at 8100 Georgia Ave.; call (301) 495–4915 or visit www.montgomerypreservation.org/BOStation.html.

The underpass on Georgia Ave. and Blair Mill Rd. benefited from the Arts on the Block program that used the talents of two dozen Montgomery County high school artists to create a paint-and-mosaic mural with a "transportation" theme. Artist G. Byron Peck led the project.

Continuing out Georgia Ave., which parallels the railroad and subway tracks, you'll come to the intersection of Georgia and Colesville Rd., and the Silver Spring subway station. As of October 2009, the area is being redesigned, reconfigured, and recreated into the Silver Spring Transit Center. It will expand the existing Silver Spring facility into a large multi-modal center to accommodate Metro and MARC rail systems, local and inter-city bus and automobile traffic, and pedestrians and bikers. Retail space is included in the design concept that is expected to be complete some time in 2011.

The **Penguin Rush Hour,** a 25-panel mural, 100 feet long and eight feet high, was installed at the underpass on Colesville Rd. at the Silver Spring station. It was part of the MetroArt I arts project (see also Prince George's County). Created by Sally Callmer of Bethesda, who previously was a miniaturist, the mural was meant as a temporary installation but became such an integral part of the community that the Montgomery County Department of Transportation purchased it as a permanent fixture. The penguin even became the unofficial mascot of Silver Spring which is why you see them here and there. Somewhere in 2005 or so, the panels were removed so Callmer could restore them, with the intent of replacing them by sometime in 2007. Oops. So, the penguins will stay in storage until the transportation center is completed and then, theoretically, the penguins will return. The mural shows penguins rushing hither and thither catching the next Metro train or departing and heading home or to work. There's a newspaper here and a briefcase there.

very
underground

The Forest Glen metro station, which is nearly 200 feet below ground level, is the deepest in the system and maybe in the world. Because of its depth, it has an elevator-only exit system. The escalators in the Wheaton metro station are 508 feet long with a vertical rise of 230 feet, and the escalators are said to be the longest set of single-span escalators in the Western Hemisphere.

A new **Silver Theater** has risen on Colesville Rd. in Silver Spring, rekindling fond memories of its earlier days when it was "kool inside." It has three sections, one with 400 seats and a 70mm screen, one with 200 seats, and one with 75 seats. There is also a gallery, a cafe, concession stands, and a lobby. In addition to classic, foreign language, and art movies, there are musical performances and lectures. When the art deco–style Silver first opened in October 1938, FDR was president. Within the early years, such movies as Little Miss Broadway, Boys Town, Snow White and the Seven

Dwarfs, The Wizard of Oz, and Gone with the Wind were shown. It's now the home of the American Film Institute (AFI) and known as the AFI Silver Theatre and Cultural Center. Check the schedule for regular film showings and the Silver Docs celebration. Located at 8633 Colesville Rd. in Silver Spring; call (301) 495-6720 or visit www.afi.com.

Just off the east side of Georgia Ave., in Silver Spring, is a statue of Norman Lane (1911–1987), known as the "unofficial mayor" of Silver Spring. The bronze statue honors Lane who spent some twenty years walking the streets, doing odd jobs, taking blooms from the Bell Flowers dumpster and giving them to women, sleeping on the street or in back of nearby auto body repair shop, and just being nice to people. The statue was created by his friend, artist Fred Folsom, and was dedicated in 1991. The plaque quotes Lane's most oft-said remark, "Don't worry about it."

In 1887 a resort hotel and retreat was built in the Forest Glen area of Silver Spring. Over the years it also served as a finishing school for girls and a convalescent center for World War II soldiers. Known as the **National Park Seminary**, it has a number of exotic buildings in a variety of architectural styles. After the buildings became neglected, they became the passion for preservationists. Tours are offered, usually the fourth Sat of the month from Mar through Nov. The guided walking tours start at 1 p.m., last about 90–120 minutes and can include some slightly rough terrain. A reservation is not required although a $5 donation is suggested. Located at 2755 Cassedy St (watch out for resident parking only signs), call (301) 589-1715 or visit www .saveourseminary.org.

The **Bethesda Urban District** area has nearly 200 restaurants, from traditional to trendy, from down-home to deluxe. More than fifty sculptures and murals are tucked into little nooks and crannies or out in plain sight in the district. One of these is the **Pioneer Lady statue,** or Madonna of the Trail, symbolizing the importance of these roads even in their early days. Harry Truman dedicated the statue on April 19, 1929, in honor of the pioneer spirit and the National Pike, which connected the country from this spot on the East Coast to the town of Upland, California, on the West Coast. This was the last of twelve statues to be installed. The other statues were erected (chronologically) in Springfield, Ohio; Wheeling, West Virginia; Council Grove, Kansas; Lexington, Missouri; Lamar, Colorado; Albuquerque, New Mexico; Springerville, Arizona; Vandalia, Illinois; Richmond, Indiana; Washington, Pennsylvania; and Upland, California. The memorial (which faces east, whereas most of the other statues face west) is dedicated to the pioneer mothers of the covered-wagon days.

The engraving reads: OVER THIS HIGHWAY MARCHED THE ARMY OF MAJOR GENERAL EDWARD BRADDOCK, APRIL 14, 1755, ON ITS WAY TO FORT DUQUESNE, AND [THIS IS] THE FIRST

MILITARY ROAD IN AMERICA, BEGINNING AT ROCK CREEK AND POTOMAC RIVER, GEORGETOWN, MARYLAND, LEADING OUR PIONEERS ACROSS THE CONTINENT TO THE PACIFIC.

The *Pioneer Lady* statue is located between the post office and the Hyatt Regency Hotel at the corner of Wisconsin Ave., East-West Hwy., and Old Georgetown Rd. in Bethesda. The statue was reinstalled in 1986, after years in storage due to subway and hotel construction.

Then, perhaps like the pioneers before her, who settled and moved, moved and settled, the poor *Pioneer Lady* or Madonna of the Trail statue had another unsettling moment. In Dec 2004 she began to lean. A little forward and a little to the port. Off to storage, again, while the statue's owners, the Maryland State Society of the Daughters of the American Revolution, and other government bodies determined that a sinkhole from a water main break had caused the sudden Pisa-like appearance. She's safely back in place now. At least until the next problem comes along.

amusicand culturehaven

Wheaton, a few miles north of Silver Spring, is the twelfth Arts and Entertainment District in the state. Joining Silver Spring and Bethesda, it's the third district in Montgomery County. Wheaton is known as a hub of music and culture, with its many ethnic and family-owned restaurants and Chuck Levin's Washington Music Center. An Arts Network of seventy-plus members identifies local arts and entertainment resources and develops programs that enhance the arts base. Two reasons this designation is so valuable is that artists working in the districts can receive an income tax break and developers who create art space can be exempt from paying certain property taxes.

Although probably not connected, the **A. Mario Loiederman Middle School**, in the Silver Spring/Wheaton area, a magnet school for the performing and visual arts, is on its way to producing tomorrow's creative geniuses. They're campaigning the Board of Education and the County (and anyone else who will listen) for funds to build a black box theater and rising high school student Rockzana Flores and her sister Sabrina have suggested that the students from the Construction and Development Program at the Thomas Edison School of Technology design and build an arts space for the school.

Stretching the connection even more are two donations made to the school by Washington Wizard basketball star Gilbert Arenas who donated $2800 in 2008 (he gave $100 for each of 28 points he scored against Atlanta on Mar 7). Admittedly, he does this every year with the school principal submitting the school's name and then hope that the school is drawn from the hatful of entries. Loiederman was selected again in 2009 and received $2,100.

The school is located at 12701 Goodhill Rd., call (301) 929-2282 or visit www .montgomeryschoolsmd.org/schools/loiedermanms.

For more information about the public art, contact the Bethesda Urban Partnership and request a copy of the Discovery Trail brochure, 7700 Old Georgetown Rd., Bethesda; (301) 215-6660; www.bethesda.org.

Take Old Georgetown Rd. west out of Bethesda, just outside the Belt-way, and you can stop by the *Dennis and Phillip Ratner Museum,* a walk through the Hebrew Bible via visual arts. Phillip is a multimedia artist (sculp-ture, painting, etched glass, tapestry, drawing, and graphic arts) and native Washingtonian; his work is in the permanent collections of the Smithsonian Institution, the U.S. Supreme Court, the Library of Congress, the White House, and many other places. His cousin Dennis is the founder and chairman of the Hair Cuttery, the nation's largest privately owned salon chain with more than 800 salons internationally. He—and therefore his corporation—is heavily involved in community and cultural affairs.

The museum's collection includes examples of Phillip's sculptures, draw-ings, paintings, and graphics, and exhibits of the works of professional and student artists, from various institutions and from seminars in the museum. This facility is open Sun from 10 a.m. to 4:30 p.m. and Mon through Thurs from noon to 4 p.m. It is closed on all holidays and during the month of August. Located at 10001 Old Georgetown Rd., Bethesda; call (301) 897-1518 or visit www.ratnermuseum.com.

For years the locals knew that *Uncle Tom's Cabin,* of Harriet Beecher Stowe fame, sat behind a wall of trees on Old Georgetown Rd. in Bethesda. The 13-by-17-foot, eighteenth-century cabin was the home of Josiah Henson (1789–1883), but it was attached to a privately owned three-bedroom house sitting on an acre of land, and few people had a chance to see it. When Hilde-garde Mallet-Prevost died in 2005, at the age of one hundred, the Montgomery County Planning Board bought the home and had a deed transfer celebration on January 16, 2006. It was attended by Joseph Henson, a distant relative of Josiah's, and Greg Mallet-Prevost (Hildegard's son), a number of local elected officials and about one hundred interested bystanders—the first members of the public to see the inside of the home and cabin.

Now called the *Josiah Henson Site,* the home is opened periodically with notices on the Web site and in local papers. It's hoped that it will be opened on a regular basis by 2012. The area is part of the National Park Ser-vice National Underground Railroad Network to Freedom program. Located at 11420 Old Georgetown Rd., Bethesda; call (301) 650-4373 or visit www .montgomeryparks.org/PPSD/Cultural_Resources_Stewardship/heritage/uncle_ toms_cabin.shtm.

A local tradition was rescued from oblivion in mid-2007, when **Barry's Magic Shop,** which had been headquartered for years in Wheaton and had been taken by "eminent domain," relocated to a store near White Flint Mall. Owner Barry Taylor, with his wife Susan Kang at his side, has mentored untold future and current Houdinis and who will almost always be willing to entertain and amaze you with "just one more little trick." The new facility has a 32-seat "magic theater" where parties can be held on Sun or other days after the store is closed. The shop is open weekdays from 11 a.m. to 7 p.m. and Sat from 11 a.m. to 6 p.m, and is located at 5544 Nicholson Lane. Call (301) 933-0373 or visit www.barrysmagicshop.com for more information.

Just a half-mile outside the beltway in North Bethesda is **Strathmore,** where you can see an art exhibit, take lessons, attend concerts and performing arts programs, or just sit in a statuary garden. Eliot Pfanstiehl is the president and chief executive officer who has seen the growth from a large mansion to a facility that now includes the Gudelsky Gazebo, the Dorothy M. and Maurice C. Shapiro Music Room, the Strathmore Tea Room, the shop, the Gudelsky Concert Pavilion, and the Music Center at Strathmore. During his tenure, more than 5,000 artists have appeared. Check the Web site and sign up for notices of upcoming activities.

The complex is connected to the Grosvenor-Strathmore Metro station via an elevated pedestrian walking. It's named the Carlton R. Sickles Memorial Sky Bridge, after the late Congressman Sickles (1921–2004) who was instrumental in the creation of the D.C. Metro.

frommymouth toyourear

Yes, those of you who have been around this area a long time may remember Eliot Pfanstiehl's Dad, the late Cody Pfanstiehl, the public relations "voice" of the DC area Metro system and his late wife, Margaret Rockwell Pfanstiehl, who started the Metropolitan Washington Ear, a service that provides audio readings of newspapers, magazines, and certain theatrical productions for the visually impaired. He used to say that Washington's mouth married Washington's ear.

Strathmore is located at 5301 Tuckerman Lane, call (301) 581-5100 (ticket office), (301) 581-5108 (tea reservations), (301) 581-5200 (administration) or visit www.strathmore.org.

If you like nature or have children who have excess energy to burn (and how many children fit into that category?), be sure to visit the **Cabin John Regional Park,** part of the Maryland–National Capital Park and Planning Commission park system. (There's also Wheaton Regional, in Wheaton; Watkins Regional, in Kettering; and Cosca Regional, in Clinton.)

Cabin John covers more than 500 acres, with an ice skating rink, hiking trails, sports fields, indoor and outdoor tennis courts, picnic tables and pavilions, a nature center, and most important for the moment, an **Action Playground.** Designed by Heidi Sussman, this playground is an elaborate obstacle course covering more than a half acre of ground. There's a section for toddlers, one for preschoolers, one for older children, and places for parents to sit. (Sussman also designed the play area for Wheaton Regional Park.) Your dog is invited to the park daily from sunrise to sunset (closed every Tues from 9 to 11 a.m. for park maintenance). There's an area for large dogs and another one for smaller dogs. The dog park is at 10900 Westlake Dr., Rockville; Cabin John Regional Park is at 7700 Tuckerman Lane; (301) 299-0024; www.mncppc.org.

Many environmental problems can be caused by importing, accidentally or intentionally, foreign species of trees, plants, fish, and other beings that end up thriving around here and destroying indigenous species because the imported version has no natural enemies. **AW Landscapes Garden Center** owners concentrate on a wide selection of native and native species plants in their design build company. As they say, "A beautifully designed and constructed landscape provides greater enjoyment of your property, while increasing the value of your home." They work with master plans, hardscapes, water features, drainage corrections, and more. Of more immediate nature is the wonderful and unique garden gift shop. The garden center is open Wed through Mon from 9 a.m. to 5 p.m. It's located at 25110 Old Hundred Rd., Comus; (301) 349-2605; www.awlandscapes.com.

fitzgeralds' restingplace

F. Scott and Zelda Fitzgerald, once residents of the area, are buried in the St. Mary's Church cemetery in Rockville, located at the corner of Viers Mill Rd. and State Rte 355 (Rockville Pike); (301) 762-0096.

Northeast of Rockville is the little town with the theater that has the big reputation. The **Olney Theatre Center** opened in 1942 as a stop on the summer "straw hat" circuit, closed because of the war, and then reopened in 1946 with Helen Hayes starring in Good Housekeeping. Other luminaries who have graced its stage include Tallulah Bankhead, Gloria Swanson, and Bea Lillie. The late Reverend Gilbert Hartke, head of Catholic University's drama department, took over the management in 1953, providing exposure for his students as well as for Carol Channing, John McGiver, and Frances Sternhagen.

Also known as the State Summer Theatre of Maryland, Olney Theatre Center started a new tradition in 1989 with the annual production of *The Butterfingers Angel, Mary & Joseph, Herod the Nut,* and *The Slaughter of 12 Hit Carols in a Pear Tree,* a Christmas entertainment by noted playwright William

Gibson. The theater also is known for the elected officials it attracts, particularly on opening night, both to see the outstanding presentations and to be seen. The Victorian farmhouse (circa 1880) next door is the Actors' Residence, where housing is provided for the cast in season. Actually, two casts stay there at one time, one for the show in production and one for the show in rehearsal. On opening night post-performance festivities take place here.Located at 2001 Olney-Sandy Spring Rd., Olney; (301) 924-3400 (box office), (301) 924-4485 (administrative office); www.olneytheatre.org.

White's Ferry, well west of the Beltway, connects Maryland (near Poolesville), to Leesburg, Virginia. There used to be 100 ferries crossing the river, so White's probably is more important these days than when it began operation in 1828, for it is the only river crossing between the American Legion Bridge on the Washington (or Capital) Beltway to the south and east, and the Point of Rocks bridge to the north and west. Regular commuters and tourists can easily tell when there is a major backup on the Beltway because these back-country roads become filled with drivers escaping the jam. The ferry General Jubal Early (named for a Confederate leader) runs the 1,000-foot crossing on a cable propelled by a diesel tug in about three minutes. It's operational from 5 a.m. to 11 p.m., weather and river conditions permitting, on a demand basis. A country store selling sundries and souvenirs is open on the Maryland side spring through fall. It's located at 24801 White's Ferry Rd., Dickerson; call (301) 349-5200 for additional information.

Just up the ramp from White's Ferry landing is the ditch that was once the *Chesapeake & Ohio Canal* and is now the longest and thinnest National Historical Park in the country, narrowing to less than 50 feet at one point. There was a time when there were twenty trading posts along the 185-mile canal, which ran from Cumberland to Washington, D.C., roughly paralleling

Panning for Gold

Minute quantities of gold have been found along the Potomac River, near Great Falls, and in the Piedmont regions. If you'd like to try your hand at panning, or at least see where some gold has been mined, stop by the Chesapeake and Ohio (C&O) *Canal Park and Great Falls Tavern Museum,* near the intersection of MacArthur Blvd and Great Falls Rd. Park in the C&O Canal parking area and follow the unmarked trail to the Maryland Gold Mine, which was worked until the 1920s. No one has become rich with Maryland gold, but one can try. For more information about the history of gold finds in the state and rules and regulations about prospecting, write to the Maryland Geological Survey, 2300 St. Paul St, Baltimore 21218; or call (410) 554-5500 or visit www.mgs.md.gov.

the Potomac River. In 1988 conservationists spent three months clearing away foliage and found the 150-foot foundation of a nineteenth-century depot and the Granary. From the Civil War until 1924, canal boats headed down to Washington, D.C., where they would tie up to a three-story wooden storage building called the Granary to load up with grain from area farms. In the more than sixty years since the canal closed, the Granary and canal have been neglected and overgrown by trees and shrubbery.

Other parts of the canal are alive and thriving, although hurricanes often wreak havoc upon the waterway. About four million people visit some part of the park, with May through Oct the busiest time. The 14 miles between Georgetown (in Washington, D.C.) and Great Falls sees the most visitors, so if you're looking for solitude in your nature walks, biking, or horseback riding expeditions, aim toward the upper areas. Primitive camping areas are located approximately every 5 miles, from Swain's Lock (mile 16) to Evitts Creek (mile 180), on a first-come, first-served basis, no permits needed (except for a group area at mile 12). Each site has a chemical toilet, pump water (May to Nov), picnic table, and fire ring with cooking grill.

takefatherhurley, thenturnleft

As you travel along Interstate 270, you may see a sign for Father Hurley Blvd and wonder who he is to deserve such recognition. Actually, he's now Monsignor Leonard Hurley, founding pastor of Mother Seton Parish in Germantown, which is located on the forenamed road.

Hurley, now in his late-70s, worked with the county (or maybe they worked for him) in the 1980s on development controls and ordinances. In 1987 the county renamed Germantown Drive in his honor.

The park is open from sunrise to sunset with six visitor centers, Georgetown, Great Falls Tavern, Brunswick, Williamsport, Hancock, and Cumberland to welcome you. Mule-drawn canal boat rides are available at Georgetown and Great Falls spring through fall. Besides the canal towpath, other hiking trails at Great Falls include the Gold Mine, River, Woodland, Berma Rd., Angler's Spur, and the appropriately named Billy Goat Trail. For information contact the C&O Canal Headquarters, 16500 Shepherdstown Pike, Sharpsburg; (301) 739-4200.

Canal barge rides are available at Great Falls and in Georgetown (Washington, D.C.) from Wed through Sun from early Apr through the end of Oct. The narrated tours last about an hour and cost $5. Contact the visitor center for specific days and times; 11710 MacArthur Blvd, Potomac; (301) 767-3714; www.nps.gov/choh/planyourvisit/publicboatrides.htm

Frederick County

Abutting the northwest border of Montgomery County and going north to the Pennsylvania state line, with the Potomac River on its southern border, Frederick County is steeped in history. The county claims the largest number of Main Street Maryland communities within its borders. Main Street activities can be found in downtown Frederick, Brunswick, Middletown, Mt. Airy, and Thurmont. The Main Street designation, says Amy Seitz, director of Community Access & Partnership, tells you that you "can expect a pedestrian-friendly historic downtown with distinctive architecture, locally-owned shops and restaurants, and a sense of community."

The county also is home to the restored train depot and museum at Brunswick; the Barbara Fritchie and Roger B. Taney homes; wineries and orchards; the Catoctin Mountains (where Camp David, the presidential retreat, is located); the Grotto of Lourdes and the National Shrine of St. Elizabeth Ann Seton; the Lilypons Water Gardens; Gov. Thomas Johnson's Rose Hill Manor and Schifferstadt Architectural Museum; many churches and steeples; and, of course, that picturesque stopping point, Sugar Loaf Mountain.

A 40 foot statue, "To Lift a Nation," by sculptor Stan Watts, of Salt Lake City, Utah, was dedicated in Emittsburg on November 5, 2007 at the National Emergency Training Center. It was based on a photo taken by Thomas E. Franklin, and the statue supposedly contains rubble from the Ground Zero site. It's dedicated to the firefighters who perished on September 11, 2001. Reportedly, there was a small problem with the funding because someone was pulling a Ponzi scheme, but the deal for the statue stipulated that it has to remain at the park. As the park is on federal property, it is subject to whatever security levels are in effect at the time of your visit. Call (301) 447-1000 for current information. You will need a driver's license or photo ID at the campus entrance. The statue is located at 16825 South Seton Ave.; Emittsburg; visit www.firehero.org for more information.

Frederick, about equidistant from Washington, D.C., and Baltimore—or about an hour's drive from either city—is another of the state's designated Arts and Entertainment Districts. The city's leaders and citizens have worked hard to revitalize the downtown area,

soundspretty fishytome

The brook trout is native to the streams of Catoctin. It isn't really a trout as the name implies. Rather, according to the National Park Service, it is a charr, a close cousin to the trout in the salmon family. Brown and rainbow trout are also in the Catoctin's streams, but are not native to the eastern United States.

preserving a fine collection of Federal, Georgian, and Victorian buildings. Among the highlights is the **Weinberg Center for the Arts,** housed in a renovated 1926 movie theater. The city has museums, photography studios, and about a dozen art galleries. As mentioned elsewhere, the Arts and Entertainment District designation provides a property tax credit for developers and business owners who renovate buildings for arts-related purposes. The National Trust for Historic Preservation also has chosen Frederick as a Distinctive Destination.

Frederick is known for its *churches.* Ten, plus one synagogue, are noteworthy for their histories and architectural styles dating from the Colonial, Revolutionary, and Civil War eras. Tours are available during the year, and a brochure is available from the Frederick Visitor Center that details the history of each house of worship. A special event for all the houses of worship is the Candlelight Tour held in Dec; each is decorated for the holiday and hosts are on hand to greet visitors and answer questions. Special music and presentations are provided at various churches throughout the evening, and free parking is available. Hospitality rooms are located at a number of places, and the one at Trunk Hall in the Evangelical Lutheran Church is wheelchair accessible.

Many prominent Marylanders now reside in **Mount Olivet Cemetery,** including Francis Scott Key, Barbara Fritchie, and Gov. Thomas Johnson, along with veterans of the American Revolution, the Civil War (more than 800 Confederate soldiers), and World War II, as well as more than 30,000 other people. A statue of Key stands more than 9 feet tall on a monument that is 16 feet high and 45 feet around; you can't miss the statue because it welcomes you at the main entrance. The U.S. flag standing by him flies twenty-four hours a day in honor of his writing the words to "The Star-Spangled Banner." Much of the money collected for the $25,000 monument was donated in dimes and dollars by people all over the country.

when is a stone bridge not a stone bridge?

The **Community Bridge mural project** created the illusion of 3,000 stones, none of which are alike, a gate, a fountain, and numerous other items suggested by the community, both nearby and from afar. William M. Cochran was the primary muralist in this 2,500-square-foot trompe l'oeil, but many others helped. Pam Jaffee painted almost all of the ivy, a feat that took her almost six months to finish. The project started in February 1993 and took five years to complete. Located on South Carroll St in Frederick; call (301) 228-2888 or visit http://bridge.skyline.net.

Little green-and-white signs direct you to the graves of Governor Johnson and Barbara Fritchie, which are across the road from each other. Johnson was a Revolutionary War patriot, born in Frederick County in 1732 (the same year as George Washington), and was a prominent member of the Continental Congress. He was the first governor of the state of Maryland and associate justice of the U.S. Supreme Court. Fritchie was made immortal by John Greenleaf Whittier's poem, "The Ballad of Barbara Fritchie," about her bravery against Gen. Stonewall Jackson, when, at the age of 95, she waved the Union flag and dared soldiers to "Shoot if you must, this old gray head, but spare your country's flag." It's said that the feisty Fritchie so impressed Jackson that he ordered his troops to spare her and her home. A monument of Maryland granite with the Whittier poem on a bronze tablet was unveiled on September 9, 1914. The cemetery is considered one of the most beautiful and distinguished in this part of the country. Mount Olivet Cemetery is located at 515 South Market St; (301) 662-1164; www.mountolivetcemeteryinc.com.

onsecond thought…

Thurmont originally was called Mechanicstown because Jacob Weller, a mechanic of German descent, settled here with his family in 1751.

If you've ever heard an entire community a-twitter about something local, you can only begin to realize the excitement as two local "boys," Bryan and Mike Voltaggio, diced and sauced and wowed their ways to be among the final three contestants on season six of Bravo channel's Top Chef program. Bryan, after working through Charlie Palmer's Aureole and Charlie Palmer Steak, opened his dream restaurant, *VOLT,* in Frederick in July 2008. His younger brother, Michael is chef de cuisine at the Langham Huntington Hotel & Spa, in Pasadena, California. As young as VOLT was, it had already become difficult booking a reservation. Once the shows were broadcast and even after Bryan came in second, it was almost impossible unless you wanted to eat at 9 p.m. on a weeknight. For an extraordinary experience, book Table 21, a 21-course tasting menu for up to four guests with seating in the kitchen for $121 per person. Sat seat-ins are set for 5:30 and 8:30 p.m. and Wed through Sun seating is 7 p.m. The "boys" have set up a Web site, www.voltaggiobrothers.com so you can keep up with their activities. VOLT is located at 228 North Market St, Frederick. Call (301) 696-8658 or visit www.voltrestaurant.com.

Between Frederick and Thurmont is the old ***Catoctin Furnace.*** For 125 years Catoctin Village was a prosperous iron-making community. Started by a group of men that included the future first governor of Maryland, Thomas

Johnson, the stack went into blast in 1776 to produce pig iron, tools, and household items, including the popular ten-plate stove. Bombshells for 10-inch mortars were produced toward the end of the Revolutionary War. By the mid-eighteenth century, the owner of the furnace had eighty houses for his workers, a sawmill, gristmill, company store, farms, ore railroad, three furnace stacks (including an anthracite coal stack), and more than 11,000 acres of land. By 1903 the furnace ceased to operate, although ore was taken out of this area until 1912. Cunningham Falls State Park, (301) 271-7574. The furnace, remaining houses in Catoctin Village, and Harriet Chapel can be seen along State Rte 806, on the east side of U.S. Hwy. 15, about 12 miles north of Frederick.

Frederick County has enough winter that **covered bridges** were necessary to assure safe passage over waterways. Bridges otherwise would have become frozen, slick, and impassable. Three covered bridges remain in Frederick County. The first is **Loy's Station.** This 90-foot-long bridge, built between 1850 and 1860, crosses Owens Creek and is surrounded by a five-and-a-half-acre park. It's located on Old Frederick Rd., off State Rte 77, about 3 miles from Thurmont. Call (301) 271-1843 for more information.

Roddy Road Covered Bridge (1856), north of Thurmont off US 15, is considered the best looking of the state's remaining bridges by covered-bridge fans. It is a single span, about 40 feet long, with a 13⅔-foot roadway. It is a fine example of basic king-post truss design, though steel stringers were installed later. Surrounding the bridge, which crosses Owens Creek, is a seventy-acre natural area for picnicking and gentle afternoon outings. Call (301) 271-1843 for more information.

The **Utica Covered Bridge,** at 101 feet, is the largest of the three. Built in 1850, it was moved in 1889 and has been structurally reinforced with concrete piers and steel-beam supports. The bridge crossed the Monocacy River until a summer flood in 1889 lifted the span from its abutments and placed it down on the river several yards away. Instead of replacing the still-intact bridge on its supports, it was dismantled, moved, and reassembled over Fishing Creek at Utica Mills. The bridge is located on Utica Rd. off Old Frederick Rd., which is off US 15. For more information about the covered bridge, call (800) 999-3613 or (301) 600-4047 or visit www.fredericktourism.org.

Frederick County's fertile ground attracted many settlers, and you can still see and enjoy the fruits of many hard workers at a number of orchards.

Catoctin Mountain Orchard is known for its diversity and quality of all types of berries, soft fruits, apples, and vegetables. Cortland, Red and Golden Delicious, Stayman, York, and Ida Red apples are available in autumn. You can pick your own blackberries, black raspberries, sour and sweet cherries, and strawberries, but call ahead for picking days and hours. Catoctin Mountain Orchard also offers preserved fruit and jam, packed in appealing, reusable containers, freshly baked pies, cobblers, and turnovers.

The orchard is open 9 a.m. to 5 p.m. daily June through Jan, and Fri and Sat Jan through Mar. The orchard is on US 15, 15036 North Franklinville Rd., and the mailing address is 15036 North Franklinville Rd., Thurmont. Call (301) 271-2737 or visit www.catoctinmountainorchard.com.

Pryor's Orchard has a modern storage facility housed in a rustic barn-type market, complete with racks of antlers and an antique cider press. Pryor's seventy-three-acre orchard is one of the oldest in the Thurmont area and a favorite of local canning enthusiasts. Pryor's is noted for its many varieties of peaches, summer and fall apples, and pears. You can pick your own blueberries and sour and sweet cherries. The orchard is open from June 15 through Nov 15. Pryors Orchard has the largest eastern cottonwood tree in the state. You can see it looming over their house when you drive into the market place at 13841 B. Pryor's Rd., Thurmont; call (301) 271-2693 or visit www.pryors orchard.com.

Scenic View Orchard has a fine selection of produce, including peaches, plums, nectarines, pears, apples (and cider), melons, sweet corn, green beans, and other vegetables. It is open daily 10 a.m. to 6 p.m. July 15 through Nov 1, with some out-of-season availability. Located at 16225 Sabillasville Rd., Sabillasville; call (301) 271-2149 or visit www .scenicvieworchards.com.

pickyourown

You can buy fresh fruits and vegetables or pick your own at sixty or seventy farms and orchards in fourteen counties across the state, from Anne Arundel to Washington. Write to Marketing Resource and Development Group, Maryland Department of Agriculture, Annapolis 21401, for a copy of the current Pick Your Own and Direct Farm Markets in Maryland brochure. Or stop by a library or county extension office to pick up a copy.

Thurmont is also the gateway to *Camp David,* the Presidential retreat. It was originally called High Catoctin and was one of three camps built by the Civilian Conservation Corps during the Depression. The other two camps are Misty Mount (available for individual and group camping) and Greentop (used by the Baltimore League of the Handicapped since 1937). The camp buildings were constructed from local timber. High Catoctin was renamed Shangri La by Franklin Delano Roosevelt and then renamed Camp David by Dwight D. Eisenhower.

You can't visit Camp David, but you can stop by the *Cozy* restaurant and see the *Camp David Museum* in Thurmont. The camp's history is revealed

Footprints in the Park

Frederick County is considering constructing a park to showcase Maryland's earliest dinosaur footprints, on a two-acre lot near Emmitsburg. That's where 200-million-year-old footprints of three ancient reptiles were found, according to paleontologist Peter M. Kranz. The footprints are believed to be the tracks of atreipus, a 4-foot-long herbivore; coelophysis, a carnivore that was a little larger than the atreipus; and a prosauropod, a vegetarian that was an ancestor of the brontosaurus and the Astrodon johnstoni, Maryland's official state dinosaur. They're the only footprints in Maryland from the Triassic period.

here, with pictures and memorabilia of presidents, from Hoover to today, including campaign buttons and coffee mugs. Almost all of the items were given to the Cozy by the press corps and foreign dignitaries. The Cozy, started by Wilbur R. Freeze in 1929, is the oldest family-owned restaurant in the state, and contains an inn, shops, and, of course, a restaurant. It is located at 103 Frederick Rd.; call (301) 271-4301 or visit www.cozyvillage.com.

A couple of campgrounds offer a place to spend a night or two and Frederick is close enough to Washington and Baltimore to be used as a base, if you wish. You'll find 40 miles of the 2,170-mile Appalachian Trail follows the county's western border, mostly along South Mountain. *Gathland State Park* is a good place to start your long hike or short walk. The ATC visitor center and trail store is in Harpers Ferry, West Virginia. 799 Washington St; (304) 535-6331; www.appalachiantrail.org.

Catoctin Mountain Park has scenery, wildlife, historic buildings, hiking trails, fly-fishing, camping, and you can stay in an historic cabin in Camp Misty Mount. Located at 6602 Foxville Rd., Thurmont; (301) 271-3140 (reservations), (301) 663-9388; www.nps.gov/cato/index.htm.

Gambrill State Park has overlooks, a campground with 34-campsites and 4camper cabins open seasonally, and miles of hiking, biking, and horse trails. Located at 8602 Gambrill Park Rd., Frederick; (301) 271-7574, (888) 432-2267; www.dnr.state.md.us/publiclands/western/gambrill.html.

Crow's Nest Lodge campground has 110 campsites located along Big Hunting Creek, a mountain trout stream that flows through the Catoctin Mountains. Each spacious campsite is designed to accommodate a large tent, tent trailer, or up to a 40' travel trailer. Most of the sites are shaded, and many have water and electricity. Pets are welcome, as long as they are on a leash at all times. Located at 335 West Main St; Thurmont; call (301) 271-7632.

Ole Mink Farm Recreation Resort has luxury log cabins with one, two, or four bedrooms, and other lodging options. Located at 12806 Mink Farm Rd., Thurmont; (301) 271-7012, (877) 653-6465; http://oleminkfarm.com.

Places to Eat in the Capital Region

BETHESDA

Perhaps 200 restaurants are in and around the Bethesda Triangle (at the intersection of Old Georgetown Rd., Wisconsin Ave., and East-West Hwy.), catering to just about every taste you can imagine. Because of this competition, it's easy to find an excellent place to eat within your budget, from inexpensive to extremely pricey. However, because it's a competitive business, restaurants do open and sometimes close quickly. Most of these have been around for ages although a few are new. It's still wise to call to check hours and reservation requirements. Here are a few suggestions:

Balducci's
10323 Old Georgetown Rd.
(301) 564-3100
www.balduccis.com

Benihana of Tokyo
7315 Wisconsin Ave.
(301) 652-5391

Gifford's Ice Cream Co., (and other locations)
7237 Woodmont Ave.
(301) 907-3436
www.giffords.com

sweetgreen
4831 Bethesda Ave.
(301) 654-7336
www.sweetgreen.com

BETHESDA NORTH

Meritage
Marriott Hotel and Conference Center
5701 Marinelli Rd.
(301) 822-9234

Tastee Diner of Bethesda
7731 Woodmont Ave.
(301) 652-3970
www.tasteediner.com

BOWIE

Grace's Fortune
15500 Annapolis Rd.
(301) 805-1108
www.gracesrestaurants.com

Old Bowie Town Grille
8604 Chestnut Ave.
(301) 464-8800
www.oldbowietowngrille.com

BROOKEVILLE

Sunshine General Store
22300 Georgia Ave.
(301) 774-7428

COLLEGE PARK

Noodles & Company
7320 Baltimore Ave.
(301) 779-5300
www.noodles.com

CROFTON

Jasper's
1651 Rte 3 North
(301) 261-3505
www.jaspersrestaurants.com

FORT WASHINGTON

Proud Mary Restaurant
13600 King Charles Terrace
(301) 292-5521
www.proudmaryrestaurant.com

FREDERICK

Brewer's Alley Restaurant & Brewery
124 North Market St.
(301) 631-0089
www.brewers-alley.com

Café 611
611 North Market St.
(301) 631-1460
www.cafe611.com

Isabella's Taverna & Tapas Bar
44 North Market St.
(301) 698-8922
www.isabellas-tavern.com

La Paz Mexican Restaurant
51 South Market St.
(301) 694-8980
www.lapazmex.com

Mangia e Bevi, Ristorante Italiano
8927-J Fingerboard Rd.
(301) 874-0338
www.mangiaebevi.us

GAITHERSBURG

O'Donnell's Sea Grill
311 Kentlands Blvd.
(301) 519-1650
www.odonnellsrestaurant
.com

GERMANTOWN

Seafood in the Buff
20220 Frederick Rd.
(240) 375-9223
www.seafoodinthebuff.biz

GREENBELT

Jasper's
7401 Greenbelt Rd.
(301) 441-8030
www.jaspersrestaurants
.com

HYATTSVILLE

Wild Onion Café
6504 America Blvd.
(301) 209-0630

LARGO

Gladys Knight & Ron Winans Chicken & Waffles
860 East Capital Centre Blvd.
(301) 808-6402
www.gladysandron.net

Jasper's
9640 Lottsford Court
(301) 883-2199
www.jaspersrestaurants
.com

OXON HILL

Grace's Mandarin
188 Waterfront St.
(301) 839-3788
www.gracesrestaurants
.com

Moon Bay Coastal Cuisine
Gaylord National Resort
201 Waterfront St.
(301) 965-5400
www.gaylordnational.com

RIVERDALE

Calvert House Inn
6211 Baltimore Ave.
(301) 864-5220
www.calverthouseinn.com

ROCKVILLE

Bean Bag
1605 East Gude Dr.
(301) 261-4794
www.thebeanbag.com

Royal Dragon Restaurant
4832 Boiling Brook Parkway
(301) 468-1922
www.royalkosherrestaurant
.com

Yuan Fu Vegetarian Restaurant
798 Rockville Pike
(301) 762-5937

SILVER SPRING

General Store and Post Office Tavern
6 Post Office Rd.
(301) 562-8787

Parkway Deli
8317 Grubb Rd.
(301) 587-2675
http://theparkwaydeli.com

Ray's the Classics
8606 Colesville Rd.
(301) 588-7297

Places to Stay in the Capital Region

Most hotels and motels in the Greater Washington area belong to the major hotel chains, including Best Western, Comfort Inn, Days Inn, Doubletree, Econo Lodge, Hampton Inn, Hilton, Holiday Inn, Marriott, Ramada Inn, Sheraton, and Red Roof Inn. Fortunately, you can also find wonderful individually owned hotels and inns. If, for some strange reason, you're bypassing all the wonderful things you can do and see in Maryland and you're headed toward the attractions of Washington, you'll probably be staying in Prince George's or Montgomery County, and you'll want one that's near a subway station, or that provides shuttle service to a subway.

Adventure Theatre
Glen Echo
(301) 634-2270
www.adventuretheatre.org

Airmen Memorial Museum
Suitland
(301) 899-3500
(800) 638-0594
www.afsahq.org/AMM/amm-htm/
mwelcome.htm

Antique Carousel
Watkins Regional Park
Kettering
(301) 218-6757
www.pgparks.com

Beall-Dawson House & Park
Rockville
(301) 762-1492
www.montgomeryhistory.org

Beltsville Agricultural Research Center
Beltsville
(301) 504-9403
www.ars.usda.gov/is

BlackRock Center for the Arts
Germantown
(301) 528-2260
www.blackrockcenter.org

Brookside Gardens
Wheaton Regional Park
Wheaton
(301) 962-1400
www.brooksidegardens.org

Catoctin Wildlife Preserve and Zoo
Thurmont
(301) 271-3180

Clara Barton National Historic Site
Glen Echo
(301) 492-6245
www.nps.gov/clba

Clearwater Nature Center
Clinton
(301) 297-4575
www.pgparks.com

Darnall's Chance House Museum
Upper Marlboro
(301) 952-8010
www.pgparks.com

Delaplaine Visual Arts Center
Frederick
(301) 698-0656
www.delaplaine.org

Dorsey Chapel
Glenn Dale
(301) 464-5291
www.pgparks.com/places/
eleganthistoric/dorsey_intro.html

Frederick Keys Baseball
Frederick
(301) 662-0013
www.frederickkeys.com

Glen Echo Park
Glen Echo
(301) 492-6282
www.nps.gov/glec

Gudelsky Gallery
Silver Spring
(301) 649-4454
www.mcadmd.org

Imagination Stage
Bethesda
(301) 280-1660
www.imaginationstage.org

Lamar House
Middletown
(301) 371-7090
www.cmhl.org/lamar.html

Lilypons Water Gardens
Buckeystown
(301) 874-5133
(800) 999-5459
www.lilypons.com

Marietta House Museum
Glenn Dale
(301) 464-5291
www.pgparks.com

Martin F. O'Rourke Memorial Railroad Library at Bowie Tower Huntington Railroad Museum
Bowie
(301) 805-4616
(301) 262-6200
www.cityofbowie.org

McCormick-Goodhart Mansion
Langley Park
(301) 431-4185
www.casademaryland.com

McCrillis Gardens and Gallery
Bethesda
(301) 949-8230
www.brooksidegardens.org

Monocacy National Battlefield
Frederick
(301) 662-3515
www.nps.gov/mono

Montpelier Cultural Arts Center
Laurel
(301) 953-1993
www.pgparks.comsmart.net/~parksrec/montarts.htm

Museum of Frederick County History
24 East Church St
(301) 663-1188
www.hsfcinfo.org

National Archives at College Park
College Park
(202) 501-5205
www.nara.gov

National Capital Trolley Museum
Silver Spring
(301) 384-6088
www.dctrolley.org

National Museum of Civil War Medicine
Frederick
(301) 695-1864
www.civilwarmed.org/

National Shrine–St. Elizabeth Ann Seton
Emmitsburg
(301) 447-6606
www.setonshrine.org

Northampton Plantation Slave Quarters Archeological Site
Mitchellville
(301) 627-1286
www.pgparks.com/places/eleganthistoric/northampton_intro.html

Poplar Hill on His Lordship's Kindness
Clinton
(301) 856-0358
www.poplarhillonhlk.org

Roger Brooke Taney & Francis Scott Key Museum
Frederick
(301) 228-2828

(continued on next page)

OTHER ATTRACTIONS WORTH SEEING IN THE CAPITAL REGION (CONT.)

Rose Hill Manor Park
Frederick
(301) 228-2828
www.rosehillmuseum.com

Sandy Spring Museum
Sandy Spring
(301) 774-0022
www.sandyspringmuseum.org

Sandy Spring Slave Museum & African Art Gallery
Sandy Spring
(301) 384-0727
www.sandyspringslavemuseum.org

Schifferstadt Architectural Museum
Frederick
(301) 663-3885
www.smallmuseum.fredericklandmarks
.org/schifferstadt.htm

Strathmore Hall Arts Center
North Bethesda
(301) 581-5200
www.strathmore.org

Surreybrooke
Middletown
(301) 371-7466
www.surreybrooke.com

Watkins Regional Park
Upper Marlboro,
(301) 390-9258
www.pgparks.ccom

BRANDYWINE

Cedarville State Forest
10201 Bee Oak Rd.
(301) 888-1410
(888) 432-2267
www.dnr.state.md.us

BUCKEYSTOWN

Inn at Buckeystown
3521 Buckeystown Pike
(301) 874-5755
(800) 272-1190
www.innatbuckeystown
.com

CASCADE

Cascade Inn
14700 Eyler Ave.
(301) 241-4161
(800) 362-9526
www.thecascadeinn.com

CLARKSBURG

Little Bennett Regional Park
23701 Clarksburg Rd.
(301) 972-9222
www.mc-mncppc.org

CLINTON

Cosca Regional Park
11000 Thrift Rd.
(301) 868-1397
www.pgparks.com

COLLEGE PARK

Cherry Hill Park
9800 Cherry Hill Rd.
(301) 937-7116
(800) 801-6449
www.cherryhillpark.com

DERWOOD

Reynolds of Derwood Bed & Breakfast
16620 Bethayres Rd.
(301) 963-2216
www.reynolds-bed
breakfast.com

FREDERICK

Hill House Bed & Breakfast
12 West Third St.
(301) 682-4111
www.hillhousefrederick
.com

Morningside Inn
7477 McKaig Rd.
(301) 898-3920
www.morningside-inn.com

GAITHERSBURG

Gaithersburg Inn
104 Russell Ave.
(301) 330-1331
www.gaithersburginn.com

GREENBELT

Greenbelt Park
6565 Greenbelt Rd.
(301) 344-3948
(Park headquarters)
(301) 344-3944
(Ranger station)
(800) 367-2265
www.nps.gov/gree

ROCKVILLE

Cabin John Regional Park
Robert C. McDonell Campground
7701 Tuckerman Lane
(301) 495-2525
www.montgomery
parks.org

Parklawn Campsites
12724 Viers Mill Rd.
(301) 495-2525
www.montgomeryparks
.org

SHARPSBURG

Antietam's Jacob Rohrbach Inn
138 West Main St.
(301) 432-5079
www.jacob-rohrbach-inn
.com

TAKOMA PARK

Davis Warner Inn
8114 Carroll Ave.
(301) 408-3989
(888) 683-3989
www.daviswarnerinn.com
www.inntravels.com/usa/
md/dwi.html

THURMONT

Cozy Inn
105 Frederick Rd.
(301) 271-4301
www.cozyvillage.com

UPPER MARLBORO

Watkins Regional Park
301 Watkins Park Dr.
(301) 249-6900
www.pgparks.com

SOUTHERN MARYLAND

→

Civilization (or at least suburban sprawl) has entered Southern Maryland and now parts of Charles, Calvert (sometimes pronounced "Cawlvert" or "Calvit" by the locals), and St. Mary's counties probably have changed almost equally because of avulsion and accretion (erosion and accumulation of land) and developmental encroachment since the first English colonists settled here in the mid-1600s.

As you drive down these roads, you will see signs of early settlements established by brave men and women who came seeking new lives, religious freedom, and adventure. Dozens of churches, some dating from the early seventeenth century, dot the historic landscape.

Water has made its influence felt, of course; and you'll find many waterside communities, places to buy and eat fresh seafood, and aquatic research centers. In Southern Maryland I looked for markets that keep a community alive, and I found several community craft centers and talented artisans. I hope you will take the time to enjoy the maritime influence and the fine and unusual dining surrounding, or perhaps surrounded by, this rich coastal area.

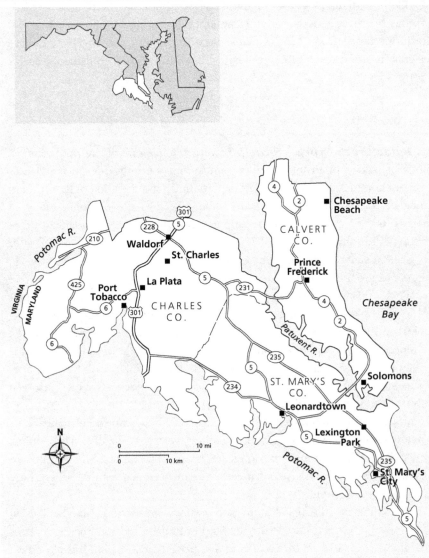

Potomac R.

210

VIRGINIA
MARYLAND

425

Port
Tobacco

6

6

301

228

301

Waldorf

La Plata

5

St. Charles

CHARLES
CO.

231

5

234

235

5

ST. MARY'S
CO.

Leonardtown

Lexington
Park

5

4

2

Chesapeake
Beach

CALVERT
CO.

Prince
Frederick

4

2

Patuxent R.

Chesapeake
Bay

Solomons

235

Potomac R.

St. Mary's
City

5

N

0   10 mi
0   10 km

Bikers particularly enjoy the terrain of Southern Maryland, and a bicycle map has been created just for you, highlighting the sights through ten loops. The loops range from 7 to 58 miles. Bike stores and points of interest are designated along the various routes. Contact any of the tourism offices for a copy.

Calvert County

The ***Battle Creek Cypress Swamp Sanctuary*** has one of the northernmost stands of bald cypress trees in the country and the only one on Maryland's western shore. Forget the images of cypress trees and the Old South, for there is neither Spanish moss hanging from these boughs nor Southern belles in hoop skirts. The cypress in this swamp are thought to be descendants of trees growing here some 5,000 to 15,000 years ago, shortly (relatively speaking) after the glaciers started receding. Some of the trees reach more than 100 feet in height and are 4 feet in diameter.

Within this one-hundred-acre nature sanctuary is an interpretive center and a great place for nature photography in the spring (when violets, may-apples, and pink lady's slipper orchids are in bloom) and early summer when the blooms are most profuse. Bring fast film and a tripod, because the light is heavily filtered through the canopy. With its rich wetlands, look for such species as sweet gum, ash, southern arrowwood, and spicebush. You'll also see tulip tree, mountain laurel, and Virginia pine.

Just take the 1,700-foot boardwalk through the swamp to get really close to nature. However, you don't want to get too close to some of it. Those thick, fuzzy vines climbing the trees along the boardwalk through the swamp are poison ivy, and they are just as dangerous as their cousin with the three shiny leaves if you are allergic to it.

The sanctuary, the first Nature Conservancy preserve in Maryland, is at 2800 Grays Rd. off Sixes Rd. (State Rte 506) in Prince Frederick. It's open Tues through Sat from 10 a.m. to 4 p.m. and Sun from 1 to 4:30 p.m. It is closed on

AUTHOR'S FAVORITES SOUTHERN MARYLAND

Battle Creek Cypress Swamp
Sanctuary

Calvert Marine Museum

Flag Ponds Nature Park

Historic St. Mary's City

Mon, and on Thanksgiving, Christmas, and New Year's Day. Call (410) 535-5327 or visit www.calvertparks.org.

If you want to hobnob and brush shoulders with the movers and shakers of Calvert County, you probably should find your way to **Stoney's** (there are three of them and the address, phone number, and URL are at the end of the paragraph). Sit down for a crab cake or oyster sandwich (you might hear that pronounced "arester," but no matter how you say it, they'll understand you). Seasonal hours apply, so check for days and times. There are three locations: Stoney's Kingfishers Seafood (14442 Solomons Island Rd., Solomons; 410-394-0236); Stoney's Solomons Pier (14757 Solomons Island Rd. South, Solomons Island 410-326-2424); and Broomes Island Marina (39393 Oyster House Rd., Broomes Island; 410-586-1888); or visit them on the Web at www.stoneyssea foodhouse.com.

Francis and Ann Koenig donated the thirty-acre park known as **Annmarie Garden** to the people of Calvert County, so it's there for everyone to enjoy. Located at the headwaters of St. John Creek in Solomons, the park was dedicated in October 1993. There's a range of sculpture and botanical treasures here, starting with the glazed ceramic gateposts, perhaps the largest and most complex hand-built enterprise ever attempted by a U.S. pottery studio. It consists of seven tons of ceramics in 630 pieces.

oysterlegacy

Solomons was named for Isaac Solomon who opened an oyster cannery here in 1867.

The first major permanent installation was a tribute to the oyster tonger, without whom we wouldn't have those succulent morsels. Maryland artist Antonio Tobias Mendez created the statue that was dedicated at Artsfest '94, an annual weeklong September event that combines the visual and performing arts. There's also the holiday Garden in Lights. Among the flora attractions are more than 460 azaleas. Another special treat is the Surveyor's Map, a floating walkway that's more than 300 feet long, ending at a lookout within the tree canopy.

Annmarie Garden is open daily from 9 a.m. to 5 p.m. Located at 13480 Dowell Rd., Dowell; call (410) 326-4640 or visit www.annmariegarden.org.

Contained within the 327-acre park known as **Flag Ponds Nature Park** are wooded uplands, ponds, swamps, freshwater marshes, sandy beaches, and part of Chesapeake Bay. Here you can clearly see the difference between the uplands and the wetlands, between the Cliffs of Calvert and Chesapeake Bay. Wildlife abounds, including fox, muskrat, otter, turkey, whitetail deer, and pileated woodpecker. Special facilities include three miles of gentle hiking trails, rare plants such as the blue flag iris (from which the park derives its name), pond observation decks, picnic sites, a beach, a fishing pier, and a visitor center with wildlife exhibits.

One building remains from what was once a thriving "pound net" fishery that supplied trout, croaker, and herring to the bustling Baltimore markets during the first half of the twentieth century. Flag Ponds is open daily from 9 a.m. to 6 p.m. and on weekends from 9 a.m. to 8 p.m. during the summer. From Labor Day through Memorial Day the park is open on weekends from 9 a.m. to 6 p.m. and closed during the week. From Apr through Oct, there is a daily vehicle charge of $4 for residents and $6 for nonresidents, or a seasonal pass for $15 and $20, respectively. Nov through Mar the charge is $3 for both residents and nonresidents. Located at 1525 Flag Ponds Parkway, Lusby; call (410) 586-1477 or visit www.calvertparks.org.

Instead of being a day late and a dollar short, Otto Mears and a group of Denver railroad financiers decided in 1890 that they'd build a new resort on the Chesapeake Bay so Washingtonians could escape the notoriously hot and humid summers. They built the railroad to Chesapeake Beach, a 1,600-foot boardwalk that had a band shell, dance pavilion, roller coaster, and a mile-long pier for tourist boats from Baltimore. The resort opened on June 9, 1900. A carousel opened in 1929 and it's believed that Gustav A. Dentzel, the premier carousel maker, created many of the carved animals. North Beach, a mile to the north, was created to house the workers.

The Depression was one factor that led to the resort's demise and that was compounded by the introduction of the automobile, then World War II, gas rationing, and the rest is history. You can learn more about the history at the **Chesapeake Beach Railway Museum** and see old photos, a diorama, archaeological finds, a carousel animal, railroad equipment, and the amazing growth that has now come to this area. The museum is open daily Apr 1 through Oct 31 from 1 to 4 p.m. with extended weekend hours; and on weekends and byappointment at other times. Located at 4155 Mears Ave.; call (410) 257-3892 or visit www.cbrm.org.

Jefferson Patterson Park and Museum always offers something interesting pertaining to the history and archaeology about the area, the War of 1812, and the environment, so it's no surprise that still another attraction has been added. "Patuxent Encounters: The Patuxent Indians and Captain John Smith" is part of the regional observation of Smith's voyages of the Chesapeake Bay. Additions to the Woodland Indian hamlet are in the works so you can learn more about the traditional and contemporary American Indian ways of life.

Sukeek's Cabin site represents a previously enslaved family's first home as free people after the Civil War. The 560-acre park that covers 9,000 years of human history is set along two-and-a-half miles of the Patuxent River and St. Leonard Creek. There's an active calendar of events, including heritage celebrations, children's activities, tours, concerts, dances, lectures, and education programs. The park is open Wed through Sun, from 10 a.m. to 5 p.m. from Apr 15 through Oct 15. It's located at 10515 Mackall Rd., St. Leonard; call (410) 586-8501 or visit www.jefpat.org.

A little south of the Calvert Cliffs power plant is *Calvert Cliffs State Park,* a 1,460-acre wooded area that brings you to cliffs formed more than 15 million years ago. The cliffs hold more than 600 species of fossils. To seek your own 15-million-year-old fossils, take the approximately 2-mile hike down to the beach (and 2 miles back up, of course). Fishing and youth group camping are other activities available. The park is open daily from sunrise to sunset. Admission is $5 per car. Located at 1650 Calvert Cliffs Parkway, call (410) 394-1778 or visit dnr.maryland.gov/publiclands/southern/calvertcliffs.html.

Continuing south on State Rte 4 will bring you to Solomons where you can spend countless hours at the award-winning *Calvert Marine Museum and Lighthouse.* The information there is proof that a museum can be fun, fascinating, and fact filled. This museum has grown from a drop of water splashed about by LeRoy "Pepper" Langley in 1970, to a huge reservoir of information and fun. Stop by the Children's Discovery Room, where there is a pile of earth from Calvert Cliffs that you can dig in to find fossils. It can be difficult and time-consuming to search for fossils at outdoor sites, but not here. One shark tooth per person, please. This room is more fun than a bushel of crabs that has just been dusted with seasoning. New programs have been established for Sea Squirts (toddlers aged 18 months to 3 years), Little Minnows (preschoolers ages 3 to 5), and Young Salts (children 5 to 7). These are drop-in programs open to CMM members only.

The *Drum Point Lighthouse* out back is one of the old screw-pile, cottage-style lighthouses that used to protect the watermen of the bay. The two-story, hexagon-shaped structure was built in 1883 to mark the entrance of the Patuxent River from the Chesapeake Bay. A crane and barge moved the stilted cottage to its current location in 1975. Take a few minutes to walk through the lighthouse (watch your head when going up and down the steps), and mentally transport yourself to the time when people lived here and tended the light. It is romantic to think of the "good old days" when there were lightkeepers, but most don't think this remote lifestyle is very attractive these days.

The **William B. Tennison** treasure is an old bugeye (a type of boat) that takes people on cruises around the bay. This bugeye is a Chesapeake Bay sailing craft built in 1899 at Crabb Island by B. P. and R. L. Miles. Her hull is

MARCH

Maryland Day
St Mary's City
(240) 895-4990
(800) 762-1634
www.stmaryscity.org

APRIL

John Wilkes Booth Escape Route Tour
Clinton
(301) 868-1121
www.surratt.org

MAY

Criterium Bicycle Races
Leonardtown
(410) 394-2770
www.paxvelo.com

Piney Point Lighthouse Waterfront Festival
Piney Point
(301) 769-2600
www.stmarysmd.com/recreate/museum

Quilt and Needlework Show
Sotterley Plantation
Hollywood
(301) 373-2280
(800) 681-0850
www.sotterley.org

Solomons Maritime Festival
Solomons
(410) 326-2042
www.calvertmarinemuseum.com

JUNE

African-American Family Community Day
St. Leonard
(410) 586-8501
www.jefpat.org

Blue and Gray Days
Point Lookout State Park
(301) 872-5688
www.pllps.org

Southern Maryland Soap Box Derby
Leonardtown
(301) 994-1185
http://smdsbd.com

St. Mary's County Crab Festival
Leonardtown
http://stmaryscrabfestival.com

JULY

African-American Family Community Day
St. Leonard
(410) 586-8501
www.jefpat.org

Calvert County Jousting Tournament
Port Republic
(410) 586-0565
www.christchurchcalvert.org/Jousting_Tournament.htm

AUGUST

Bassmaster Elite
Smallwood State Park
Marbury
(301) 645-0558

Cancer Gala
Chesapeake Beach
(301) 855-8351 ext 108
www.rodnreelcancergala.org

Jousting Tournament
Port Republic
(410) 586-0565
www.christchurchcalvert.org/Jousting_
Tournament.htm

SEPTEMBER

Calvert County Fair
Barstow
(410) 535-0026
www.calvertcountyfair.com

Charles County Fair
La Plata
(301) 932-1234
www.charlescountyfair.com

Maryland Lighthouse Challenge
Various locations
(410) 326-2750
www.cheslights.org

Southern Maryland Amish 100
Leonardtown
(301) 757-4353
www.paxvelo.com

St. Mary's County Fair
Leonardtown
(301) 475-2256
www.somd.com/smcfair

OCTOBER

Blessing of the Fleet
Colton's Point
(301) 769-2222
www.7thdistrictoptimist.org

Patuxent River Appreciation Days
Solomons
(410) 326-2042 ext 17
www.pradinc.org

St. Mary's County Oyster Festival
Leonardtown
(301) 863-5015
www.usoysterfest.com

NOVEMBER

CAASA's Step-by-Step 5K Fun Run/Walk
Solomons
(410) 535-3733
www.ecalvert.com/content/tourism/
calendarofevents

Veteran's Day Parade
Leonardtown
(301) 475-9791
www.leonardtown.somd.com

DECEMBER

Christmas Doll & Train Exhibit
Colton's Point
(301) 769-2222
www.stmarysmd.com

Maryland State Police Shiver in the River
Newburg
(410) 789-6677
www.somd.org

Victorian Christmas
Waldorf
(301) 274-9358
www.somd.lib.md.us

"chunk built," or made of nine logs, rather than by a plank-and-frame method of construction. Originally rigged for sailing, she was converted to power in 1907, and a new, larger cabin was added aft. You can cruise on the *Tennison* and see the Governor Thomas Johnson Bridge, the Solomons Island and Chesapeake Biological Laboratory, and the U.S. Naval Recreation Center at Point Patience. This allows you to view the inner harbor and Patuxent River as you can never see them from land. The one-hour cruise starts Wed through Sun at 2 p.m. May through Oct. A 12:30 p.m. cruise is offered on Sat and Sun in July and Aug. You can charter the boat for your own event. Fares are $7 per adult and $4 per child (five to twelve).

Periodically, the museum holds special programs. It might be a Rolling Stones Experience concert with covers of "I Can't Get No Satisfaction," "Beast of Burden," and "Angie." Another day might bring such local authors and illustrators as James Tigner, Jr., Kristina Henry, Elaine Ann Allen, and Marcy Dunn Ramsey. Or, listen to a summit discussion about the "State of the River: Local Challenges of Sea Level Rise and Climate Change."

The Calvert Marine Museum is open daily 10 a.m. to 5 p.m. except New Year's Day, Thanksgiving, and Christmas. The museum closes at 3 p.m. on concert dates. A wheelchair is available, but the lighthouse is not wheelchair accessible. Admission is $7 for adults, $2 for children 5 to 12, and $6 for seniors fifty-five and older. Located at 14150 Solomons Island Rd.; call (410) 326-2042 or visit www.calvertmarinemuseum.com.

The ***Cove Point Lighthouse*** was off-limits to visitors for years. The Calvert Marine Museum owns it now and has regularly scheduled shuttle service from the museum to the lighthouse. Cove Point was lit for the first time in December 1828 and wasn't converted from kerosene to electricity until almost a century later. It was nearly another sixty years before it was fully automated, in 1986. The 40-foot tower and lightkeeper's house were constructed of locally made bricks.

After the Calvert Marine Museum Society acquired the light from the U.S. Coast Guard in 1996, there was a massive amount of repair work to be done on the buildings, fencing, grounds, security, and other facilities so it could be open for your visit. Because the light is still operational (it's the oldest continuously working lighthouse in Maryland), visitors are only allowed inside the base, but you can look up the spiral stairway to the lantern room.

The lighthouse is open daily from 10 a.m. to 4 p.m. June through Aug and on weekends and holidays in May and Sept. Admission is $3. Check with the Calvert Marine Museum for details about the shuttle bus schedule; call (410) 326-2042 for additional information.

Charles County

The population, major occupations, and pastimes have changed enormously in the past decade as parts of the area are becoming suburbs of Washington, D.C. Whereas most of the usual tourist attractions were centered in La Plata and Waldorf, you can find something interesting to do almost anywhere. It just depends on your interests.

People will acknowledge that baseball games can be slow and last forever. Some think the same about the crusade to bring minor league baseball to Charles County. It took 23 years from inception to the first "Play Ball!" The baseball proposal first surfaced in 1985 with the thought of creating a home for a Class A team. Land was donated, construction had been started, league approval had been received, and hiring was underway. Then, the 1986 county election saw the ouster of three county commissioners who backed the project. Fast forward to 2004 and tobacco is no longer king. Quality-of-life issues are becoming more important in attracting new businesses and upscale residents. The **_Regency Furniture Stadium_** opened on Fri, May 2, 2008, with seating for 4,500 "Crustacean Nation" members (fans). It is expected to generate $27 million in ticket prices, tax revenues, and tourism expenditures. Their first season saw them win 74 games and lose 66 games for a winning percentage of .529. They came in second in the Liberty Division. The Blue Crabs play in the

Neighbor to Neighbor

On Sunday, April 28, 2002, an F-4 force tornado (with winds of 207–260 mph, strong enough to level well-constructed homes and hurl cars) touched down in the town of La Plata, killing four people and injuring about one hundred others. This tornado caused more damage than any storm since the 1926 tornado that killed fourteen schoolchildren. Dozens of businesses and a number of homes and churches in the storm's 26-mile path were damaged or destroyed. Business and personal papers were found 50 miles away, across the Chesapeake Bay in Dorchester and Talbot Counties. Many of the papers have been returned, many accompanied by personal notes of sympathy.

The entire community, including people living far beyond the La Plata boundaries, helped the town get back on its feet. On July 3, a little more than two months after the devastation, the Waldorf Jaycees sponsored a "Charles County Cares—Neighbor to Neighbor" dinner that netted $195,000 to be distributed to the American Red Cross, the Children's Aid Society, the Tri-County Youth Services Bureau, and the county's nonprofit relief fund. La Plata is bouncing back, supported by emergency funding and the great spirit and help of "neighbors" everywhere.

Atlantic League of Professional Baseball, an eight-team league that was formed in 1998. Located at 11765 St. Linus Dr., Waldorf; call (301) 638-9788 or visit www.somdbluecrabs.com.

St. Ignatius Catholic Church near Port Tobacco was established in 1641 by Father Andrew White, who sailed with other Jesuits on the Ark and the Dove to help found a new colony. Some years ago a tunnel was discovered leading from the basement of the servants' quarters to the Potomac River, 120 feet below. No one knows whether this was part of the Underground Railroad, a convenient way to load and unload boats from the river below (particularly during inclement weather), or an escape route in the days when Jesuit priests had to make a fast departure.

Stop by the church to see a relic of a Cross now encased in glass and silver. It was brought over by Father White (who wore it around his neck). Take a little time to admire a mahogany table made in Santo Domingo, and view the needlepoint kneelers made by the parishioners. Stroll around the grounds and see animals at the working farm run by the resident Jesuits. Catch the Way of the Cross garden, the historic herb and butterfly garden, and the outdoor Shrine of Our Lady. When you've done that, take a few minutes to just admire the view of the Potomac River. Following the 1773–1805 suppression of Jesuits, the men who stayed at St. Ignatius took their vows again in 1805 under a White Russian superior, thus making St. Ignatius and the residence the oldest in the United States and probably the world.

Tours of the church, Manor House, and parish grounds may be arranged through the hospitality group. St. Ignatius Church, 8855 Chapel Point Rd., Port Tobacco; (301) 934-8245; www.chapelpoint.org.

Settled in 1634, Port Tobacco was once Maryland's second-largest seaport and was even found on early world maps. The town was the original county seat.

A courthouse was constructed in Port Tobacco in 1729, but was replaced when the county seat moved to La Plata. The original *Port Tobacco courthouse* has been restored and is open Apr through Oct, Mon, Sat, and Sun from noon to 4 p.m. and by appointment. Located on Chapel Point Rd., Port Tobacco; call (301) 934-4313.

Nearby is the *Port Tobacco One-Room Schoolhouse,* built in 1876 and used until 1953. The Charles County Retired Teachers' Association restored the building in the 1990s and furnished it with items from the 1800s. The schoolhouse is open on weekends from noon to 4 p.m. Apr through Oct, and also on Mon from noon to 4 p.m. June through Aug, and by appointment. Located on Chapel Point Rd., Port Tobacco; call (301) 932-6064 or (301) 934-8836.

A few miles southwest, in Welcome, is the home and workshop of Steve and Kris Crescenze, restorers and builders of all things related to carousels, including animals and decorations. As **Restorations by Wolf,** they have also restored some of the creatures and features on the 1905 Dentzel carousel (formerly of Chesapeake Beach) at Watkins Regional Park in Largo.

Their love affair with carousels began in the late 1980s when the Crescenzes bought two carousel figurines to display in a curio cabinet. Now their home looks like a huge curio cabinet inside a never-ending carousel. Figures are in every nook and cranny, including a pig, a giraffe, a lion, and, of course, horses—everywhere except in one room filled with Coca-Cola memorabilia.

If you've ever picked up a copy of Carousel News & Trader magazine you may well have seen a picture of their work; they've been on more than a dozen covers. Yes, a carousel coffee-table book is on Steve's mind. Located at 8480 Gunston Rd., Welcome; call (301) 932-2734 or visit www.carousel restorations.com.

Mount Carmel Monastery was the first convent for religious women in Colonial America, founded on October 15, 1790. It was started by four Carmelite nuns, three of whom—Ann, Ann Theresa, and Susan Mathews—along with the Reverend Charles Neale were natives of Charles County. The group set up temporary quarters at Chandler's Hope, then owned by the Neale family. Father Neale donated 860 acres to the Carmelites to build their monastery. Two of the original convent buildings have been restored and are open to visitors during the summer season. The other buildings are still used as an active convent and a gift shop. The monastery is open daily in the summer from 9 a.m. to 4 p.m. Mass is said daily at 7:15 a.m. and on Sun at 8 a.m. Located at 5678 Mount Carmel Rd., La Plata; call (301) 934-1654 or visit www.erols.com/carmel-of-port-tobacco.

britishinvasion

Benedict is also notable as the landing site for 4,500 British troops in August 1814. Local historians say it is the only small town on U.S. soil that has been invaded by foreign troops, for these were the troops who marched on to the nation's capital. The British troops returned to Benedict with their wounded burying two of their soldiers at Old Fields Chapel cemetery in Hughesville. During the Civil War, Camp Stanton was established here for recruiting and training African-American infantrymen to serve in the Union Army.

In your travels through the county, you may see evidence of tobacco, an important (and maybe the most important) crop in this area for 300 years. It takes 250 man-hours to produce one acre of tobacco (less labor-intensive crops may take as little as four man-hours), and Maryland tobacco is air-dried in a "stick" of tobacco made up of individually harvested leaves. By contrast, in Virginia the entire tobacco plant is cut at one time and is flue-cured by heat in three days. During the three- to six-month drying or curing process, each stick of tobacco will lose more than one-and-a-half gallons of water.

However, Maryland initiated a tobacco-farm buyout program and nearly 75 percent of the tobacco growers in the state, primarily in the southern counties, have agreed to the buyout. This means they get paid for not growing the tobacco while the state helps them find other productive cash crops. Some farmers are experimenting with vineyards, Christmas trees, and fruit orchards. The tobacco barns were built with vertical boards that could be propped open so the tobacco could be "air cured." That means they aren't insulated and, other than a tobacco barn museum, it has been difficult finding new uses for them. Eleven have been places on an endangered building list.

Pope's Creek is the best place to go for crabs and a view of the Potomac River. The three-mile drive off US 301 down Pope's Creek Rd. is also a little history lesson, for it was along this route that John Wilkes Booth found refuge after assassinating Abraham Lincoln. Two historical markers designate where he stopped along Pope's Creek Rd. for three days and where he crossed the Potomac into Virginia.

Bass-ically Speaking

For the past dozen years or so, Smallwood State Park has been the home of the *National Bass Tournament,* attracting pros and amateurs from the United States, Canada, and other countries. In 1854 the Potomac River was stocked with thirty bass brought from Ohio, spawning a major industry. Today the Potomac ranks as one of the country's premier largemouth bass fisheries. Winning strings regularly exceed fifty pounds. Included in the challenge of the competition is the ever-changing hydrilla (an underwater plant that provides cover for the bass population) and the timing of the tides.

The year 2005 was a spectacular one for bass fishing and Charles County. The Forrest Wood (FLW) tour came to Smallwood and brought in tons of money (well, $4.6 million worth anyway) with food and lodging accommodations, souvenirs, and other necessary boat supplies. There is also another revenue source, said Joanne Roland, former tourism director for Charles County and coordinator of the event: Several anglers arrive a week before the event, go to the nearby Maryland Airport to rent a pilot and plane, and fly over the Potomac River to see how the hydrilla is growing and to note any changes in the river.

As you may have read or heard, the Northern Chinese Snakehead was introduced into the Potomac and many feared they would devour the bass fingerlings or feed on the same parts of the lower food chain. There were some who thought the bass might do that to the snakeheads. So far, neither one seems to be bothering the other.

Down at Pope's Creek are the shells of oysters eaten over the centuries, first by Charles County Native Americans, then by settlers, and today by travelers. These shells cover some thirty acres to a depth of 15 feet in some places.

If you prefer eating crabs and oysters to looking at old shells, stop by **Captain Billy's** for some crabs served in a traditional style. The tables are covered with paper and piles of those tasty crabs; a pitcher of beer accompanies the feast. Here you can learn why Maryland is called the Land of Pleasant Living. You may have seen Captain Billy's featured on an episode of "The Best of . . ." on The Food Network or check the restaurant's Web site for the history of this traditional eatery. Note that the restaurant is closed from late Nov through mid-Feb. Call (301) 932-4323 or visit www.captbillys.com.

Captain Bill opened **Robertson's Crab House** prior to Captain Billy's so you have a choice. I'm sure you'll hear comments and preferences for one over the other. It's your decision. Of course, Robertson's is open all year. It's located at 11455 Pope's Creek Rd.; Newberg; call (301) 934-3300.

The old building on your right as you drive along Pope's Creek Rd. to the water is an old Rural Electrification Administration powerhouse with lovely arched windows reminiscent of the Palladian style.

The bridge across the Potomac, three miles downriver, is the Governor Harry W. Nice Bridge. It opened in 1940, replacing Laidlow's Ferry, and was the first crossing of the Potomac River south of the nation's capital. The 1938 groundbreaking was presided over by President Franklin D. Roosevelt. The bridge is 1.7 miles long and narrower than many bridges (11' each lane), and rises 135 feet above the water. More than 6.8 million vehicles traveled across the bridge in 2008. The toll, collected southbound only, is $3 for a passenger car with a 60 percent savings for those using Maryland-issued E-ZPass.

Dr. Samuel A. Mudd's house, where John Wilkes Booth was treated by the country doctor after Booth shot President Abraham Lincoln, is now a museum with costumed docents leading tours. The two-story, three-part early Victorian frame farmhouse, built about 1754, is furnished with original and

hearthetrain acomin'

On January 1, 1873, the first trains started running on the Pope's Creek Line of the Baltimore & Potomac Railroad. Although it was created so goods could be transported from Charles and Prince George's Counties to Baltimore and is used today to transport coal to the power plant on the Potomac, the line also allowed a "spur" to be run from Bowie to Washington, D.C., something that would otherwise have been prohibited because this new line provided competition to the Baltimore & Ohio line between the two cities.

family pieces from that period. It is open for tours Wed and Sat, Apr through Nov from 11 a.m. to 4 p.m. and by appointment. Periodically special events are scheduled that might be a Civil War encampment or exhibits of women's clothing of the period. Admission is $5 for adults and $2 for children ages 6 to 16. The home is a stop on the Civil War Trail. It's located at 3725 Dr. Samuel Mudd Rd., Waldorf; call (301) 274-9358 or (301) 645-6870; or visit www.somd .lib.md.us/museums/mudd.htm.

St. Mary's County

St. Mary's County is almost all off the beaten path even when you are on their most-traveled roads. The county offers many different attractions that draw thousands of people each year, yet it remains primarily historic and underdeveloped. From the Naval Air Test and Evaluation Museum (connected with the Naval Air Station, Patuxent River), to the Old Jail Museum, to Point Lookout State Park with its terrific camping area and beaches, to the crafts at Cecil's Old Mill, you can spend a good deal of time down here.

For more than 80 years, from 1851 through 1932, the Blackistone Lighthouse on St. Clements Island kept a searching eye along the Potomac River, and then it burned in 1956. After an almost untold amount of work, beginning in Apr 2007, the light and building have been reconstructed as part of a state park. Original drawings and specifications and photographs helped people make it as accurate as possible. It took more than a year, but it opened in June 2008. The island is where Maryland was founded in 1634 and the state operates it as a park. A seasonal water taxi runs to the island from the **St. Clements Island Museum,** 38370 Point Breeze Rd., Colton's Point. Call (301) 769-2222 or visit www.co.saint-marys.md.us/recreate/museums/stclementsisland.asp.

The **Three Notch Trail,** a 28-mile recreational (pedestrian, bicycle, and equestrian) trail along a railroad right-of-way, was begun in June 2006. Starting from Hughesville (in Charles County) and running to Lexington Park (to the Patuxent River Naval Air Station), the trail will connect the Northern County Senior Center in Charlotte Hall, the Charlotte Hall Library, St. Mary's County Farmers' Market, Charlotte Hall Veterans Home, the new St. Mary's County Welcome Center, the Northern Senior Center, and link the villages of New Market and Charlotte Hall. The first two phases are constructed of asphalt and are 10 feet wide in most sections. Split-rail fencing and various plantings offer buffers for the trail in some sections. Benches are provided along the way and the trail complies with the Americans with Disabilities ACT (ADA).

You have a chance to "adopt" part of the trail or sponsor mile-marker signs, so call the Department of Recreation, Parks, and Community Services if you're interested; (301) 475-4200, ext. 1811; they're also looking for volunteers for trail upkeep and other functions. Visit their Web site at www.co.saint-marys .md.us/recreate/facilities/threenotchtrail.asp for more information.

"People" watchers try to drive by the home of **Ross in the Garden** to catch up on what he is doing. A "friend" of Alan Spence, he's mostly at his spot in the garden from spring through fall, and you can follow his exploits as his wardrobe changes periodically. According to Spence, Ross had a guitar, microphone, and lawn chair set up for a while for anyone who wanted to listen, request a song, and perhaps sing along with him. He's been seen bringing fish home from an outing, riding a unicycle, plowing the garden, riding a sawhorse, and reminding people to vote. He helped conduct the orchestra one night during the summer concert series in St. Mary's City. There was a thought about him participating in the Governor's Cup race (from Annapolis to St. Mary's City via sailboat), but a storm was threatening with lightning, etc., and you know how scarecrows get when it rains. When Ross is out and about, you can see him in front of the Spence home on Rte 5, on the right hand side, about a hundred yards or so after you leave St. Mary's College of Maryland heading toward Leonardtown. Visit www.rossinthegarden.com for additional information.

The summer concert that Ross "helped" conduct is part of the St. Mary's College of Maryland free **River Concert Series,** held on Fri nights during June and July. Under the direction of music director Jeffrey Silberschlag, the maestro privilege is periodically part of the annual auction held at the March gala to raise funds for the county's Arts Outreach program. Barbara Bershon has all the details about what is being auctioned and whether this is one of the auction items that will be up for bid.

During the 2009 season, audiences were treated to a Maryland 375 birthday celebration, Terrae Maraie, a Fifies 4th of July, and an evening of Rodgers and Hammerstein. You can choose your seating to be with the serious listeners, the casual listeners, and serious socializing people. The outdoor concerts overlook the St. Mary's River and begin a 7 p.m. The grounds open at 5 p.m. There's also a Wednesday night film series. Call (240) 895-4107 or (240) 895-2024; or visit www.riverconcertseries.com.

As water is such an important part of St. Mary's County, it's understandable that locals and tourists were pleased when the **Leonardtown Wharf Public Park** was opened in May 2008. The park offers a kayak launch, boat tie ups, and a waterfront promenade. Starting a McIntosh Run at the lower end of town, you can paddle through 400 pristine acres to the edge of Breton Bay, and arrive at the new park. Located on Business Rte 5, Leonardtown; call (301) 475-9791 or visit www.somd.com/leonardtown.

Historic **St. Mary's City** was the first proprietary colony in America and the first capital of Maryland. Starting in 2002, historic masons and carpenters started rebuilding the brick chapel of 1667 on its original foundation. It was completed in 2009 and serves as an interpretive exhibit commemorating the founding place of the Roman Catholic church. Located on Rte 5 and Rosecroft Rd.; call (800) 762-1634 or (240) 895-4967; or visit www.stmaryscity.org.

Fortunately, you can still find numerous traces of Colonial times in and around this area, particularly the **Sotterley Plantation,** an eighteenth-century Tidewater plantation overlooking the Patuxent River. The Sotterley tale is one of inspiration, for it has gone from America's most endangered historic site to its most promising. This plantation, the only remaining Tidewater plantation in Maryland open to the public with a number of visitor and educational programs, is older than Mount Vernon and Monticello. Over the years the property had decayed, and it was feared it would have to be shut down. However, John Hanson Briscoe, great-grandson of a Sotterley slaveholder, and Agnes Kane Callum, great-granddaughter of a Sotterley slave, spearheaded the campaign for funds and restoration and with the help of people across the country and the foundation's trustees. Sotterley's grounds are open Tues through Sun from 10 a.m. to 4 p.m. It is closed from Oct 31 to May 1, although special tours may be arranged. Admission is $2 per person Mon through Fri during the off-season. In-season admission rates are $7 for adults and $5 for children 6 through 16 to tour on Sat and Sun. Located at 44300 Sotterley Lane, Hollywood; call (301) 373-2280 or (800) 681-0850; or visit www.sotterley.org.

hello
hollywood

Plenty of movies supposedly are set in Maryland (remember *Annapolis?*), but 2006 saw a movie made at Sotterley Plantation that stood in for the deep south during the time of slavery. *Prince Among Slaves* follows the life of Abdul Rahman, an African prince who was sold into slavery in 1788. A ninety-minute documentary was shot for PBS, airing in the fall of 2007, and the production crew was definitely enamored with the area on the water, without modern skyscrapers in the background, plenty of horses and antique equipment available, and some terrific talent.

The **Patuxent River Naval Air Museum** is the country's only museum highlighting naval aviation research and development, and testing and evaluation. Seventeen aircraft tested at the station are exhibited outside. Inside is a collection of 1,300 models, samples of helmets used over the years, and displays of crew systems, cockpits, and a time line of aviation history. A library is available for research. Located at 22156 Three Notch Rd., Lexington Park, call (301) 863-7418 or visit www.paxmuseum.com.

At the *St. Clements Island Potomac River Museum* you can discover the landing site of Maryland's first European settlers. St. Mary's City is a small town—just St. Mary's College of Maryland, a post office, Trinity Episcopal Church, and Historic St. Mary's City, an outdoor living-history museum. Scant development and modernization has meant that St. Mary's is the only early permanent English settlement that has remained largely undisturbed. That makes it is a favorite of archaeologists, who have uncovered millions of artifacts in a relatively short time.

George McWilliams III (a former area native who has retired to West Virginia) created the 20-by-8-foot oil-on-canvas mural depicting the landing of the first colonists to found the colony of Maryland in 1634. However, the people in the painting are more modern residents, including Kim Cullins, marketing and program specialist for the St. Clements Museum (she's standing in the group of three behind the men carrying the cross), and the two people standing next to her are McWilliams' parents. McWilliams went to St. Clements Island in March and took pictures so he'd know how the sky and trees looked at that time of the year. Including research, it took him a year to complete the painting.

You can see the replica of the square-rigged **Maryland Dove,** one of the two ships that brought the first settlers and supplies from England; the reconstructed State House of 1676; the Godiah Spray Tobacco Plantation; archaeological excavations; the Margaret Brent Memorial Garden; and a visitor center with an archaeology exhibit hall, guided walking tours, and museum gift shop. It's difficult to believe you're barely an hour from Washington, D.C. (well, depends on the traffic), while walking through this seventeenth-century capital. The 800 acres of unspoiled tidewater landscape whisper tranquility.

The museum is open daily and weekends from 10 a.m. to 5 p.m. from late Mar through Sept, and then Wed through Sun from noon to 4 p.m. the rest of

Be My Loveville Valentine

In 1989 Eva C. Hall decided the postmark from her zip code, 20656, should be red and have a cherubic arrow-shooter aiming toward a heart, particularly around the first half of February. It's understandable; 20656 is Loveville, named after Kingsley Love, the town's first postmaster. Hall has worked at the post office for thirty years, and she receives mail from around the world so special cards and letters will have a special stamp for Valentine's Day. About 30,000 pieces of mail will be hand-stamped at this post office, which normally sees about 400 pieces a day. Most come from visitors from nearby Washington, Virginia, Pennsylvania, and, of course, Maryland, but other letters have come from as far away as Japan. The post office is at 27780 Point Lookout Rd., Loveville 20656. Call (301) 475-5243.

the year. Located at 38370 Point Breeze Rd., Colton's Point; call (301) 769-2222 or visit www.stmarysmd.com/recreate/museums/stclementsisland.asp

With more miles of shoreline than square miles of land and a college campus full of students, you know this has to be a good party town (the college shudders at that reputation) that is surpassed by its academic reputation. However, one can study only so long. St. Mary's College of Maryland was formerly St. Mary's Female Seminary, and it is considered one of the best buys in education, with an excellent teacher-student ratio and a small enrollment of about 1,300 students. It's considered the Public Honors College, which, as a student or parent of a student, that is the reputation that should interest you. The cafeteria is open 24 hours when school is in session. Visitors can also access the exercise room and swimming pool with a pass. Located at 18952 East Fisher Rd., St. Mary's City; call (240) 895-2000 or visit www.smcm.edu.

A major social and sailing event is the annual August overnight ***Governor's Cup Yacht Race*** down the Chesapeake from Annapolis to St. Mary's (current capital to first capital). When the race is over and the boats have been rafted, there's live music, food vendors, and an awards ceremony. Among the crew members on the 148 boats in 2006 were Maryland Special Olympics sailors who joined the thrill of this oldest and longest race on the Chesapeake. None of them had ever participated in an overnight race before. National sailors consider the annual Governor's Cup one of the ten best sailing parties of the year (there's that reputation again). The water is also perfect for those interested in sailboarding. With St. Mary's mild winters, students can enjoy boating about six months of the school year. Call (240) 895-3039 or (240) 895-2000; or visit www.smcm.edu/govcup.

The ***Freedom of Conscience Statue*** at the entrance to the college was erected by the counties of Maryland and symbolizes the religious freedom on

Buzzy's Country Store

As you head toward Point Lookout, at the very southern tip of St. Mary's, you're likely to find Ridgell's Country Store. It's been there since about Civil War days. Clarence "Buzzy" Ridgell, its proprietor since 1953 died June 11, 2009, at the age of 84. His oldest son, J. Scott Ridgell now runs the place. This is where you come for beer, souvenirs, pennants, bait, wine, friendship, and other "stuff." Among other things (Buzzy was a St. Mary's county commissioner in the 1960s), he collected several hundred hats over the years, most of them hanging from the ceiling. They were from as far away as Australia and Russia. Stop by, say hello to Bruno, the eighth Saint Bernard (all named Bruno, even the females, which this one happens to be) to greet customers. Located at 12665 Point Lookout Rd., Scotland; call (301) 872-5430.

Tasty Treat

Stuffed baked ham is a traditional meal in these parts and one of the best places to try it is at Raley's Town and Country Market in Ridge. An average twenty-pound ham will include about ten pounds of cabbage, a pound or so of kale, three pounds of onions, some crushed red pepper, and some black pepper. The fat is trimmed off the bone and removed, and slits (about 1–2 inches deep) are made in the ham. Then the shredded veggies are stuffed into the slits and where the bone was. The stuffed ham is baked for about five hours. It's usually very salty, so eat with fresh biscuits to cut the salty taste. Raley's Town and Country Market, Point Lookout Rd., Ridge; (301) 872-5121.

which the state was founded. In 1649, at the request of town officials from St. Mary's City, a guarantee of freedom of conscience to all Christians (freedom of other religions came later) was enacted by the state legislature.

Buying locally is today's black in culinary talk. Even those who have been buying from farmers and farmers' markets for years probably have not heard of the **Circle C Oyster Ranch.** Bring your cooler and some ice so you'll have a place to stow the oysters that you "pick." You can watch or assist the oyster harvesting from floats at St. Jerome's Bay. The experience is available all year on Mon, Wed, Thurs, and Fri from 8 a.m. to 4 p.m. and on weekends by appointment. Located at 49944 Airedele Rd., Ridge; call (301) 872-4177 or visit www.oysterranching.com.

All is not water, water, everywhere, in St. Mary's County; some of the area is devoted to produce farms. One major enticement of the county is the **Charlotte Hall Farmers Market,** with its Amish goods, produce, antiques, and curios. As with most farmers' markets, the earlier you arrive, the better the selection. The market is open year-round on Wed, Sat, and Sun. Mon through Sat, Apr through Oct, from 8 a.m. to 5 p.m. Located at 30030 Three Notch Rd., Charlotte Hall; call (301) 884-3966.

The **Captain Tyler passenger ferryboat** runs between Point Lookout State Park and Smith Island, on weekends May through Oct. The cost is $30 for the daytrip up to $299 per couple for the overnight package, with overnight accommodations at the Cove or the Paddlewheel Motel. Call (410) 425-2771 or visit www.smithislandcruises.com.

The lighthouse at **Point Lookout State Park** at the confluence of the Potomac River and Chesapeake Bay is considered the most haunted lighthouse in America. Paranormal aficionados say male and female apparitions appear and disappear. Doors open and close without reason. Voices, snoring, and footsteps are heard. The light was the first permanent one built on the Potomac River. The grounds are available for picnicking, swimming, fishing, and enjoying the nearby campground with its 143 wooded sites (26 with full hook-up and 27 with electric). Mosquito protection is recommended during the biting season. A boat launch facility and fish-cleaning station are available. The park is open daily from sunrise to dusk. It's located at 11175 Point Lookout Rd., Scotland; call (301) 872-5688 or visit www.dnr.state.md.us/publiclands/southern/pointlookout.html.

The **Piney Point Lighthouse Museum and Historic Park** is where you can see exhibits describing the construction and operation of the lighthouse (which was in use from 1836 through 1964) and the role of the U.S. Coast Guard. You can learn about the Piney Point that was a socially elite getaway where Presidents James Monroe, Franklin Pierce, and Theodore Roosevelt visited. Other notables included Daniel Webster, Daniel C. Calhoun, and at a later time, Kate Smith. It was damaged during Hurricane Isabel's visit in 2003, so the reconstructed building sits on higher ground. Guided tours are available by reservation at (301) 769-4723. The museum, maritime exhibit, lighthouse, and store are open Fri through Mon from 10 a.m. to 5 p.m. from May through Oct. The grounds, with picnic tables, are open daily from dawn to dusk. You can visit the park by boat and tie up at a pier that is handicap accessible. Admission is $3 for adults, $1.50 for children 6 to 18, free for children under 5. Located at 44701 Lighthouse Rd., Piney Point; call (301) 994-1471 or visit www.co.saint-marys.md .us/recreate/museums/ppl.asp.

vacation
destination
fitforapresident

The Piney Point Lighthouse was known as the Lighthouse of Presidents because starting with James Madison, presidents and other notables spent their summers at Piney Point.

The **Black Panther** is a U-1105 German submarine from the World War II era that featured a rubber coating that made it "invisible" to the detection devices of the day. The sub was captured at the end of the war, and after going over it with a fine-toothed comb, the United States Navy sank it off the coast of Piney Point. Now it's Maryland's first Historic Shipwreck Diving Preserve and a National Historic Landmark. Call (301) 769-2222 or visit www.co .saint-marys.md.us/recreate/museums.

While driving through Great Mills, stop by **Cecil's Old Mill and Country Store,** one of Maryland's first industrial districts (circa 1900). You'll find locally made crafts and original artworks. It's open Mon through Sat from 10 a.m. to 5:30 p.m. and on Sun from 11 a.m. to 5:30 p.m. Located at 20853 Indian Bridge Rd.; call (301) 994-1510 or visit www.cecilscountrystore.com/index.html.

Places to Eat in Southern Maryland

ABELL

Morris Point Restaurant
38869 Morris Point Rd.
(301) 769-2500
www.morris-point.com

BROOMES ISLAND

Stoney's Seafood House
39393 Oyster House Rd.
(410) 586-1888
www.stoneysseafoodhouse
.com

CALIFORNIA

Tavern at the Village
23154 Wetsone Lane
(301) 863-3219
www.thetavernatthevillage
.com

CHESAPEAKE BEACH

Abner's Crab House
3748 Harbor Rd.
(301) 855-6705
(410) 257-3689
www.abnerscrabhouse
.com

Rod 'n Reel Smokey Joe's
4165 Mears Ave.
(301) 855-3089
www.chesapeakebeach
resortspa.com/dining.html

COBB ISLAND

Captain John's Crab House
16215 Cobb Island Rd.
(301) 259-2315
www.cjcrab.com

HOLLYWOOD

Bruster's Ice Cream
23825 Mervell Dean Rd.
(301) 373-5000
www.brusters.com

LA PLATA

Crossing at Casey Jones
417 East Charles St.
(301) 932-6226
www.thecrossingatcasey
jones.com

LEONARDTOWN

Café des Artistes
41655 Fenwick St.
(301) 997-0500
www.cafedesartistes.ws

Corbels
22770 Washington St.
(301) 997-0008
www.corbelsrestaurant
.com

Do Dah Deli
25470 Point Lookout Rd.,
Unit 3
(301) 475-3354
http://dodahdeli.com

Olde Town Pub
22785 Washington St.
(301) 475-8184
http://oldetownpub.com

LEXINGTON PARK

Tides Restaurant & Oyster Bar
46580 Expedition Dr.
(301) 862-5303
www.thetidesrestaurant.net

MECHANICSVILLE

Bert's 50s Diner
28760 Three Notch Rd.
(301) 884-3837
www.berts50sdiner.com

PINEY POINT

Evans Seafood Restaurant
16800 Piney Point Rd.
(301) 994-9944
www.evansseafood
restaurant.com

PRINCE FREDERICK

Adams, the Place for Ribs
2200 Solomons Island Rd.
(410) 586-0001
www.adamsribsprince
frederick.com

RIDGE

Spinnaker's Restaurant
16244 Millers Wharf Rd.
(301) 872-5020
www.pointlookoutmarina
.com/spinnakers

ST. MARY'S CITY

Brome Howard Inn
18281 Rosecroft Rd.
(301) 866-0656
www.bromehowardinn
.com/restaurant.htm

SOLOMONS

Catamarans Restaurant
14470 Solomon Island Rd.
(410) 326-8399
www.catamarans-
restaurant.com

Naughty Gull Restaurant and Pub
450 Lore Rd.
Spring Cove Marina
(410) 326-4855
www.naughtygullpub.com

Places to Stay in Southern Maryland

CHESAPEAKE BEACH

Chesapeake Beach Resort Spa and Hotel
4165 Mears Ave.
(410) 257-5596
(866) 312-5596
www.chesapeakebeach
resortspa.com

LA PLATA

Best Western Hotel— La Plata Inn
6900 Crain Hwy.
(301) 934-4900
(877) 528-1234
www.bestwesterninn.com

Part of Plenty B&B
8664 Port Tobacco Rd.
(301) 934-0707
(800) 520-0708
http://partofplenty.com

LEXINGTON PARK

The Miller House
46090 Wilson Court
(301) 863-5730

PINEY POINT

Camp Merryelande Vacation Cottages
15914 Camp Merryelande Rd.
(301) 994-1722
(800) 382-1073
www.campmd.com

River Creek Lodge
16680 Piney Point Rd.
(301) 994-1234
www.rivercreeklodge.com

PORT REPUBLIC

Cottages of Governors Run
2847 Governors Run Rd.
(410) 586-2346
(877) 586-1793
www.baycottages.com

PRINCE FREDERICK

Cedar Hill Country Estate
455 Barstow Rd.
(410) 474-4684
www.cedarhillplantation
.com

RIDGE

Scheible's Motel
48342 Wynne Rd.
(301) 872-0025
http://scheibles.homestead
.com/motel.html

Woodlawn Historic Bed & Breakfast
16040 Woodlawn Lane
(301) 872-0555
www.woodlawn-farm.com

ROSE HAVEN

Herrington On the Bay
7151 Lake Shore Dr.
(301) 855-8435
(800) 213-9438
www.herringtononthebay
.com

ST. LEONARD

Matoaka Beach Cabins
4510 Matoaka Lane
(410) 586-0269
www.matoakabeachcabins
.com

ST. MARY'S CITY

Brome-Howard Inn
18281 Rosecroft Rd.
(301) 866-0656
(888) 801-0656
www.bromehowardinn.com

SCOTLAND

St. Michael's Manor B&B
50200 St. Michael's Manor Way
(301) 872-4025
www.stmichaels-manor
.com

SOLOMONS

Arban Yacht Boat and Breakfast
13101 Windjammer Ave.
(443) 404-1559
(410) 326-6714
www.arbanyachtcharters
.com

Back Creek Inn B&B
210 Alexander Lane
(410) 326-2022
www.bbonline.com/md/
backcreek

OTHER ATTRACTIONS IN SOUTHERN MARYLAND

African-American Heritage Society Museum
La Plata
(301) 843-0371
www.potomacheritage.org/pathfind/afri.asp

Chesapeake Beach Water Park
Chesapeake Beach
(410) 257-1404
www.chesapeakebeachwaterpark.com

Disc Golf Course, John G. Lancaster Park
Lexington Park
(301) 863-8400, ext. 3570
www.stmarysmd.com/recreate

Greenwell State Park
Hollywood
(301) 373-9775
www.greenwellfoundation.org

Jefferson Patterson Park and Museum
St. Leonard
(410) 586-8500
www.jefpat.org

Joseph C. Lore & Sons Oyster House
Solomons
(410) 326-2042
www.calvertmarinemuseum.com

King's Landing
Huntingtown
(410) 535-2661
(410) 535-5327
www.calvertparks.org/Parks/KingsLanding/KLPhome.htm

Middleham Chapel
Lusby
(410) 326-4948
www.middlehamandstpeters.org

Skipjack Tours
Piney Point
(301) 994-2245
www.skipjacktours.com

St. Mary's River State Park
Leonardtown
(301) 872-5688
www.dnr.maryland.gov

Thomas Stone National Historic Site
Port Tobacco
(301) 392-1776
www.nps.gov/thst

Tudor Hall
Leonardtown
(301) 475-2467
www.co.saint-marys.md.us

Bowen's Inn, Inc.
14630 South Solomons Island Rd.
(410) 326-6790

Locust Inn Rooms
14478 South Solomons Island Rd.
(410) 326-9817

Solomons Holiday Inn Select
155 Holiday Dr.
(410) 326-6311
(800) 356-2009
www.ameritel.net/hisolomons

Solomons Victorian Inn
125 Charles St.
(410) 326-4811
www.solomonsvictorianinn.com

EASTERN SHORE

→

Welcome to the Eastern Shore, the middle part of the **Delmarva Peninsula** (DELaware, MARyland, and VirginiA). This is where you see as well as hear about those unfamiliar boats, the skipjack, the bugeye, and the bungy. You will also see "June bugs," the thousands of kids who invade the ocean beaches and boardwalks every summer to work at jobs and on tanning.

Explore and enjoy the dissimilarities you will find within a few short miles. Find budding artists at the Dorchester Arts Center. Search for bald eagles and great blue herons, mingle with area residents at the general store, and see centuries-old homes that have not needed restoration because they have been so well maintained over the years. Ride the ferryboats, eat at some of the best seafood restaurants in the country, and examine the fine local examples of duck-decoy carving.

Take time to locate the Mason-Dixon line; it surprises many people that it separates Pennsylvania and Maryland and it also delineates the Delaware-Maryland border. Be sure to get some sand between your toes and contemplate the treasures of America in Miniature. On the eastern side of the Chesapeake Bay lies the Eastern Shore, a very distinct and separate entity

EASTERN SHORE

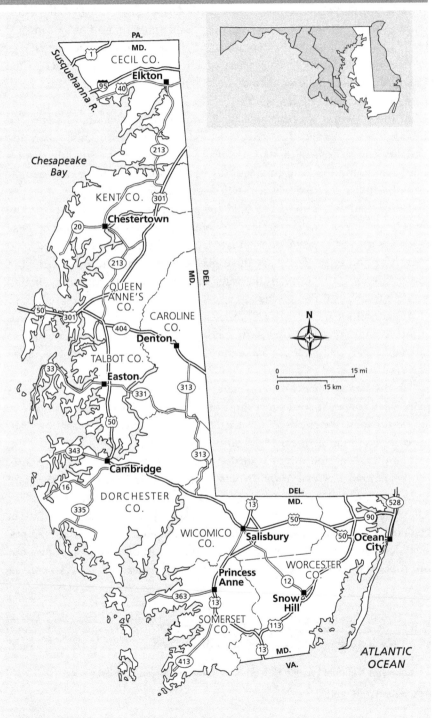

PA.
MD.
CECIL CO.
Elkton
Susquehanna R.
1
95
40
213
Chesapeake Bay
KENT CO.
301
Chestertown
20
213
QUEEN ANNE'S CO.
MD.
DEL.
CAROLINE CO.
50
301
404
Denton
TALBOT CO.
33
Easton
331
313
50
343
313
Cambridge
16
DORCHESTER CO.
335
N
0   15 mi
0   15 km
DEL.
MD.
13
WICOMICO CO.
50
Salisbury
90
528
50
Ocean City
Princess Anne
WORCESTER CO.
12
13
Snow Hill
363
SOMERSET CO.
113
13
413
MD.
VA.
ATLANTIC OCEAN

from the "western shore." People here are dedicated to the ways of the watermen and to the riches the land can bring, although farming here means just about anything that grows (except tobacco). Some of these idyllic places have become harder to find as civilization or urbanization has crept over to the Eastern Shore and huge condominium communities have sprung up almost every place that land meets water.

At the eastern end of the William Preston Lane Jr. Memorial Bridge—the Chesapeake Bay Bridge (U.S. Hwys. 50 and 301)—is Kent Island, where the first European settlement in Maryland was founded in 1631. When the settlers came, they found the Nanticoke and Choptank tribes, which are now immortalized by Indian lore exhibits and two rivers named after the tribes.

History surrounds the bay's little towns and 500 sheltered harbors. The bay is home to boat builders, sailors, fishermen, and sportsmen. Some of these waterways are still as secluded as in the days when pirates and buccaneers hid in the bays and inlets. Some say there may still be buried treasure stashed in the sand dunes. At other times the waterways can compete with traffic-bound interstate freeways for congestion.

Hunters flock here every fall, for this is a major stop for migrating birds on the Atlantic flyway. To conserve and protect those birds that are not so abundant, nearly $2 million has been raised for conservation projects along the flyway.

On the flat-as-a-pancake terrain are farmlands, stately manors, and, once again, small towns. It seems that most of Maryland is filled with small towns. And, fortunately, the towns of the Eastern Shore are always sponsoring festivals celebrating the richness of the land or the sea.

Many crafters and artisans are located along the Lower Eastern Shore, and the *Lower Eastern Shore Heritage Council* (LESHC) has a brochure listing artists, galleries and museums, and a calendar of art-related events. For example, there are coppersmiths, paper makers, painters, and specialists in ceramics. How much better to pick up some memorable item for a souvenir or home decor item, than to buy a dirty-language T-shirt or to cocoon yourself in your room should it happen to rain for your entire vacation. You can contact

AUTHOR'S FAVORITES EASTERN SHORE

Blackwater National Wildlife Refuge	Ward Museum of Wildfowl Art
Plumpton Park Zoo	

the Council at 212 West Main St, Salisbury; (410) 677-4707; www.lowershore heritage.org.

Another Eastern Shore campaign, started in 2009, is "Eat, Drink, Buy Art," designed to entice you from the Western Shore to visit and explore the talented people who live here. Nine communities—Berlin, Cambridge, Chestertown, Easton, Elkton, Denton, Princess Anne, Salisbury, and Snow Hill—have united to promote the a combination of outstanding restaurants, galleries, shops, events, and artists that you might not otherwise notice. A brochure and Web site (www.eatdrinkbuyart.com) allow you to search their database for just what you want.

For the past few years Maryland has provided a booklet called *The Bay Game* to help youngsters (and their parents) spend meaningful and educational time while traveling from the Bay Bridge to the Ocean. *The Bay Game* contains puzzles, a bookmark, games, and more. In 2002 the booklet introduced Cooper and Hanna, two water droplets that tell their story of traveling through the Chesapeake Bay watershed. The booklets are sometimes available at tollbooths, or download a copy from the Web site. Call (877) 620-8367, ext. 8016 or visit www.dnr.state.md.us/baygame.

Our Eastern Shore excursion starts at the top of the bay and works its way down and to the east, over to the Atlantic Ocean.

Cecil County

Starting at the top of the state, at the head of the Chesapeake Bay, we begin at Cecil County.

If you have seen such movies as The Manchurian Candidate (at least the original), Guys and Dolls, The Philadelphia Story, Pillow Talk, and Solid Gold Cadillac, then you have heard people talking about eloping to Elkton or going to "that town in Maryland" to get married. Until the late thirties, Elkton was known as the Marriage Capital of the World. Tens of thousands of couples were wed here, and one can assume most of them were eloping. They came to Elkton because it was the first county seat south of New York that did not require a waiting period or blood test before the ceremony was performed. The practice lasted until 1939 when the state legislature enacted a 48-hour waiting law. The reputation continued, though, at least in films.

Only one wedding chapel remains, the ***Little Wedding Chapel.*** This is where Babe Ruth and Joan Fontaine were married (no, not to each other), among dozens of notables, and this is where nearly 1,000 couples are still married each year. Located at 142 East Main St, Elkton; call (410) 398-3640 or (302) 740-1846 or visit www.historiclittleweddingchapel.com.

filmscene sightings

You'll see Elk Neck State Park, North East, twice during Clint Eastwood's film, Absolute Power. He plays Luther Whitney, whose estranged daughter Kate (played by Laura Linney), regularly jogs in the park. And, if you happened to catch Dead Man's Curve (1998), the lighthouse scene was shot at the Elk Neck Lighthouse in Elk Neck State Park.

For a post vow exchange meal, head to the *Howard House Tavern,* a business that's been around since 1853 and has the photos and keepsakes to prove it. Lunch and dinner feature Maryland seafood and shellfish, housemade soups, and burgers that are half-price on Monday. It's located at 101 West Main St; call (410) 398-4646 or visit www .howardhousetavern.com.

Fair Hill Nature and Environmental Center is a facility located in the northern half of the 5,600-acre Fair Hill Natural Resources Management Area in northeastern Cecil County. One of the state's remaining covered bridges is at Fair Hill, which was a 7,000-acre estate owned by William DuPont Jr. The entire Maryland portion was purchased by the state as a Natural Resource Area. In the northern reaches of the property, near the Pennsylvania border, is the 1850s covered bridge. The headquarters building was formerly used by DuPont as his hunting lodge and

A Beloved Place

Fair Hill Nature and Environmental Center will look familiar to those of you who saw the Oprah Winfrey film Beloved—about half of the movie was shot on the property. According to Carol Cebula, who was office administrator at Fair Hill at the time, the house was built from scratch and was "aged" for the movie. Only those rooms used in the movie were actually decorated; the rest were left bare. The back of the house was constructed of plywood so the cameras could have access for filming.

The movie's other buildings, particularly the log structures, were imported from North Carolina, where they had been dismantled and shipped to Maryland to be reassembled. The farm animals were brought in and the garden was planted.

A barn, smokehouse, outhouse, corn crib, carriage shed, and other farm structures were built, two wells were drilled, telephone cables were installed, the heating and air conditioning were upgraded, roadways were laid, and a new Chevy Tahoe was given to the center. In all, Fair Hill received about $1 million in cash and donated items.

All of this for about two weeks' worth of shooting! Ed Walls, the former Fair Hill manager, was in the movie as a ticket taker in the carnival scene and was the only staff member who had a part in the film.

is next to the covered bridge over Big Elk Creek. There are two Mason-Dixon line markers on the property.

This is an outdoor education school with programs designed to encourage awareness, understanding, and appreciation of the natural world, our natural resources, and the impact of people on the environment. The indoor and outdoor classrooms are open Mon through Fri and on occasional weekends and evenings for members of the Fair Hill Environmental Foundation Inc. (a private, nonprofit support group) and for groups by reservation. Program subjects might include bird identification, wildflowers, marsh studies, landscaping, animal designs for survival, aquatic studies, basic entomology, clean water watch, ecology, forestry, and soil studies.

tri-statearea

Located in the northeastern corner of Maryland, midway between Baltimore and Philadelphia, Cecil County is the only Maryland county that is considered part of the Wilmington, Delaware, New Jersey, and Maryland primary metropolitan statistical area.

Foxcatcher Farms Covered Bridge, one of Maryland's six remaining original covered bridges (there were 70), is located on this property and is available to those who enjoy horseback riding, biking, or hiking. It was built over the Big Elk Creek in 1860 and in 1994 it received the State's Historic Civil Engineering Landmark award. Visit the Web site at www.mdcoveredbridges.com/foxcatcherfarms.html.

The Fair Hill Nature and Environmental Center's operating hours vary according to the time of the year, generally meaning they're open weekdays from about 9 a.m. to 2:30 p.m. or so. However, during other hours, weekends, and other non-open days, board members and some staff might be working there and will open the doors so you can visit. Located at 630 Tawes Dr., Elkton; call (410) 398-4909 or visit www.fairhillnature.org.

Across State Rte 273 is the ***Steeplechase Track at Fair Hill,*** an exact replica of Aintree, where England's Grand National is held. Since it opened in 1933 there have been a number of steeplechase races annually, and the May event is the only steeplechase in the United States that permits pari-mutuel wagering. Call (410) 398-6565 or visit www.fairhillraces.org.

The National Steeplechase and Hunt Association moved its headquarters from Belmont, New York to Fair Hills, in June 1989. Call (410) 392-0700 or visit www.nationalsteeplechase.com for more information.

Detouring a little before heading down the Eastern Shore, you can visit another covered bridge (or "kissing" bridge) in Cecil. ***Gilpin's Falls covered bridge*** has a 119-foot span and a 13-foot roadway, and it is adjacent to State Rte 272 over Northeast Creek, ½ mile north of Bayview. You'll have to look

dueling
newspapers

quick, though, because it's been vandalized and weather-beaten and may be beyond repair. Reportedly, the bridge's arches were made from single timbers, which were curved to shape by balancing them on stumps and pulling their ends down. The bridge was constructed in the 1850s, abandoned in the 1930s, and left to disintegrate until 1959, when it was restored. Traffic along Rte 272 bypasses the bridge, which is within a few yards of the roadway. For more information, visit www.mdcovered bridges.com/gilpinsfalls.html.

If your children think ice cream comes from a store and not from a cow, stop by **Kilby Cream** in Rising Sun. Since 2005, the Kilby family has been making its own delicious ice cream. How can you resist such flavors as "udderly chocolate," "chocolate raspberry," "tractor tracks," "mango," and "fear the turtle"? They also have locally made soups and fresh sandwiches from Rumbleway Farm. The candy is from LUMU Candy and the blueberries are from Spring Valley Farm. Oh, and the strawberries are from Walnut Springs Farm. They've transformed the old milkhouse at the end of the lane into a ceramic studio with regularly scheduled workshops. A second shop, **Kilby's Canal Creamery** is open seasonally in Chesapeake City. They're open Thurs through Sun from 11:30 a.m. to 7 p.m. Stop by Kilby Cream at 129 Strohmaier Lane; or call (410) 658-8874 or visit www.kilbycream.com.

The **Day Basket Factory** was established in 1876 in the town of North East and still makes oak splint baskets the old-fashioned way. Shortly after the Civil War, Edward and Samuel Day came to North East from Massachusetts to make their baskets because the wood was plentiful, the transportation was good, and the demand for their wares, particularly from cotton pickers, was great. Business boomed, and during World War I the factory had thirty-five people on its payroll turning out 2,000 baskets a week. There are now four or five basket makers there who produce old-time baskets, from lunch and market styles to fruit and bread baskets. Antiques are tucked into nooks surrounding the baskets.

Water Power

The Susquehanna River separates the western border of Cecil County from the eastern border of Harford County. At one time there were two covered bridges crossing the Susquehanna River, but the last one was flooded with the construction of the **Conowingo Hydroelectric Plant.** Built in 1928, Conowingo is one of the largest hydroelectric plants in the northeast and the biggest fish lift in the United States. Tours are available for school groups only, grades 5 through 12. The enormous dam forms a freshwater lake 14 miles long, impounding some 105 billion gallons of water. It is a noted fishing spot. There's a public swimming pool, open from Memorial Day through Labor Day. The plant is located on U.S. Hwy. 1 in Conowingo. Call (410) 457-5011 for more information.

The shop is open Mon through Sat from 11 a.m. to 5 p.m. from June 1 to Labor Day and at various times during other seasons. You may not see workers in the factory on Sat, though. Located at 714 South Main St, North East; call (410) 287-6100 or visit www.daybasketfactory.com.

Plumpton Park Zoo, the second-largest zoo in Maryland, is a rural zoological garden that features plants and exotic and native animals, including emus, wallabies, llamas, bison, Persian sheep, Chinese deer, miniature donkeys, pygmy goats, wild turkeys, and Australian black swans in a country setting.

Eighteenth-century buildings and ruins are on the grounds, including the 1734 mill that houses the gift shop. The zoo has an adopt-an-animal program, with prices ranging from $25 for an Amazon parrot or Australian black swan to $250 for a giraffe or a Siberian tiger, with options in between.

Plumpton Park Zoo is open daily from 11 a.m. to 4 p.m. Apr 1 through Sept 30, and on Mon, Wed, and Fri from 11 a.m. to 3 p.m. in Oct, weekends in Nov, weather permitting. It's closed Dec 1 through Mar. Admission is $11.95 for adults, $10.95 for seniors sixty and over, and $7.95 for children 2 through 12. Group tours are available by reservation. Located at 1416 Telegraph Rd. (Rte 273), Rising Sun; call (410) 658-6850 or visit www.plumptonparkzoo.org.

Heading farther south is Chesapeake City, where you'll come across the *Chesapeake and Delaware Canal.* On October 17, 1829, it made water transportation in the northern part of the Bay even more important. At that time the canal had four locks, but the Corps of Army Engineers lowered the canal to sea level in 1927, thus eliminating the need for locks.

Receiving considerably less publicity than the C&O Canal, the 14-mile C&D Canal cuts off about 350 miles of water navigation for ships. It carries 40 percent of all the ship traffic in and out of the Port of Baltimore. The

JANUARY

AGH Penguin Swim
Ocean City
(410) 641-9858
www.ocean-city.com/calendar/#jan

FEBRUARY

National Outdoor Show
Church Creek
(410) 397-8535
www.nationaloutdoorshow.org

MARCH

Bay to Ocean Writers Conference
Wye Mills
(443) 786-6938
www.baytoocean.com

Eagle Festival
Blackwater National Wildlife Refuge
Cambridge
(410) 228-2677
www.fws.gov/blackwater

St. Patty's Day Parade
Chesapeake City
(410) 885-5298
www.chesapeakecity.com/calendar2
.htm

St. Patrick's Day Parade and Festival
Ocean City
(410) 289-6156
www.ocean-city.com/calendar/#mar

APRIL

Bay Bridge Boat Show
Kent Island
(410) 268-8828
www.usboat.com

Blessing of the Boats
Smith Island
(410) 651-2968
(800) 521-9189
www.visitsomerset.com/pages/events
.html

Daffodil Show
Princess Anne
(410) 651-3803
www.teacklemansion.org

MD International Kite Festival
Ocean City
(410) 289-7855
www.ococean.com

Salisbury Festival
Salisbury
(410) 749-0144
www.salisburyarea.com

Spocott Windmill Day
Lloyds
(410) 228-7090

Spring Celebration
Berlin
(410) 641-4775
www.berlinchamber.org

**Ward World Championship
Wildfowl Carving**
Ocean City
(410) 742-4988, ext. 106
www.wardmuseum.org

MAY

1800s Festival
Fairmount
(410) 651-3945
www.visitsomerset.com/pages/events
.html

Antique Aircraft Fly-in
Cambridge
(301) 490-6759

Kent Island Days
Stevensville
(410) 643-5358

Soft Shell Spring Fair
Crisfield
(410) 968-2500
(800) 782-3913
www.crisfieldchamber.com

Springfest
Ocean City
(410) 250-0125
(800) OC-OCEAN
www.ococean.com

JUNE

Bay Music Festival
Centreville
(410) 604-2100
www.baymusicfestival.com

Chesapeake Bay Wine Festival
Stevensville
(410) 739-6943
www.chesapeakebaywinefestival.org

Chesapeake Chamber of Music Festival
Easton, Queenstown, Chestertown
(410) 819-0380
http://chesapeakechambermusic.org

Cypress Festival
Pocomoke City
(410) 957-1919
www.pocomoke.com

EagleMan Ironman 70.3
Cambridge
(410) 964-1246
www.tricolumbia.org

Eastern Shore Fishing Derby
Salisbury
(410) 548-4900, ext. 109
www.wicomicorecandparks.org

Rock Hall Annual Rockfish Tournament
Rock Hall
(410) 639-6622

Scorchy Tawes Pro-Am Fishing Tournament
Crisfield
(410) 968-2500
(800) 782-3913
www.crisfieldchamber.com/events.htm

Youth Fishing Derby
Blackwater National Wildlife Refuge
Cambridge
(410) 228-2677
www.blackwater.fws.gov

JULY

Hart's Annual Peach Festival
North East
(410) 287-2650

J. Millard Tawes Crab & Clam Bake
Crisfield
(410) 968-2500
(800) 782-3913
www.crisfieldchamber.com

Kent County Fair
Chestertown
(410) 778-0416
www.kentcounty.com

Plein Air Festival
Talbot County and Easton
(410) 822-7297
http://pleinaireaston.com

Somerset County Fair
Princess Anne
(410) 651-1350
www.somersetcountyfair.org

Talbot County Fair
Easton
(410) 822-8007
www.talbotfair.org

Tuckahoe Tractor Pull
Easton
(410) 822-9868
www.tuckahoesteam.org

(continued on next page)

AUGUST

Great Pocomoke Fair
Pocomoke City
(410) 957-1919
www.pocomoke.com

National Hard Crab Derby and Fair
Crisfield
(410) 968-2500
(800) 782-3913
www.crisfield.org

Pine'eer Arts and Craft Festival
Ocean Pines
(410) 208-3060

Pirates and Wenches Fantasy Event
Rockhall
(410) 935-3491
www.rockhallpirates.com

Queen Anne's County Fair
Centreville
(410) 310-2151
www.queenannescofair.com

Seafood Feast-I-Val
Cambridge
(410) 228-1211
www.seafoodfeastival.com

Summerfest
Denton
(410) 478-2050
www.carolinesummerfest.com

Thunder on the Narrows
Chester
(410) 643-5764

Wheat Threshing, Steam and Gas Engine Show
Federalsburg
(410) 754-8422
www.threshermen.org

White Marlin Open
Ocean City
(410) 289-9229
(800) OC-OCEAN
www.whitemarlinopen.com

Worcester County Fair
Snow Hill
(410) 957-4079
www.worcestercountyfair.com

SEPTEMBER

African-American Heritage Festival
Berlin
(410) 641-3255

Autumn in Delmar Country Craft Fair
Delmar
(410) 228-6645
(800) 239-6645

Berlin Fiddlers' Convention
Berlin
(410) 641-4775

Eastern Shore Fall Festival Championship Jousting Tournament
Ridgely
(410) 482-2176

Maryland State Surfing Championships
Ocean City
(410) 213-0515

National Hard Crab Derby and Fair
Crisfield
(410) 968-2500
(800) 782-3913
www.crisfieldchamber.com/events.htm

Port Deposit Heritage Day
Port Deposit
(410) 378-2121

Skipjack Races and Land Festival
Deal Island
(410) 784-2785
www.webauthority.net/lions.htm

Sunfest
Ocean City
(410) 250-0125
(800) OC-OCEAN
www.ococean.com

**West Wicomico Heritage Ride
Bike Tour**
Salisbury
(410) 860-2447
www.wicomicorecandparks.org

Yesterdays
North East
(410) 287-2658

OCTOBER

Artisan's Festival
Centreville
(410) 758-0835

Autumn Walk at Leaf Thyme
Elkton
(410) 398-5566

Chesapeake Wildfowl Expo
Salisbury
(410) 742-4988, ext 106
www.wardmuseum.org

Fall Into St. Michaels
St. Michaels
(800) 808-SMBA
(410) 745-0411
www.bluecrab.org/st.michaels/fism.htm

**J. Millard Tawes Oyster and Bull
Roast**
Crisfield
(410) 968-2501
www.crisfieldheritagefoundation.org

**Native American Indian Heritage
Festival & Pow-wow**
Marion
(410) 623-2660
www.indianwatertrails.com

Ocean City Oktoberfest
Ocean City
(410) 524-7020
(410) 524-6440
www.oceanpromotions.info

Olde Princess Anne Days
Princess Anne
(410) 651-2238
(800) 521-9189
www.teackle.mansion.museum

**Chestertown Historic Tea Time
House Tour**
Chestertown
(410) 778-3499
www.kentcountyhistory.org

Upper Shore Decoy Show
North East
(410) 287-2675

Wye Grist Mill Day
Wye Mills
(410) 827-6909

NOVEMBER

Waterfowl Festival
Easton
(410) 822-4567
www.waterfowlfest.org

DECEMBER

First Night Talbot
Easton
(410) 820-8822
http://easternshore.com/firstnighttalbot

22,000 vessels that use it annually make it one of the busiest waterways in the world.

The **C&D Canal Museum** in Chesapeake City, located next to the canal, reviews its history and lets you see a full-size replica of the 30' Bethany Lighthouse, in use until the canal was deepened and the locks removed. The museum is open Mon through Fri from 8 a.m. to 4 p.m. Located at 815 Bethel Rd.; call (410) 885-5621 or visit www.chesapeakecity.com/about.htm.

South Chesapeake City is on the National Register of Historic Places, with picturesque Victorian architecture, antiques, waterfront restaurants, art galleries, and inns. During season, a free ferry is available several times a day to go from south to north and vice versa.

I find the other, or north, side of the canal equally interesting—at least the views are. During the ride or walk across the Hatem bridge, 135 feet in the air, you can see the canal's course for miles. From the north side you can see the pilots on their pilot boats going to and from the ships navigating the canal. Stop by the Pilot House for information and a schedule on ships coming through. Call (410) 885-5622 or visit www.nap.usace.army.mil/sb/c&d.htm.

Kent County

Kent County has the largest proportion of farmland to total acreage of the Upper Eastern Shore counties, yet it is bordered on the north by the Sassafras River, on the south and the east by the Chester River, and on the west by the Chesapeake Bay, so you can understand its multiple focal points. There might be an Old-Fashioned Fourth festival in Rock Hall, an Eastern Shore fish fry, and a Kent County Watermen's Association workboat race and docking competition, all on the same summer weekend.

After the harvest, it is time for snow goose and deer hunting. For those who prefer architectural history to land and water sports, Chestertown, the county seat of the smallest county in the state, is said to be the tenth-favorite historic place in America because of the large number of restored eighteenth- and nineteenth-century homes. In 2007, the National Trust named the city one of America's Dozen Distinctive Destinations. They note the "historic buildings are the backdrop for visitors who enjoy ambling along redbrick sidewalks, peeking over garden walls, and exploring antiques shops, galleries, specialty stores, and sidewalk cafes. Among the town's finest historic buildings are the Hynson-Ringgold House (renowned for its unusual antler staircase and hip roof) and Wide Hall (a masterpiece of Georgian architecture), and the Custom House (intricate Flemish Bond brickwork). Chestertown is small, with fewer than 5,000 residents according to the 2000 census. However, it is the home of the renowned Washington College. It's also known for having about a half-dozen consignment shops including **Scotties Shoes & Consignments** (307 High St; (410) 778-4944) where you can buy the New York Times, greeting cards, magazines, maps, and sometimes some footwear. Sales from the **Nearly New Shop** (High & Spring Sts; (410) 778-1781) benefit the Chester River Hospital Center Auxiliary.

Sophie Kerr, who grew up in Caroline County, is known for many things. She started writing when she was 18, worked on newspapers, and then moved to New York City. According to the Washington College magazine, "she saw 23 novels, hundreds of shorts stories, and a cookbook published during her lifetime." She bequeathed $500,000 to Washington College with instructions to fund a promising graduating writer each year and provide funds for visiting writers and scholars, scholarships, library books, and literary publications. Her home is still there, privately owned and not open for tours. Learn more at www.tourcaroline.com/landmarks.shtml.

Kent Island is the eastern terminus of the almost annual Chesapeake Bay Bridge Walk. Usually held the first Sunday in May, the walk has been cancelled three times due to inclement weather in 1980, 2002, and 2007. It was cancelled in 2003 for heightened security, was cancelled in 2005 for westbound construction and then again in 2008, 2009, and 2010 because of resurfacing and reconstruction of the bridges. As many as 50,000 people participate in the 4.3 mile (or so) walk, including those using wheelchairs. It is absolutely fascinating, looking at the expansion joints, seeing the world from as much as 186 feet over the Bay, and watching the freighters and pleasure boats sailing and motoring below.

For current traffic conditions at the Bay Bridge, call 1-877-BAYSPAN. Visit www.baybridge.com to view traffic images from the bridge's approaches, sign up for e-mail and traffic alerts and learn more about the Bay Bridge Preservation Project.

When driving through Kent County, you're encouraged to take time to see such local sights as the picturesque view of waterfront homes at Chestertown; the Eastern Neck National Wildlife Refuge; the Geddes-Piper House, a Philadelphia-style town house that serves as a museum and the home of the Kent County Historical Society; the Kitty Knight House; the 3,000-acre wildlife research and demonstration area known as Chesapeake Farms, the Rock Hall Museum, the Tolchester Beach Revisited Museum, and the Waterman's Museum; and Washington College, the tenth-oldest college in this country, which George Washington helped found.

At the **Kent County Museum** are indoor and outdoor exhibits of farm machinery from the last two centuries. The county gave a group of local farmers one hundred acres, twenty-five acres of which they ran on a volunteer basis to help defray the museum's operating costs. It was started about two dozen years ago, and people from the area and as far away as Pennsylvania have donated equipment to it. Two early farm tractors mark the entrance, so you can't miss it.

Inside and outside the 40-by-150-foot building are exhibits on equipment used in planting and harvesting corn, wheat, soy, and other grains. You will see threshers, tools from preindustrial days, and modern-day combines and reapers. Other exhibits explain the work done by hand planters, automated corn planters, and tractors (the earliest tractor on display is a 1947 model).

On the first Saturday in August is a threshing dinner. Of course, if you just happen by at other times of the year when workers are planting or otherwise tending to the fields, you can watch them at work then, too. No admission is charged, but contributions are accepted. Kent Museum is open noon to 3 p.m. on the first and third Saturday of each month, May through Oct, and by appointment. Located at 13689 Turner's Creek Public Rd.; call (410) 348-5543 or visit http://kentcounty.com/farmmuseum.

Bicycle tours are popular in Kent County, and the Tourism Development Office has prepared a booklet, *The Kent County Bicycle Tour,* for your information. Included are nine routes developed by the Baltimore Bicycling Club that range from 11 to 81 miles in length. Routes include the 11-mile Pomona Warm-Up, which follows winding country roads, along the Chester River, and the 81-mile Pump House Primer through northern Kent County and Cecil County. In addition to tourism information, specific directions, maps, and a listing of restaurants, hotels, motels, campgrounds, and bed-and-breakfast establishments are available from the Kent County Tourism Development Office.

The **Kent Manor Inn & Restaurant** is intimate enough to feel like a bed-and-breakfast and large enough to have the amenities of a fine country estate. The property sits on 220 woodland acres on a tributary of the Chesapeake Bay. Its public spaces and twenty-four rooms are lovingly decorated. The original wing of the house was built circa 1820, with the center portion added just prior to the Civil War. This is the perfect place for a romantic getaway, a corporate retreat, and, perhaps best of all, an ideal place for a wedding (there's a garden house with seating for 150 guests), for it's secluded without being remote. A visit here means there's time to stroll the grounds, take a ride on the inn's paddleboats, swim in the Olympic-sized swimming pool, or enjoy a fine meal on the glass-enclosed sun porch when the weather permits.

You can get to the Kent Manor Inn via Rte 50 (12 miles from Annapolis), by plane (the Bay Bridge Airport is just across the street), or by boat (the dock is 38 57'50.34 North and 76 18'52.61 West on Thompson Creek, accessible via

Area (land): 10,455 square miles (27,077 square kilometers), forty-second in size

Capital: Annapolis

Largest city: Baltimore

Number of counties: twenty-three, plus Baltimore City

Highest elevation: Backbone Mountain, 3,360 feet (1,024 meters)

Lowest elevation: sea level, along the Atlantic Ocean

Greatest distance from north to south: 124 miles (199 kilometers)

Greatest distance from east to west: 238 miles (383 kilometers)

Coastline: 31 miles (50 kilometers) of Atlantic Ocean coastline, 3,190 miles (5,134 kilometers) of Chesapeake Bay coastline

Population: 5,699,478 (2009 estimate), nineteenth among the states

Population density: 541 persons per square mile

Population distribution: 86 percent urban, 14 percent rural

Median family income: $89,608 (family of four)

Statehood: April 28, 1788 (seventh state)

Nickname: the Old Line State, the Free State, America in Miniature

State flower: black-eyed Susan

State tree: white oak

State motto: Fatti maschii, parole feminine (Manly deeds, womanly words)

State bird: Baltimore oriole

State fossil shell: *Ecphora quadricostata*

State cat: calico

State dessert: Smith Island Cake

State exercise: walking

State horse: Thoroughbred

State dog: Chesapeake Bay retriever

State reptile: diamondback terrapin (*Malaclemys terrapin*)

State fish: striped bass (rockfish, *Morone saxatilis*)

State crustacean: Maryland blue crab (*Callinectes sapidus*)

State insect: Baltimore checkerspot butterfly (*Euphydryas phaeion*)

State dinosaur: Astrodon johnstoni

State boat: skipjack

State song: "Maryland, My Maryland"

State sport: jousting

State folk dance: square dancing

State theaters: Center Stage, Baltimore; Olney Theater Center, Olney (summer theater)

State drink: milk

Cox Creek and Eastern Bay. The dock is 3½ feet at mean low water). Located at 500 Kent Manor Dr., Kent Island, Stevensville; call (410) 643-5757, (800) 820-4511 (lodging), (410) 643-7716 (dining); or visit www.kentmanor.com.

If you'd like to see a full-size, exact replica of a 1768 schooner that plied the waters of colonial North America in the service of the Royal Navy, then head to the foot of Canon Street—Chestertown's waterfront—to see the **Schooner Sultana.** Built directly from original plans, *Sultana* was launched in 2001 and is considered to be one of the most accurate vessel replications in the world today. The *Sultana*'s mission is to provide unique, hands-on educational experiences in colonial history and environmental science throughout the Chesapeake Bay area.

So, if she's not at her home dock, she is probably sailing and visiting the ports of such neighboring Chesapeake Bay towns as Annapolis, Baltimore, and St. Michaels. *Sultana* also is available for private charters, serving up to thirty passengers. She is suitable for events including private sailing charters from two hours to five days in length, dockside receptions, festivals, and reenactments. The vessel is Coast Guard certified and is staffed by a professional captain and crew. Located at 105 South Cross St, Chestertown; call (410) 778-5954 or visit www.schoonersultana.com.

When you travel through Rock Hall, in southwestern Kent County, you may notice **Tallulah's on Main,** a gallery/gift shop and a five-suite hotel, and wonder about the name. According to Jim Messersmith, owner of Tallulah's, the famed movie star Tallulah Bankhead used to shop at this location when it was a general store; she bought her meats and gourmet items next door when it was Myer's meat market. Many of the locals still remember her frequent visits, and her grandnieces visit the gift shop and gallery. Jim says they liked the name, but "most of all felt that she needed to be honored still as a great actress and woman of our time." The folks at Tallulah's have several books about her life and wonderful stories. Tallulah's also rents a house on the beach with a beautiful due-west sunset view all year long. Located at 105 South Cross St, Chestertown; call (410) 778-5954 or visit www.Tallulahs onmain.com.

Queen Anne's County

The **Old Wye Grist Mill** is the oldest business in Queen Anne's County, in operation since about 1682 and powered by water. At least three mills (two grist and one saw) have been located in this area for more than 300 years, giving the town of Wye Mills its name. Among its historic claims is the fact that Robert Morris, financier of the American Revolution, purchased ground cornmeal from this mill to be used as provisions for George Washington's Continental army at Valley Forge in 1778.

The Wye Mill is open Fri, Sat, and Sun from 10 a.m. to 4 p.m. and by appointment from mid-Apr through mid-Nov. There is no admission charge, but donations are appreciated. Located at 28637 Queen Anne's Hwy.; call (410) 827-3850 or visit www.oldwyemill.org.

Queen Anne's is known for its sprawling countryside and 410 farms, averaging 400 acres each, terrific access to the bay and bay tributaries, and the genteel lifestyle it promotes. Kent Narrows, formerly known for its horrendous weekend beach traffic jams, has become a minor destination of its own, with plenty of historic sites, fine boating, golf, and dining.

The meeting place of the Eastern Shore since 1955, however, has been **Holly's Restaurant,** noted for having the best milkshakes (with four scoops of ice cream and three ounces of milk) and fried chicken (cooked in peanut oil, I'm told) in the state. The waitresses are friendly and the tables are wooden and devoid of such frills as tablecloths. Holly's is located at 108 Jackson Creek Rd., Grasonville; call (410) 827-8711 or visit www.hollysrest.com.

fastball foxx

James or Jimmie "Double X" Foxx was born in Sudlersville. Known for pitching right-handed for the Philadelphia Athletics, he was enrolled in the National Baseball Hall of Fame in 1951. It's said the coach in the movie *A League of Their Own* was based on Foxx.

Birdlife photographers and observers will enjoy the **Wildfowl Trust of North America's Chesapeake Bay Environmental Center** and the adjacent captive wildfowl collection in Grasonville. Surrounded by more than 500 acres of natural beauty, the center has a fascinating and colorful flock of wildfowl, including ducks, geese, and swans, and nearby are deer, red foxes, river otters, and bald eagles living in the brackish marsh, pine forest, shrub habitat, meadow, and shallow water impoundment. Special screening allows you to quietly enter blinds so you can observe wildlife without disturbing it. Nature trails, wetland boardwalks, the observation towers, and viewing blinds offer a variety of ways to see the wildlife and a panoramic view of Chesapeake Bay.

The Wildfowl Trust of North America, founded in 1979, is responsible for the center, and you can be sure of programs, guided walks, workshops, a wetland festival, and lectures promoting stewardship of our dwindling wetland resources. A gift shop and a shaded picnic area are also on-site.

The center is a half-mile from State Rte 18, off Perry Corner Rd. Admission is $5 for adults, $4 for seniors age fifty-five or older, and $2 for children age 18 and younger. Dogs are not permitted. The center is open daily from 9 a.m. to 5 p.m. It is closed Thanksgiving, Dec 24 and 25, New Year's Day, and Easter. Located at 600 Discovery Lane; Grasonville; call (410) 827-6694 or visit www.bayrestoration.org.

Talbot County

Tourists coming through this area on their way to St. Michaels—about 100,000 each year—stop to see the Chesapeake Bay Maritime Museum, the Customs House, St. Michaels Museum at St. Mary's Square, the Robert Morris Inn, and Tilghman Island. The Chesapeake Bay Maritime Museum receives by far the most tourists, and well it should.

The *St. Michaels Museum at St. Mary's Square* exhibits items of significance to the local history and culture, not just of St. Michaels, but of the land between Tilghman and Royal Oak, called the Bay 100—that portion of land that could be defended by one hundred armed men. Two buildings, originally part of a steam saw- and gristmill, are used for this museum, one of them dating from 1820 and one from 1860. The latter is referred to as the "Teetotum" building because it is shaped like a child's four-sided top of that name. In the 1820 building are artifacts from 1800 to 1850, in the kitchen area are items from 1850 to 1900, and in the Teetotum room are articles from colonial days to about 1950. The museum is open May through Oct on Fri and Sun from 1 to 4 p.m., Sat 10 a.m. to 4 p.m., and Mon from 10 a.m. to 1 p.m. Admission is $3 for adults and $1 for children (6 through 17). Call (410) 745-9561 for additional information.

Graul's Supermarket, with stores in Annapolis, Parkton, Towson, Lutherville, and Cape St. Claire, has been a favorite grocery store since 1920,

The Town That Fooled the British

The tale may be apocryphal, but the story of how St. Michaels got its nickname has been around for so long that people will swear on their mothers' graves that it's true. So you will hear that during the War of 1812, this town "was an important shipbuilding center of privateers, blockade runners, and naval barges. This activity caused an attempt by the British naval forces to destroy the shipyards and the boats under construction. On the morning of August 10, 1813, a number of British barges shelled the town and attacked a fort on the harbor side. Residents, forewarned, had hoisted lanterns to the masts of ships and the tops of the trees, causing the cannons to overshoot the town. This first 'blackout' was effective and only one house was struck. It is known as the 'Cannonball House.' St. Michaels is now known as 'The Town that Fooled the British.'"

so you can imagine the delight when a new store opened in St. Michaels. All its customers who have lived on the western side of the bay can now enjoy their favorite shopping experience where they vacation or in their new home on the Eastern Shore. The fourth generation of Grauls operates the six markets; John Evans Jr., a great-grandson of originators Fred and Esther Graul, runs this store. You'll find family recipes handed down through the generations, unmatchable friendly service, and incredibly delicious baked goods. Graul's is open Mon through Sat from 8 a.m. to 8 p.m. and Sun from 8 a.m. to 5 p.m. Located at 1212 South Talbot St, St. Michaels; call (410) 745-3537 or visit www.graulsmarket.com.

As mentioned elsewhere, six vehicular *covered bridges* still exist in Maryland. Romantic Shelters, a variation of the covered bridge and usually on private property, can be found in ten counties, including Talbot. The *Peachblossom Creek Covered Bridge* is about 50' long and is on the walking trail in the Cooks Hope Community You can see it from Rte 50, south of Easton. Visit www.mdcoveredbridges.com/romanticshelters.html for more information.

If hot (and I don't mean weather) tempts your taste buds, then a stop in St. Michaels isn't complete until you've visited *Flamingo Flats.* Their motto is: "Where taste is paramount and life's too short to eat boring food." Opened in 1988, Flamingo Flats has hot sauce and salsa specialties; cigars; a tasting bar with more than 2,000 salsas, hot sauces, marinades, and barbecue sauces; more than 500 mustards; more than 75 jars with olives as a base; and hundreds of cookbooks, gifts, and jewelry items.

Among the sauces you'll find are Chile Today Hot Tamale, Gator Hammock Gator Sauce, Jump Up and Kiss Me, Lottie's Bajan Cajan, Matouk's Hot Calypso, Ring of Fire, and Rothschild's Fiery Raspberry Salsa. If you have an asbestos tongue, step up to the tasting bar and go to town. The shop specialty is its own Cannonball sauce. Cannonball is a combination of carrots, onions, lime juice, tomato, vinegar, and habanero peppers. It's a sauce more for tasting than for destroying your intestinal lining. The store is open daily from 10 a.m. to 5 p.m. from Apr 18 through Dec 31. It is open Thurs through Mon from Jan 1 through Apr 17. Located at 100 South Talbot St, St. Michaels; call (410) 745-2053 or (800) HOT-8841; or visit www.flamingoflats.com.

As you drive southwest out of St. Michaels, and the land becomes narrower and the waters become closer, aim toward Tilghman Island and the *Phillips Wharf Environmental Center.* You can catch a cruise, charter a boat, take a water tour, and with fun and education in mind you can see the last crab shanty on Knapp's Narrows, and meet up with a blue crab, a horseshoe crab, oysters, a sea star (formerly called starfish), and other bay critters. Talk with Kelly Cox to learn more than you ever thought possible about the Bay and the area. The center is open Thurs through Mon from 10 a.m. to 4 p.m. on a volunteer basis. Call ahead. Admission is $5 for adults and $3 for children from 3 through 11. Or, take a cruise aboard the *Express Royale* or the *FUN4U* and be admitted to the center for free. Call (888) 312-7847 or visit www.pwec.org.

Bed-and-breakfast establishments seem to belong in large Victorian homes, and the ***John S. McDaniel House Bed and Breakfast,*** owned and operated by Mary Lou and Fran Karwacki, fits that description to a T. Built about 1890, the house has a high octagonal tower (a great sitting room), a hip roof with dormers, and a porch that runs across the front and part of the south side of the house. Each of the eight guest rooms is spacious and bright and equipped with air-conditioning and a ceiling fan. Fortunately, the house is located within walking distance of historic Easton. It's located at 14 North Aurora St, Easton; call (410) 822-3704 or (877) 822-5702; or visit www.bnblist.com/md/mcdaniel.

One of the ten remaining car ferries in service in Maryland is the ***Oxford-Bellevue Ferry,*** which crosses Tred Avon River and connects Oxford to Bellevue. It has been operating since 1683 and is said to be the oldest "free-running" (not cable-connected), privately owned ferry in the country.

Tom and Judy Bixler assumed ownership of the ferry in 2002. And in 2006 Judy, president, was named one of Maryland's Top 100 Minority Business Owners for the year. The program recognizes the state's best minority and women business owners and their achievements. She was cited for her business development, client satisfaction, professional affiliations, and community outreach. Besides being captain of the ferry, she's worn other hats, including president of the Oxford Business Association, a member of the advisory board of the Talbot County Board of Tourism, and a volunteer for the Festival of Trees, Oxford Invitational Fine Arts Fair, Oxford Day committee, Oxford Fire Department Building Fund, and the March of Dimes. Obviously, if you have a question about the area, good restaurants, or directions, Judy's the person to ask.

It operates from the first day of spring through the Sunday after Thanksgiving. Generally, the ferry schedule starts at 9 a.m. daily and runs until sunset, except during June, July, and Aug, when it runs until 9 p.m. The first ferry starts from the Oxford side.

It costs $10 for car and driver one-way and $16 round-trip, plus $1 per passenger each way. Bicycles are $4 one-way, $6 round-trip, and foot passengers are $3 each one-way and $5 round trip. Motorcycles are $6 one way and $9 round trip. This is a particularly photogenic ferry crossing at sunset, when the boats are all at their Oxford harbor moorings with their masts standing out against the skyline. To reach the Oxford-Bellevue Ferry from Easton, take State Rtes 333; From St. Michaels take State Rte 33 and 329 and follow the signs. Call (410) 745-9023 or visit www.oxfordferry.com.

Next to the Oxford landing is the **Customs House,** a replica of the original built in pre–Revolutionary War days when Oxford was an official port of entry. It's open on weekends when volunteers are available. Call (410) 226-5760 for more information.

For a "quiet" area, there's been a lot of activity. First, the film crew for Wedding Crashers (starring Owen Wilson, Vince Vaughn, Christopher Walken, Jane Seymour, and a number of local residents) came to St. Michaels in 2004 and there was a perceptible surge in wedding bookings, particularly at the Inn at Perry Cabin. Then, the next year Matthew McConaughey and Sarah Jessica Parker were in town for the filming of Failure to Launch.

Most recently, and perhaps the event with the longest-lasting impact, Kathy Harig opened her **Mystery Loves Company** bookstore in a century-old bank building. The store has frequent local author appearances, and as the only bookstore in Oxford, carries a full line of new and carefully read used books, not just mysteries, signed first editions, book gift baskets, and book-related gifts, children's books, and items about the Chesapeake Bay. Harig's first store was in the Fell's Point area of Baltimore, but she lives in Talbot County. The store is open Fri from 10 a.m. to 5 p.m., Sat from 10 a.m. to 6 p.m., and Sun, Mon, and Wed from10 a.m. to 4p.m. Located at 202 South Morris St; call (410) 226-0010 or visit www.mysterylovescompany.com.

Almost as good as a platter of crabs are the biscuits from **Orrell House and Bakery.** Hundreds of dozens of these heavy biscuits, which started as a source of pin money for Mrs. Orrell about fifty years ago, go out to local stores and shops around the country. The recipe, which combines flour, water, salt, lard, sugar, and baking powder, originated in Southern Maryland and the Eastern Shore during plantation days. It produces a biscuit that is soft and doughy on the inside and hard on the outside. There are some who say

wholelotta green

There are more than 240,000 acres of public land in the Maryland State Forests and Parks system, meaning there is a state forest or park within forty-five minutes of nearly every Marylander.

these biscuits are not any good until they feel like hockey pucks, and many swear by them as teething biscuits.

Believe me, just because they feel hard does not mean they have gone stale. A special pick is used to prick the tops of the biscuits (in an O and cross design) so they will not blister and burn. The bakery is open on Wed from 9 a.m. to 2 p.m. It's located at 14124 Old Wye Mill Rd. (Rte 662), Wye Mills; call (410) 822-2065.

Wye Is This Oak So Famous?

You have heard that big oaks come from little acorns, and, of course, the converse is true—little acorns come from big oaks. The Maryland Forest, Park, and Wildlife Service gather the acorns from the Wye Oak, plant them, and let them grow for a couple of years until they are established seedlings. You can purchase a Wye Oak seedling from the state for about $35 to $60 (plus tax if you live in Maryland) even though the famous oak no longer stands. They are shipped in March in time for spring planting. They cannot be shipped to Arizona, California, Florida, Louisiana, or Oregon due to quarantine restrictions. These are the cutest little trees, no bigger in diameter than your little finger, but they produce mature-size leaves, about six or seven of them the first year. They do not grow as rapidly as, say, a maple tree, but they are of substantial size within a decade. And, who knows, 400 years from now there may be a champion tree in your yard. You can also order painted Wye Oak leaves and jewelry (not from Wye Oak leaves, though). To order Wye Oak seedlings, call (800) TREES MD or order online at http://shopdnr.com; for Wye Oak items, visit www.wye-oak .com or call (301) 881-7813.

On June 6, 2002, a thunderstorm raged through Talbot County and felled the mighty Wye Oak. It was believed to be more than 450 years old and was 96 feet tall. In another word, it was HUGE. Considered to be the largest and finest white oak tree in the country, it stood in the middle of **Wye Oak State Park.** The state bought the tree and one acre around it in 1939—the first time any state ever purchased one tree just to preserve it. Over time, more land was added to make this a state park. It was the first state park to be fully accessible to the disabled.

Plans now include keeping the property as a state park, with the tree stump and a one-room schoolhouse. Fortunately, state foresters had gathered fresh buds from the tree to make clones of it. Two of the trees previously cloned from the Wye Oak have been planted at Mount Vernon, Virginia, and one probably will be planted to replace the tree that was felled.

What do you do with a downed tree that size? Well, movers built a frame around its circumference, hauled it away, and placed the remains in a warehouse (which had one of its walls removed for the tree to fit). Previously, when large branches broke off, they were carved into sculptures. A piece of lumber was sent to each county to use as they wish.

In June 1984, in the quiet hours of an early Sunday night, a thirty-five-ton limb from grand old Wye Oak crashed to the ground. Being practical, the state decided that some of the limb should be made into souvenirs, such as gavels; but 70,000 pounds of tree would make a lot of gavels. The Maryland Forest, Park, and

Wildlife Service sent a two-ton chunk of wood to sculptor Steven Weitzman to create the Wye Oak Sculpture. He carved the wood into a monument in his shop at Seneca Creek State Park in Gaithersburg. On April 3, 1985, his sculpture of two children leaning over a shovel in the act of planting a tree was moved to its permanent home at Martinak State Park, two miles east of Denton. The children, carved larger than life-size, are standing beneath a white oak tree in this 10-foot-tall statue that measures about four-and-a-half feet from front to back.

Caroline County

Caroline County is the only Eastern Shore county not directly on the ocean or the bay, but there are calm waters, such as the Choptank and Tuckahoe Rivers and Marshyhope Creek, state parks for canoeing and fishing, and an active crabbing and fishing industry. The prime interest here is agrarian, and the crops are bountiful. Corn, soybeans, cucumbers, tomatoes, peas, beans, sweet corn, cantaloupes, peaches, and melons fill the fields and make a stop at a local produce stand an essential part of anyone's visit.

Across from the Caroline County Courthouse in Denton is the **Museum of Rural Life.** The museum combines one of the original dwellings on Court House Square with new construction. There's a reception area, a gallery for rotating exhibits, and an audiovisual room. The museum explores the various aspects and changes in rural life since European settlers arrived here in the 1600s. Hundreds of artifacts, documents, and photographs have been collected. You may even uncover some of the history behind the fireworks-induced conflagration of July 4, 1865. Located at 16 North 2nd St; call (410) 479-2055 or visit www.carolinehistory.org.

Research indicates the **Linchester Historic Mill** (originally Hunting Creek Grist Mill) is the oldest working mill. The historic marker indicates it was

The Green Garden County

According to George Sands of the Caroline County Library: "On March 24, 1981, the County Commissioners of Caroline County adopted a resolution establishing an official motto for 'Caroline the Green Garden County of Maryland.' This was carried out in conjunction with the library publication of an Agricultural Directory. The research showed that at that time, Caroline County was first in Maryland in production of vegetables for markets and processing. It is among the top 3 percent in the U.S. in acreage of garden vegetables and at or near the top in Maryland and the nation in a number of related vegetable production areas. The term was coined by Bud Hutton."

known as Murray's Mill during the Revolutionary War and supplied provisions to the Continental Army. Linchester was a Colonial port of entry. It's open every weekend. Located at 3390 Linchester Rd.; Preston; call (410) 673-1910.

The historical marker next to the **Choptank Electric Cooperative** on State Rtes 404 and 328, just west of Denton, marks the modest but historic **Neck Meeting House.** Built in 1802 by members of the Society of Friends, the meetinghouse is believed to be the oldest house of worship in Caroline County. Most of the funds raised for the aluminum marker came from the recycling of aluminum cans by local residents. The Caroline County Historical Society is refurbishing the small building, and if you would like to look inside, stop by the cooperative for the key. The Society's hours are daily from 10 a.m. to 5 p.m. from Apr 1 through Nov 30 and Fri and Sat from 10 a.m. to 3 p.m. and Sun, from noon to 4 p.m. from Dec 1 through Mar 31. Located at 16 North Second St; call (410) 479-0655 or (410) 479-2055 or visit www.carolinehistory.org.

George Martinak deeded land to the state in 1961 for preservation as a recreational facility and a natural area for the enjoyment of all. The resulting effort, **Martinak State Park,** is bordered by the Choptank River and Watts Creek, and you can drop a line for bass, perch, sunfish, and catfish (a Maryland Chesapeake Bay Sportfishing License is required), camp in one of the sixty-three campsites for tent or trailer camping Apr through Oct, stay in a year-round cabin, launch your boat, rent a boat, go hiking, picnic, enjoy a ball game, or recreate on the playground. You'll also be able to see the reconstructed hull of a wrecked bungy, a type of boat used on the bay in the early nineteenth century. The park is open from sunrise to sunset daily, except Christmas week. Located at 137

ah, sweet caroline

What's in a name (to paraphrase the Bard)? Also called the Green Garden County, in the heart of the Eastern Shore, Caroline County was created in 1773 from Dorchester and Queen Anne's Counties. It's named for Lady Caroline Eden, the wife of Maryland's last Colonial governor, Robert Eden (1741–1784). Lady Caroline was the daughter of Charles Calvert, Fifth Lord Baltimore, and the sister of Frederick Calvert, Sixth Lord Baltimore.

adkins family legacy

The Adkins Arboretum at Tuckahoe State Park, west of Denton, was conceived and funded by the late Leon Andrus of Cheston-on-Wye. He suggested that it be named in honor of the Adkins family, who has produced generations of civic leaders.

Deep Shore Rd., Denton; call (410) 479-1619 or (888) 432-2267 or visit www .dnr.state.md.us.

Seven miles west of Denton, off Rte 404, is ***Tuckahoe State Park.*** Tuckahoe Creek meanders through this park, and a sixty-acre lake offers fishing and boating opportunities on twenty acres of open water. There are thirty-five campsites and four sites for youth groups. A central bathhouse with showers and toilet facilities is available. The Adkins Arboretum encompasses 500 acres of parkland and nearly three miles of walkways through the trees and shrubs. Canoes are available for rental from May to Oct. There are also other recreational options, including archery, a playground, a ball field, an equestrian center, hiking trails, a pet loop, and picnicking. Located at 12610 Eveland Rd., Ridgely; call (410) 634-2847 or visit www.adkinsarboretum.org.

Dorchester County

When you cross the Choptank River Bridge, you'll see something that looks like a large sailing yacht. It's the ***Dorchester County Visitor Center*** at ***Sailwinds Park East,*** and the mistake is understandable because the center lies amid a spectacular 110-foot fiberglass sail. Here you will find visitor information on the Eastern Shore region, a children's playground, a beach, and a boardwalk that links to the Choptank Fishing Pier. A new, permanent exhibit, "Where Land & Water Meet" was unveiled in the summer of 2008. It showcases the area's history and heritage of making a living off both the land and the water. Stunning photomurals, decoys, crab pots and agricultural tools are used to interpret how nature has played a crucial part in Dorchester's everyday life over the centuries.Located at 2 Rose Hill Pl., Cambridge, MD 21613, call (410) 228-1000 or visit www.tourdorchester.org. Such diverse events as the Seafood Festival and concerts featuring big name stars are held at the nearby ***Governors Hall at Sailwinds Park*** 200 Byrn St, Cambridge; call (410) 228-SAIL or visit www.sailwindscambridge.com.

Because Dorchester County is blessed with fairly flat terrain and lots of water, the county has created brochures of interest to boaters and birders. A bird watcher guide lists birding options at Blackwater National Wildlife Refuge and several wildlife management areas. Any of the brochures can be obtained by calling (410) 228-1000 or (800) 552-TOUR.

The ***Dorchester Arts Center*** was founded in 1970 and has between 400 and 500 members (mostly from the Cambridge area) including potters, photographers, quilters, stained-glass artists, and basket makers. They moved into new quarters, the historic Nathan Building, and now have 17,000 square feet of space with state-of-the-art classrooms, galleries, performing arts spaces,

the heart of chesapeake country

Dorchester County is located in the center of Maryland's Eastern Shore, and if you look at the shape of the county, you'll realize it's heart-shaped. That's the rationale behind the county's promotion as "the Heart of Chesapeake Country," and the state's designation as the Heart of Chesapeake Country Heritage Area.

and Studioworks, the Center's year-round gift shop. The facility is available for rent for rehearsal dinners, business meetings, and other special events. In addition to regular classes in these and other crafts, the center has two galleries where local work is exhibited and sold. Each month a new exhibit opens with a reception. During the year, the center sponsors a variety of music, dance, and educational programs, a number of which are free to the public. Each September the sidewalks along historic brick High Street, with its beautiful period homes, are festooned with the best work of 125 or more of Dorchester County artists at the Dorchester Showcase. The center is open Mon through Fri from 10 a.m. to 2 p.m. and Sat from 11 a.m. to 3 p.m. It's located at 321 High St; call (410) 228-7782 or visit www.dorchesterartscenter.org.

For more than a century, the *J. M. Clayton Company* has been stocking our favorite seafood stores, restaurants, and others with crabs and seafood, using only "blue crab crabmeat." To buy crabs, oysters, crab knives, and more, stop by their retail market Mon through Fri from 8 a.m. to 5 p.m. Plant tours are available by appointment for groups of ten or more people, $5 per person. Located at 108 Commerce St, Cambridge; call (410) 228-1661 or visit www.jmclayton.com.

Another place of interest is *Bucktown,* where Harriet Tubman lived as a child. Tubman has been called the Moses of her People because of her work in the Underground Railroad that helped free more than 300 slaves. A slave herself, Tubman ran away only to return to Delmarva nineteen times to free others. During the Civil War she served in the Union army as a nurse, scout, and spy. A birthplace marker denotes the location of the Brodess Plantation where Tubman lived with her mother and siblings. Bucktown is located on Greenbriar Rd. in Bucktown. Call (410) 288-1000 or visit www.tourdorchester.com.

A *Harriet Tubman Memorial Garden* pays tribute to Tubman with its landscaped garden, interpretive signs, and painted mural. It's on the eastbound side of Rte 50 at Washington St. For more information about Harriet Tubman and the Underground Railroad, stop by the *Underground Railroad: Harriet Tubman Museum and Educational Center.* A grant of $25,000 from the Maryland Commission for Celebration 2000 is allowing archaeologists to "locate

Annie Oakley Lived Here

As you're driving through the area, you might stop by 28 Bellevue Ave. on Hambrooks Bay in Cambridge. For about five years, beginning in 1912, this was the home of Wild West sharpshooter Annie Oakley. It was designed and built by Oakley and her husband, Frank Butler, when they retired to Cambridge. The bungalow was typical of the period, except for a few features characteristic of the Butlers' unique lifestyle. You can drive by and see the second floor balcony from which Oakley could shoot ducks on the Bay.

It makes one wonder, why here? According to Thomas A. Flowers, the Old Honker, in his book *Shore Folklore: Growing Up with Ghosts, 'n Legends, 'n Tales, 'n Home Remedies,* Oakley and Butler moved here because in her travels all over the world, she "had never seen a more beautiful spot than Hambrooks Bay." Butler was known to fish for perch in the bay, and Oakley's black-and-white bird dog Dave was known to stand so stock still that Oakley could shoot an apple off his head.

structures, graves, and artifacts associated with Tubman's life and better protect and interpret this nationally significant site." There's a gift shop with items from such countries as Kenya and Nigeria, Native American goods, and local products. There is no admission fee for the museum that is open Fri and Sat from 10 a.m. to 5 p.m. and by appointment. Located at 424 Race St, Cambridge, call (410) 228-0401 or visit www.harriettubmanbiography.com/index.html.

The **Bucktown Village Store** has other interesting stories and events regarding Tubman and the Underground Railroad. Talk with Jay or Susan Meredith at (410) 901-9255 or (410) 228-7650.

With the construction of the limited access US 50, the quaint town of Vienna was bypassed, so it takes a little bit of going off that beaten path to find its treasures. One of those gems is the **Vienna Heritage Museum,** set in a former gas station, where you can see remembrances of the rural life and industries located in and near the town, including equipment from the Elliott Island Button Factory, the oldest existing and last mother-of-pearl button factory that was in existence in the United States. It ceased operation in 1999, and the equipment was donated by the Martinak family on Elliott Island. Contact Bob Williams, the museum's proprietor, about walking tours through this quaint and historic town. Ask for a copy of a walking tour brochure.

The museum is open on the second and fourth Sunday of the month, from 11 a.m. to 5 p.m. at 303 Race St, Vienna. Call (410) 376-3840 or visit www.tour chesapeakecountry.org.

South of Cambridge is the **Blackwater National Wildlife Refuge,** a marvelous sanctuary of more than 28,000 acres. The refuge boasts the largest nesting population of bald eagles in the East, north of Florida. You can watch a sky's eye view of nesting eagles and ospreys. The eagle cam is live from Dec through July (when the eagles are at the nest) and the osprey cam is live all year although they're only there from Mar through Sept. Visit the Web site at www.friendsofblackwater.org/camcentral.html. Admission to the park is $3 per car and $1 per person on foot or bicycle unless you have a Golden Age, Golden Eagle, Golden Access, or Blackwater National Wildlife Refuge Pass, or a current Federal Duck Stamp. The visitor center has wildlife exhibits, an eagle's nest, monitors for the eagle and osprey cams, a gift shop, butterfly garden, restrooms, maps and brochures, and an information kiosk. On the second floor is a birding and natural history library. The center is open Mon through Fri from 8 a.m. to 4 p.m. and on weekends from 9 a.m. to 5 p.m. There is no admission fee to visit the new (2006) welcome center and observation deck.

mr.jim

James B. Richardson, a master shipwright known along the waterways as "Mr. Jim," built the 1971 reproduction of the Spocott Windmill, likening it to the wooden boats he has built and repaired. The mill has canvas sails with a wingspan of 52 feet. The wide sails turn a wooden shaft and a series of wooden gears that turn the upper millstone, grinding the grain against the bottom millstone. These post windmills appeared in England at the end of the twelfth century. It's estimated that there were about eighteen post windmills in the county.

Besides the bald eagle and the great blue heron, you will see black ducks, the endangered Delmarva fox squirrel, and countless other animals and birds. Do stop by in Nov and Dec when the Canada geese fly overhead. Bring your insect repellent in July and Aug. The refuge is open daily, Labor Day through Memorial Day, from dawn to dusk; the visitor center is open daily from 9 a.m. to 4 p.m. Located at 2145 Key Wallace Dr., Cambridge; call (410) 228-2677 or visit www.fws.gov/blackwater.

Six miles west of Cambridge on State Rte 343 is *Spocott Windmill*, the only existing post windmill in the state for grinding grain. There used to be eighteen of these windmills, each resting on a single pole at the base, throughout Dorchester. When you stop by, you can also see a tenant farmhouse (circa 1775), a one-room Victorian-era schoolhouse (1870), a country store museum, and a blacksmith shop. The windmill was reconstructed in 1971, based on a windmill built here about 1850 by John H. L. Radcliffe, which was destroyed in the blizzard of 1888. You're invited to tour the windmill, climb its steep steps, and dawdle around for as long as you like. Corn is ground on special occasions. Check with the Spocott Windmill Foundation about special events, such as Spocott Windmill Day. The mill is open daily from 8 a.m. to 5 p.m. Located at 1625 Hudson Rd; call (410) 476-5058 or visit www.tourdorchester.org.

East New Market, originally Crossroads, could easily be called Church-town or Churchville, for at each of the four entrances to the town stands a church. On State Rte 16 South, it is Trinity United Methodist; State Rte 16 North, St. Stephen's Episcopal; State Rte 14 West, First Baptist; and State Rte 14 East, Salem German Evangelical and Reformed Church. These churches reflect the diverse denominations represented in this area.

Indians dwelled here; the first European mention of the region was in a grant to Henry Sewell dated 1659 in London, England. The first white settler is believed to have been a Quaker, John Edmondson, who came from Virginia in the 1660s to seek religious freedom. Edmondson was followed by the O'Sullivane family, and this historic district contains almost all of their early residences.

In addition to the churches, the town is known for its historical architecture, and the entire town is designated a historic district. Colonial homes are the core of the town's architecture, but among the almost seventy-five buildings are a number from the eighteenth, nineteenth, and twentieth centuries. Many of the brick walks laid in 1884 still exist.

Wicomico County

For a long time Salisbury was known as the last great gasp going east (or the first coming west) on the way to the beach at Ocean City. Now it's a community in its own right with a world-renowned museum, a zoo that doesn't overwhelm you with its size, and some interesting shopping. You could spend your vacation here and avoid the hot, sweaty, shoulder-to-shoulder, sand- and sunblock-covered visitors catching the rays on the shore.

For an impressive look into the peninsula's past, stop by the *Edward H. Nabb Research Center for Delmarva History and Culture,* where you can find some of the nation's oldest artifacts. Genealogists from around the world visit this center at Salisbury University. The center is named for Cambridge attorney Edward H. Nabb, whose forebears came to the Eastern Shore in the early eighteenth century as an indentured servant. In endowing the center with a $500,000 challenge grant, Nabb said, "Let's face it. This [the Chesapeake Bay region] is where the United States began. There should really be a center somewhere here as a repository for that information."

Because many settlers came up the Chesapeake as they headed to their new homes, the Eastern Shore is an important national genealogical source for family history. They even have some records the Salt Lake City–based

Church of Jesus Christ of Latter-day Saints genealogical resource center supposedly doesn't have. The Nabb Center has copies of the oldest continuous sets of courthouse records in the continental United States, dating from 1632. Recognizing the center's potential, the late Wilcomb Washburn, head of the American Studies Program at the Smithsonian Institution, donated his personal library of more than 10,000 volumes before his death, and the Donner Foundation of New York has established a $75,000 Washburn memorial at the center. It is open Mon from 10 a.m. to 9 p.m., Tues through Fri from 10 a.m. to 5 p.m. during the school semester and by appointment. It may be closed during school breaks. Located at 1101 Camden Ave.; call (410) 543-6312 or visit http:// nabbhistory.salisbury.edu.

maryland's renaissanceman

The late Edward H. Nabb had a pilot's license and was the only person on Earth to receive all three of the world's top power-boating awards: induction into the Power Boat Racing Hall of Fame and American Power Boat Association Honor Squadron; and the Medal of Honor of the Union of International Motor Boating. He was one of the last people to "read" for the bar in Maryland, attending some classes, but never officially enrolling toward a law degree. For more than forty years he was a member of Maryland's oldest law firm, Harrington, Harrington and Nabb.

The **Country House** in Salisbury is the largest country store in the East and delights all the senses with sounds of soothing music, the smell of potpourri and candles, and the feel of quality merchandise. You'll discover every colonial home furnishing you could wish to find as well as beautiful decorative accessories and old-time candy. Looking for that perfect something for your kitchen, bedroom, or bathroom? It should be here. You can select from an array of curtains, lighting fixtures, pottery, collectibles, furniture, shelving, rugs, baskets, and dried flowers. There are also some Victorian-style items, and the Christmas section is open year-round.

Owners Mike and Norma Delano handpick every item in the store, and they love to stop and talk with their customers. The shop is open Mon through Sat 10 a.m. to 5 p.m.; on Fri night it's open until 8 p.m. From Thanksgiving to Christmas the store stays open until 8 p.m. Mon through Fri. Located at 805 East Main St, Salisbury. Call (410) 749-1959 or (800) 596-4666 or visit www.thecountryhouse.com.

If you hate a zoo that rambles forever and ever and tries to be encyclopedic in its collection, you'll love the smallness and intimacy of **Salisbury Zoo and Park.** Founded in 1954 by the city to advance animal conservation and environmental awareness, the zoo has about 400 mammals, birds, and reptiles native to the Americas, with exhibits of spectacled bears, monkeys, jaguars, bison, bald eagles, and a wonderful waterfowl collection. The snug twelve-acre facility embraces a branch of the Wicomico River and has plenty of shade trees, exotic plants, and wildlife, making for a cool, peaceful setting for family outings. No gift or food concessions are in the zoo, but there are plenty nearby, and picnic tables and toilet facilities are inside the park. Admission and parking are free. Pets are not permitted. The zoo is open daily from Memorial Day to Labor Day from 8 a.m. to 7:30 p.m. and until 4:30 p.m. the rest of the year. It is closed on Thanksgiving and Christmas. Group guided tours are available by appointment. Located at 750 South Park Dr., Salisbury; call (410) 548-3188 or visit www.salisburyzoo.org.

Of major note is the ***Ward Museum of Wildfowl Art,*** which houses what is perhaps the largest collection of decorative bird carvings in the world, including many antique decoys. The museum is named for internationally renowned waterfowl carvers and painters Lem and Steve Ward of Crisfield, Maryland. During their lifetimes they produced more than 25,000 decoys and decorative birds, which the men called "counterfeits." Their workshop has been re-created, and on display are more than one hundred fine examples of their old classic hunting decoys as well as their decoratives. Lem did most of the painting, while Steve did most of the carving. Steve died in 1976, and Lem died in 1984 at the age of eighty-eight.

The museum has changing exhibits featuring oils of wild animals or the art of the Northwest Indians. You can experience the story of this Native American art form, decoy carving, from its beginning to the present. And if you don't want to venture into the wetlands yourself with the bugs and the mud, in the museum you can experience the sights and sounds of the wetland habitat of native American wildfowl. Even the setting is close to spectacular. The waterfront setting overlooks a bird sanctuary where ducks, geese, herons, ospreys, and songbirds

If It Looks Like a Duck . . .

The Ward Foundation was established to save the art form of decoy carving, which has grown from the carving of working decoys designed to catch birds to the decorative carving of collector's items. The foundation's annual summer seminars at 909 South Shumaker Dr. in Salisbury offer hands-on instruction by some of the most talented artists and teachers in the field, such as Ernie Muehlmatt, Pat Godin, Bill Koelpin, Bob Guge, Larry Bath, and Jim Sprankle. Intensive weeklong sessions cover such topics as anatomy and research, shaping, texturing, burning, priming and painting, and various brush techniques. Room and board are provided on campus. For information about the seminars, contact the Ward Foundation at (410) 742-4988.

flock, as though to perform for you. An on-site gift shop has a wide selection of wildfowl-related items. The museum is open Mon through Sat from 10 a.m. to 5 p.m. and Sun from noon to 5 p.m. Guided group tours are available. Admission is $7 for adults, $5 for seniors age sixty and older, $3 for college students (with valid ID), and for children age 3 through 12. Ward Museum members and Salisbury University students, faculty, and staff (with ID) are free. Located at 909 South Shumaker Dr.; call (410) 742-4988 or visit www.wardmuseum.org.

If you have ever heard the railroad expression about "highballing it down the road" and wondered what it meant, take a visit to Delmar to see the *High Ball.* (Delmar lies in both Delaware and Maryland; State St straddles the border. There was a time when the two halves—two mayors, two town councils, two school systems—fought over municipal functions, but things have been patched up for some time.)

Along the tracks near State Street you will see a large white ball, which was raised on high to signify that the line was clear, giving rise to the term "highballing." A small museum is housed in the library, on the Delaware side of town, at 101 North Bi-State Blvd; (302) 846-9894; www.delmarlibrary.org.

Driving along the flat stretch of State Rte 54 west of Delmar near Mardela Springs, you will parallel the southern end of the north-south section of the *Mason-Dixon line.* One could even say this is the cornerstone of the Mason-Dixon line. A double crownstone was installed in 1768 by Charles Mason and Jeremiah Dixon to settle the boundary disputes between the Penn and Calvert families, whose coats of arms it bears. There is a small parking lot and a brick and wrought-iron pavilion protecting the stones.

Called the Middle Point monument because it marks the middle of the Delmarva Peninsula, the crownstone also is a triangulation point of the National Geodetic Survey. The stone was broken off at ground level by vandals in 1983, and another stone originally set by Colonial surveyors in 1760 was defaced by removal of the Calvert coat of arms. The Maryland Department of Natural Resources and Delaware's State Boundary Commission jointly replaced the monument on October 24, 1985. Call (410) 548-4914 for additional information.

Two ferryboats continue service in this part of Maryland, survivors of the many that once linked water-isolated communities on the Wicomico River, between Wicomico and Somerset Counties. Both are small, both are free, and both operate all year, weather conditions and tides permitting.

The *Upper Ferry* crosses between Allen and State Rte 349 in Salisbury and takes about three minutes. It is an outboard motor–propelled cable ferryboat with no name. A ferry has been running here since at least 1897; the current one has a capacity of two cars plus six passengers, with a maximum vehicle size of five tons gross weight. Bicycles are permitted.

The **Whitehaven–Mt. Vernon Cable Ferry,** called the Whitehaven Ferry, is 6 miles downriver from the Upper Ferry and connects Whitehaven to Widgeon; it has been operating since 1690. The modern ferryboat, the *Som-Wico,* takes about five minutes for a crossing and can hold three cars plus ten passengers. Bikes are permitted. The ferry schedules vary seasonally, although you can sort of figure from about 7 a.m. until 6 p.m. Check the Web site for details. Call (410) 548-4872 or visit www.wicomicocounty.org/pubwrk/roads.htm.

Worcester County

The town of Berlin in eastern Worcester (pronounced like "rooster") County has no connection to the city in Germany; instead, it is a corruption of Burley Inn, the name of the site on which it was constructed. A guided map for a ***Berlin walking tour*** includes a town park and monument dedicated to Comm. Stephen Decatur, a native of Berlin. The oldest homes were built during the Federal period, later homes adopted the Victorian style, and twentieth-century homes are typified by the "bungalow." The walking tour brochure can be picked up at local Berlin businesses.

Berlin is another designated Maryland Arts and Entertainment District. The town has five working galleries, numerous specialty shops, multiple performance art venues, and annual arts festivals and a fiddlers' convention. The Berlin A&E committee meets the second Fri of each month at 9 a.m. in the Berlin Town Hall. You're invited to attend if you're a local artist who would

Laying Back in Berlin

"People tell us they've gone to Ocean City for thirty years and never stopped in Berlin," says Debbie Frene, owner of Victorian Charm, a boutique that sells scented candles, handbags, and other accessories. Dating to the 1790s, Berlin offers the quintessential day trip for those suffering from sunburn, boredom, or other summer-resort afflictions. Berlin is a little bit of St. Michaels or Chestertown on the far eastern shore, and is just seven miles west of Ocean City. Runaway Bride, the hit movie with Julia Roberts and Richard Gere, was set here, and scenes from Tuck Everlasting were also shot here, albeit after re-creating the look of older days (yes, they dumped tons of dirt on the streets to do so).

You can simply prowl the ultra-quaint streets lined with boutiques like Victorian Charm, the Globe (a fabulous restaurant/art gallery in an old theater), and the cafe and antiques store at An a Fare to Remember. Victorian Charm is located at 100 North Main St; call (410) 641-2998 or (866) 641-6416; or visit http://victoriancharm.biz.

like to be included in the program, or one who's considering moving to the Berlin area. (410) 641-2998; www.berlinmdarts.org.

The *Calvin B. Taylor House Museum* is set in a typical Federal-style post-and-beam house. It was built about 1825 and now is used as the town museum. The gable-front house features a Palladian window with Victorian glass, restored wood graining, and a magnificent front doorway with butterfly medallions, sunbursts, and fluted, engaged columns. The house was supposed to be destroyed and replaced by a new post office and parking lot, but it was saved in 1981 by the Berlin Heritage Foundation. With $100,000 in private donations from the community, the house was restored from its dilapidated condition. Although Robert J. Henry, who was instrumental in bringing the railroad to Berlin, lived in the house, the most famous occupant was Calvin B. Taylor, the founder of the Calvin B. Taylor Banking Company, which is still in existence. Much of the house and appointments are original to the times that various occupants lived in the house, including C.B. Taylor's bank desk, with its hidden doors on the side and front.

The house is open Mon, Wed, Fri, and Sat, mid-May through the end of Oct, from 1 to 4 p.m. and for special events. There is no admission charge, but a $2 donation is suggested. Located at 208 North Main St, Berlin; call (410) 641-1019 or visit http://taylorhousemuseum.org.

In the middle of the historic district is the *Atlantic Hotel,* a faithfully restored 1895 Victorian hostelry that was rescued from the depths of distress and even the depths of "modernization" to once again become this showpiece. This latest venture is credited primarily to John Fager, owner of Fager's Island (restaurant and boutique hotels) in Ocean City. Now, the hotel that was named to the National Register of Historic Places in 1980, has new iron beds that replicate the old beds that the same company made in the mid-1800s. Antiques once again fill the rooms, sitting side-by-side 300 count linens and a flat screen television. It is safe to sit on the front-porch rocking chair and imagine slower times. The Atlantic Hotel and all of Berlin will look familiar to you if you saw the Richard Gere and Julia Roberts movie Runaway Bride. The town was called Hale in the movie and all the shops were renamed; only the Atlantic kept its own identity. Located at 2 North Main St, Berlin; call (410) 641-3589 or (800) 814-7672; or visit www.atlantichotel.com.

Seven miles east of Berlin is *Assateague Island National Seashore* and the *Assateague State Park,* reached by State Rte 611. Nearly two million people visit this seashore annually. A two-room visitor center is open for interpretive classes and exhibits, which include a small touch tank of marine life. During a visit here you can take a guided walk; view a demonstration on how to catch blue crabs, clams, and ribbed mussels; or join a naturalist at the

Old Ferry Landing to explore the width of Assateague Island. You will travel by foot and bike or car from the salt marsh to the pounding surf, discovering relationships between the various barrier island life zones. During the summer you can swim and surf at lifeguard-protected beaches. Surfing, surf fishing, mats and floats are allowed outside the areas with lifeguards.

The famed *Chincoteague ponies* can be seen on Assateague, for two herds of the wild ponies make their home here. The herds are separated by a fence at the Maryland-Virginia state line. Managed by the National Park Service on the Maryland side, horses are often seen around roads and campgrounds. The horses sold at auction every July are on the Virginia side. No road connects the two states within the park. Supposedly, the horses are descended from domesticated stock that grazed on the island as early as the seventeenth century; Eastern Shore planters put them here to avoid mainland taxes and fencing requirements. Smaller than "normal" horses, these shaggy, sturdy ponies are well adapted to their harsh seashore environment. Marsh and dune grasses supply the bulk of their food, and they obtain water from freshwater impoundments or natural ponds. Although they appear tame, they are unpredictable and can inflict serious wounds by kicking and biting. The Park Service strongly recommends that you do not pet or feed the ponies. While at the park, you may see great blue herons, snowy egrets, dunlins, American widgeons, black-crowned night herons, peregrine falcons, and numerous other birds on the Maryland side.

Legend has it that Edward Teach (Blackbeard the Pirate) kept one of his fourteen wives, a base of operations, and buried treasure on Assateague.

The Barrier Island Visitor Center at Assateague Island National Seashore is open daily from 9 a.m. to 5 p.m.; 7206 National Seashore Lane, Berlin; call (410) 641-1441, (800) 365-2267; or visit www.nps.gov/asis. The Assateague State Park is Maryland's only ocean park. Located at 7307 Stephen Decatur Hwy., Berlin; call (410) 641-2120, (888) 432-2267; or visit http://dnr.maryland .gov/publiclands/eastern/assateague.html.

The *Viewtrail 100* signs you will see on secondary state and county roads mark a scenic bicycle trail, which is maintained by the Worcester County Tourism Department. You can join the trail in Berlin as it sweeps down to Pocomoke City, past the access to Furnace Town, Nassawango Creek Cypress Swamp, Milburn Landing on the north bank of the Pocomoke River, and many other interesting attractions.

The *Delmarva Discovery Center* explores the river ecology of the *Pocomoke River* and the town's relationship to it. Among the exhibits are sound recordings, dioramas, ship models, canoes, and duck decoys. The themes include Native People, shipbuilding and woodworking, and fishing

FAMOUS SONS AND DAUGHTERS OF MARYLAND

Karen Allen, movie actress (1955–)

George Armistead, Lt. Col. Defended Fort McHenry (1780–1818)

Benjamin Banneker, astronomer, essayist, surveyor, and mathematician (1731–1806)

Henry Blair, inventor (1807–1860)

Eubie Blake, musician (1883–1983)

John Wilkes Booth, actor and assassin of Abraham Lincoln (1838–1864)

James M. Cain, author (1892–1977)

Charles Carroll, American Revolutionary War leader and signer of the Declaration of Independence (1737–1832)

John Carroll, clergyman (1735–1815)

Samuel Chase, jurist, lawyer, and signer of the Declaration of Independence (1743–1811)

Kevin Clash, voice actor (Elmo, Baby Sinclair) (1960–)

Bosley Crowther, movie critic (1905–1981)

Stephen Decatur, naval hero (1779–1820)

John Dickinson, patriot and lawyer (1732–1808)

Divine (Harris Glenn Milstread), actor (1945–1988)

Frederick Douglass, statesman and abolitionist (1818–1895)

Ethel Ennis, singer (1934–)

Olivia Floyd, Confederate agent and messenger (1825–1906)

Jimmie Foxx, baseball player (1907–1967)

Francis "Frank" Francois, politician (1934–)

Mary Katherine Goddard, first woman postmaster (1738–1816)

Thomas Alan Goldsborough, jurist and politician, (1877–1951)

Martha Grimes, novelist (1931–)

Robert "Lefty" Grove, baseball player (1900–1975)

Alan Frank Guttmacher, physician (1898–1974)

Dashiell Hammett, author (1894–1961)

John Hanson, politician and farmer (1715–1783)

Frances Ellen Watkins Harper, author, orator, social reformer, and suffragist (1825–1911)

Matthew Henson, first explorer to reach the North Pole (1866–1955)

Calvin Hill, professional football player (1947–)

Alger Hiss, public official (1904–1966)

Johns Hopkins, merchant, banker, philanthropist, and founder of hospital bearing his name (1715–1783)

Harry Roe Hughes, governor (1926–)

William "Judy" Johnson, baseball player (1899–1989)

Al Kaline, baseball player (1934–)

Sophie Kerr, author, (1880–1965)

Francis Scott Key, poet and attorney (1779–1843)

Ellis Larkins, pianist, recording artist (1923–2002)

Barry Levinson, film producer (1942–)

F. Richard Malzone, park planning master (1930–2008)

Thurgood Marshall, Supreme Court justice (1908–1993)

Barbara Ann Mikulski, United States Senator (1936–)

Dr. Samuel A. Mudd, physician charged and pardoned in Lincoln assassination plot (1833–1883)

Edward Norton, actor (1969–)

Charles Wilson Peale, portraitist (1741–1827)

Margaret Gillian Rockwell Pfanshtiel, Founder, Metropolitan Washington Ear (1932–2009)

Michael Phelps, Olympic gold medal swimmer (1985–)

Mary Pickersgill, maker of the "Star Spangled Banner" (1776–1857)

Emily Post, journalist and etiquette expert (1872–1960)

Clarence "Buzzy" Ridgell, elected official (1924–2009)

George Herman "Babe" Ruth, baseball player (1895–1948)

Pat Sajak, TV personality (1946–)

Paul S. Sarbanes, United States Senator (retired) (1933–)

Dr. Nancy Churchman Sawin, illustrator and historian (1917–2008)

Gina Schock, drummer, The Go-Go's (1957–)

Elizabeth Bayley Seton, first American-born saint of the Roman Catholic church (1774–1821)

R. Sargent Shriver Jr., diplomat and director of the Peace Corps (1915–)

Wallis Warfield Simpson, Duchess of Windsor (1896–1986)

Upton Sinclair, writer and social critic (1878–1968)

Gen. William Smallwood, American Revolutionary War hero and Maryland governor (1732–1792)

Thomas Stone, one of four Maryland signers of the Declaration of Independence (1743–1787)

Helen Taussig, pediatric cardiologist (1898–1986)

Harriet Tubman, abolitionist and organizer of the Underground Railroad (1820?–1913)

Leon Uris, author (1924–2003)

Captain Quentin R. Walsh, Coast Guard, (1910–2000)

John Waters, film producer (1946–)

Donald A. Westcott, lobbyist (1933–2005)

and industry. The Center is in the middle of an aquarium exhibit which has included the arrival of the tank, the scenic treatment of it, prepping the tank for fish (as this is being written), sturgeon being introduced, and the exhibit opening. Weekly art classes are offered, and other events are scheduled on a regular basis. Guided cruises on the Pocomoke are available at 1 p.m. Thurs through Sun from Apr through Oct. The Center is open Wed through Sat from 10 a.m. to 4 p.m. and Sun from noon to 4 p.m. Admission is $10 for adults, $8 for seniors (60 and over) and students (with ID), and $5 for children (4 through 17). A combination Center and cruise package is $18 for adults, and $9 for children. Located at 6 Market St; call (410) 957-9933 or visit http://delmarva discoverycenter.org.

The Pocomoke River is the northernmost swamp river on the East Coast, and along its banks are descendants of cypress trees that were used to make our country's first ships. Here you can view eagles, egrets, hawks, and vultures, as well. For more Maryland bike trail information, call (800) 252-8776.

The **Beach to Bay Indian Trail** is a self-guided driving and boating trail that goes from Smith Island in the Chesapeake Bay in Somerset County up to Princess Anne, Pocomoke City, Snow Hill, Berlin, and Ocean City. It was opened in 1988 and is jointly sponsored by Somerset and Worcester Tourism, Ocean City, the State of Maryland, the Department of Transportation, and the Department of Natural Resources.

A carved-wood relief sculpture in polychrome, called **The Power of Communication,** hangs over the postmaster's door in the Pocomoke City Post Office. Perna Krick of Baltimore executed the commission in 1940. The figure of a Native American with an airplane reflects the history of the area, from early tradition to the development of communication, from primitive methods to present-day service. Ms. Krick was born in Ohio in 1909 and attended the Dayton Art Institute. She studied under J. Maxwell Miller at the Rinehard School of Sculpture in Baltimore, receiving two European traveling scholarships. By the time she received this commission from the Federal Works Agency, her work had been exhibited at the Baltimore Art Museum, the Pennsylvania Academy of Fine Arts, and the Architectural League in New York.

Ocean City is a family-oriented town on the ocean. It lies seven miles east of Berlin. Thousands of college kids come here every summer to work and vacation. There is plenty to do, from kite flying (probably my favorite activity), to boating, fishing, golfing, and beach-related activities. As with any resort, there are dozens (if not hundreds) of restaurants, eateries, bars, and food stands along the 3-mile boardwalk, and you have to try some of the famous saltwater taffy and Thrasher's French fries with vinegar. Rather than trying to drive through traffic, which can be terrible in the summer, try the bus. As they say in Ocean City, "Avoid the fuss, take the bus." Ride all day, 24 hours a day, for only $2. Ocean City buses also run to and from the West Ocean City Park and Ride facility. The buses run every 10 minutes from 6 a.m. to 3 a.m. and every 20 minutes from 3 a.m. to 6 p.m. Scheduled times vary in the off season. Call (410) 723-1606 for the schedule. There is also a boardwalk tram that runs the entire length of the boardwalk, 2.5 miles, between the Inlet and 27th St Mon through Fri from 11 a.m. to midnight daily during the summer. Weekend service is offered in the spring and fall from 10 a.m. to midnight, weather permitting. The schedule varies by season. The tram fare is $3 per ride, per person. Call (410) 723-1606 or visit http://ococean.com/travel-tools/getting-around-oc.

One of the traditional sights from Ocean City to Rehoboth Beach is the airplanes flying advertising banners about 200 feet above sea level. Robert Bunting of Berlin bought a small crop duster in 1982 and started airplane advertising by flying up and down the beach with banner messages. **Ocean Aerial Advertising** is so popular that seven banner-bearing, single-engine aircraft are used for this kind of advertising. Each banner must have forty or fewer letters. Some carry marriage proposals for which they offer a special rate; others tell you about the newest restaurant in town. If you go watch the ground crew rig the planes, you will see them set the banner between two upright poles that are 6 feet apart. (It is said that if the ground crew is feeling prankish, they will close the poles to only 2 feet apart.) Then the plane flies about 85 miles per hour to pick up the banner. Usually the pilot makes it on the first trip, but it has taken as many as six tries to hook a banner. You are looking at some first-class flying. Between Memorial Day and Labor Day, each pilot logs about 500 hours, flying from 10 a.m. to 4 p.m. seven days a week, and together the pilots can fly as many as 110 banners in one day, although the average is about 45 to 50. Call (410) 641-2484 or visit www.ocean-city.com/aerial.htm.

There may be a gazillion places to stay while in Ocean City, but you'll be hard-pressed to find a place more charming or host and hostess so memorable as Vicky and Charlie Barrett and their **Inn on the Ocean.** As the name indicates, the inn is the only one on the ocean. That means you're steps from the beach and boardwalk, but it's set back enough to be quiet and peaceful.

A large wraparound veranda allows for people-watching at your leisure and a setting for the humongous breakfast (during warm weather). A fireplace in the living room warms the soul and the body during the winter. Each of the six guest rooms has a ceiling fan, TV/VCR, and private bath and is decorated with luxury and comfort in mind. Bicycles and beach equipment are complimentary so you don't have to worry about packing all that "stuff." The bed-and-breakfast was constructed in 1938 and features Victorian-style architecture. An active community member, Vicki was cochair of the OC Beach Birds art project in 2003 where eighty 5-foot fiberglass birds were transformed into unusual works of art by regional artists and displayed throughout the city. This is similar to the Chicago cows, the DC party animals (elephants and donkeys), and panda-mania exhibits. The birds were auctioned after the exhibit with the proceeds going to public art in Ocean City. Located at 1001 Atlantic Ave.; call (410) 289-8894 or (888) 226-6223; or visit www.bbonline.com/md/ontheocean.

The Ocean City restaurant that is almost always the first on anyone's list is **Phillips Crab House.** Eating at this restaurant, which was started by Shirley and Brice Phillips from Hooper's Island on Chesapeake Bay, has been a ritual in Ocean City since 1956. The two of them have become such an institution and such an integral part of their community that they were honored in 1989 by the Ocean City Good Will Ambassadors Grand Ball and again in 2000 by the Maryland Tourism Council during National Tourism Week, as the most prominent tourism industry family. Phillips has branched out with several locations, including Atlantic City, Baltimore, Myrtle Beach, Philadelphia, Rockville, and Washington, D.C. The Ocean City location is the one to visit. It was a shingle-covered shack in the boonies when it opened. Now it is in the middle of everything that is happening and can seat 1,400 diners at one time. Despite its size, you will have to arrive early or plan to wait a while, because there is always a line for dinner. This is where you come to eat crabs, piled in mounds on broad sheets of paper that cover tables that once held sewing machines.

If steamed crabs, spiced shrimp, and crab cakes don't appeal to you, you can opt for fried chicken or Virginia baked ham served with corn on the cob, watermelon, and cole slaw. A children's menu is also available. Located at Twenty-first St and Philadelphia Ave. in Ocean City; call (410) 289-6821 or visit www.phillipsseafood.com.

Ocean City has been named one of America's greatest golf hometowns by *Golf Digest* magazine, which compared 244 counties based on the number and quality of courses, golf days per year, and course congestion in the golf criteria, and crime rates, airport access, off-course amenities, and cost of living in the non-golf category. With nearly two dozen courses within a thirty-minute drive, it's easy to understand why the area was honored. The **Greater Ocean City Golf Association** markets packages with the courses and accommodations, so you can have your golf and ocean or bay vacation created for you. Located at 9935 Stephen Decatur Hwy., #141; call (410) 213-7050 or visit www.oceancitygolf.com.

Those of you who served aboard the **USS Blenny SS-324,** a World War II submarine that was built in 1944 and saw battle in the Java and South China

Seas, will find her serving a new function as a reef in the Atlantic Ocean about 15 miles off Ocean City. The *Blenny* was scuttled in 1989 also about 15 miles offshore. It acts as a base for algae and soft coral growth, which will attract small fish and then larger fish, fishermen, and divers.

Ocean City is not just for summer fun. It is a year-round community that sponsors a great number of activities during the winter season, including workshops, entertainment, an annual Christmas parade, a traditional lighting and trimming of a 30-foot tree on the beach, and the placement of holiday decorations throughout the town. Call (800) 62-OCEAN or visit www.ococean.com.

One of the unfortunate duties of Ocean City residents is lifesaving, for some people will do stupid things, and some people will be the victims of circumstances even without being stupid. The **Ocean City Life-Saving Station Museum,** located on the south end of the boardwalk, shows some early lifesaving equipment and sands from around the world, shipwreck artifacts, antique bathing suits, models of old Ocean City hotels and businesses, photos of famous storms, and tales (not tails) of mermaids.

The museum is open daily June through Sept from 10 a.m. to 10 p.m., in May and Oct from 10 to 4 p.m. and various times the rest of the year. Admission is $3 for adults and $1 for children (6 to 12). It's located at 813 South Atlantic Ave.; call (410) 289-4991 or visit www.ocmuseum.org.

Somerset County

Skipjacks (working sailboats) can be seen in the watermen's villages of Deal Island, Chance, and Wenona. Over Labor Day weekend, they gather to compete in the Tangier Sound off Deal Island in the annual Skipjack Races.

With a little time, you also might want to stop by the **Teackle Mansion** in Princess Anne on a Sunday afternoon. This is a very elaborate example of the Federal style of architecture in 1802 and then in 1818 and 1819, erected by Littleton Dennis Teackle (1777-1848), an influential man of the early 1800s. Teackle and his wife Elizabeth Upshur Teackle (1783-1835) moved to this area from Accomack County in Virginia, shortly after they were married in 1800. Teackle was a merchant, statesman, and entrepreneur, owning agriculture and timber lands, and trading with merchants in England and the Caribbean. He established the Bank of Somerset in 1813 and served for many years in the Maryland House of Delegates.

The mansion was sold and eventually became apartments, until Maude Jeffries and her sister Catherine Ricketts founded Olde Princess Anne Days Inc. The funds this organization raised bought and restored the mansion and has supported its continued renovation. The mansion is open Wed, Sat, and Sun from 1 to 3 p.m., Apr through Dec. Group tours may be arranged for other times. Located at 11736 Mansion St, Princess Anne; call (410) 651-2238 or (800) 521-9189; or visit www.teacklemansion.org.

The Teackle Mansion is also the home of the Somerset County Historical Society. Call (410) 651-2238 for more information.

The ***J. Millard Tawes Historical Museum*** in Crisfield exhibits items pertaining to the late Maryland governor J. Millard Tawes (governor from 1959 until 1967), the history and development of the Crisfield seafood industry, local art and folklore, and the anthropological history of the area. For a broader look, take one of the walking tours of Crisfield offered between Memorial Day and Labor Day. The museum is open daily from 10 a.m. to 4 p.m. from Memorial Day to Labor Day and until 2 p.m. the rest of the year. Admission is $3 for adults and a combined admission and walking tour is $5. Located at 3 Ninth St; call (410) 968-2501 or visit www.crisfieldheritagefoundation.org.

While you're in town, you also might want to try some seafood, for Crisfield is the self-proclaimed Crab Capital of the World. An alternative activity is a boat ride out to Smith or Tangier Island. See how the residents on these islands have lived for centuries and enjoy the fruits of their labor, particularly the Smith Island Cake, the Maryland state cake.

As mentioned several times, the Eastern Shore is home to incredibly talented artists. Perhaps it's something in the air or the water. The ***Somerset County Arts Council*** helps promote the artists and you can see some of their work at the Council's ***Burton Ave Gallery*** in Crisfield and you can buy or take lessons. Among the artists involved with the council include local residents and others who live on the peninsula. Some of them are Mark A. Pleasanton and Teresa L. Clauss, Alane Ortega, Bill Sailer (www.lighthouseart.org), Melissa Bailey-White & Frank White (www.chesapeakejewelers.com), Laura Ellison, Ernie Satchell, Michel Demanche, C.D. Clarke (www.cdclare.com), Lynne Fowler, R. Donald White (www.whitescooperworks.com), Barb Dougherty (www.artandinfo.com), Sandy Darrow (www.bayartcollections.com), Rich Smoker, Jerome F. Ryan, Fred Ropko and Marge Violetta, Nancy Mysak, and Knute Aspenberg (see next paragraph). The Gallery is open Mon through Sat from 10 a.m. to 4 p.m. It's located at 26430 Burton Ave.; call (410) 968-2787 or visit www.myfairladybandb.com/attractions.html.

Knut Aspenberg loves making models of working and pleasure boats, using basswood, mahogany, oak, poplar, and pine. He loves working with old and abandoned furniture in which the wood has been seasoned. With a series of saw cuts, a 2-inch board in real size becomes a ¹⁄₁₆-inch replica on a ³⁄₈-inch-to-a-foot scale. His work is available at the ***Annapolis Marine Art Gallery*** in Annapolis. Or, you can commission him to re-create your boat. Send photos or take a visit so he can take the measure of your boat and note any special details. It may take six months or so, but you will treasure the miniature as much as (or more than) you do the full-sized version. Located at 10577 Harrison Point Rd., Chance; call (410) 784-2130.

Two of Maryland's ten ferries—the Whitehaven and Upper Ferries—operate between Somerset and Wicomico Counties. Check the Wicomico County section for additional details.

Places to Eat on the Eastern Shore

BERLIN

Drummer's Cafe
2 North Main St.
(410) 641-3589
www.atlantichotel.com/
drummers-cafe

Ruth's Chris Steakhouse
11401 Maid at Arms Way
(888) 632-4747
www.ruthschris.com

CAMBRIDGE

Bistro Poplar
535 Poplar St.
(410) 228-4884
www.bistropoplar.com

Canvasback Restaurant & Pub
420 Race St.
(410) 221-7888

Port Side Seafood Company
201 Trenton St.
(410) 228-9007
www.portsideseafood.com

CHESTER

Adam's Ribs
100 Abruzzi Dr.
(410) 643-5050
www.adamsribs.com

CHESTERTOWN

Brooks Tavern in the Radcliffe Mill
870 High St.
(410) 810-0012
www.brookstavern.com

Imperial Hotel
208 High St.
(410) 778-5000
www.imperialchestertown
.com

CRISFIELD

Cove Restaurant
718 Broadway St.
(410) 968-9532

Olde Crisfield Crab and Steakhouse
(open seasonally)
204 South Tenth St.
(410) 968-2722

Watermen's Inn
901 West Main St.
(410) 968-2119
www.crisfield.com

DENTON

Eastern Shore Diner and Restaurant
23823 Shore Hwy.
(410) 479-1445
www.theeasternshore
restaurant.com

Lily Pad
104 South Second St.
(410) 479-0700
www.lilypadcafe.com

Market Street Public House
202 Market St.
(410) 479-4720
www.publichouseonline
.com

EASTON

General Tanuki's
25 Goldsborough St.
(410) 819-0707
www.generaltanukis.com

Inn at Easton
28 South Harrison St.
(410) 822-4910
(888) 800-8091

Legal Spirits Tavern
42 East Dover St.
(410) 822-0765
www.shoreboys.com

MARYLAND TOURISM OFFICES

Maryland Office of Tourism, 401 East Pratt St, 14th Floor, Baltimore 21202; (410) 767-3400, (866) 639-3526; http://visitmaryland.org.

Maryland Tourism Council, 1205 Stonewood Court, Annapolis 21409; (410) 974-4473; www.mdtourism.com.

Allegany County Convention and Visitors Bureau, 13 Canal St, Suite 306, Cumberland 21502; (301) 777-5132, (800) 425-2067; www.mdmountainside.com.

Annapolis and Anne Arundel County Visitors Bureau, 26 West St, Annapolis 21401; (410) 280-0445 ext. 19, (410) 974-8188; www.visitannapolis.org.

Baltimore Area Convention and Visitors Association, 100 Light St, 12th floor, Baltimore 21202; (877) 225-8466; http://baltimore.org.

Baltimore County Convention and Visitors Bureau, 44 West Chesapeake Ave., Towson 21204; (410) 296-4886, (800) 570-2836; www.visitbacomd.com.

Calvert County Department of Economic Development and Tourism, 205 Main St, Courthouse, Prince Frederick 20678; (410) 535-4585, (800) 331-9771; www.ecalvert.com/content/tourism/index.asp.

Caroline County Economic Development Corporation, 15 South Third St, Denton 21629; (410) 479-0655; www.tourcaroline.com.

Carroll County Visitor Center, 210 East Main St, Westminster 21157; (410) 848-1388, (800) 272-1933; www.carrollcountytourism.org.

Cecil County Tourism, Office of Economic Development, Perryville Outlet center, 68 Heather Lane, Suite 43, Perryville 21903; (410) 996-6290, (800) CECIL-95; www.seececil.org.

Charles County Tourism, 103 Centennial St, Suite C, La Plata 20646; (301) 645-0551, (800) 766-3386; www.thenationsbackyard.com/tourism.

Dorchester County Tourism, 2 Rose Hill Place, Sailwinds Park, Cambridge 21613; (410) 228-1000, (800) 522-TOUR; www.tourdorchester.org.

Tourism Council of Frederick County Inc., 19 East Church St, Frederick 21701; (301) 600-4047, (800) 999-3613; www.visitfrederick.org.

Garrett County Chamber of Commerce, 15 Visitors Center Dr., McHenry 21541; (301) 387-4386 ext. 13, (800) 800-5557; www.garrettchamber.com

Mason's
22 South Harrison St.
(410) 822-3204
www.masonsgourmet.com

Out of the Fire
22 Goldsborough St.
410) 770-4777
www.outofthefire.com

Peacock Restaurant and Lounge at the Inn at 202 Dover
202 Dover St.
(410) 819-8007
www.innat202dover.com

Portofino
4 West Dover St.
(410) 770-9200
www.portofinoeaston.com

Restaurant Local
Tidewater Inn
101 East Dover St.
(410) 822-1300
www.tidewaterinn.com

Hagerstown/Washington County Convention and Visitors Bureau, Elizabeth Hager Center, 16 Public Sq., Hagerstown 21740; (301) 791-3246 ext.15; (301) 791-3246; www .marylandmemories.org.

Harford County Tourism Council Inc., 220 South Main St., Aberdeen 21014; (410) 683-3327, (888) 544-4695; www .harfordmd.com.

Howard County Tourism, P.O. Box 9, 8267 Main St., Ellicott City 21043; (410) 313-1900, (800) 288-TRIP; www .visithowardcounty.com.

Kent County Office of Tourism, 400 High St., Second Floor, Chestertown 21620; (410) 778-0416; www .kentcounty.com.

Conference and Visitors Bureau of Montgomery County, 111 Rockville Pike, Suite 800, Rockville 20852; (240) 777-2060, (877) 789-6904; www .visitmontgomery.com.

Ocean City Office of Tourism/CVB, 4001 Coastal Hwy., Ocean City 21842; (410) 723-8600, (800) OC-OCEAN; www.ococean.com.

Prince George's County Conference and Visitors Bureau Inc., 9200 Basil Court, Suite 101, Largo 20774; (301) 925-8300; www.visitprincegeorges.com.

Queen Anne's County Department of Business and Tourism, 425 Piney Narrows Rd., Chester 21619; (410) 604-2100; www.discoverqueenannes.com.

St. Mary's County Division of Travel and Tourism, P.O. Box 653, Governmental Center, 23115 Leonard Hall Dr, Leonardtown 20650; (301) 475-4200, (800) 327-9023; www.stmarysmd .com/tourism.

Somerset County Tourism, 11440 Ocean Hwy., mile marker 19, Princess Anne 21853; (410) 651-2968, (800) 521-9189; www.visitsomerset.com.

Talbot County Office of Tourism, 11 South Harrison St., Easton 21601; (410) 770-8000; www.tourtalbot.org.

Wicomico County Convention and Visitors Bureau, 8480 Ocean Hwy., Delmar 21875; (410) 548-4914, (800) 332-TOUR; www.wicomicotourism.org.

Worcester County Tourism, 104 West Market St, Snow Hill 21863; (410) 632-3110, (800) 852-0335; www .visitworcester.org.

Scossa
8 North Washington St.
(410) 822-2202
www.scossarestaurant
.com

Thai Ki
216 East Dover St.
(410) 690-3641
www.thaiki.com

The Wedge
17 Goldsborough St.
(410) 770-3737

FRUITLAND

Restaurant 213
213 North Fruitland Blvd.
(410) 677-4880
www.restaurant213.com

GRASONVILLE

Fisherman's Inn and Crab Deck
3116 Main St.
(410) 827-6666
www.crabdeck.com

Harris' Crab House
433 Kent Narrows Way
North
(410) 827-9500
www.harriscrabhouse.com

Holly's
108 Jackson Creek Rd.
(410) 827-8711
www.hollysrest.com

GREENSBORO

Harry's at the Goldsborough House
116 West Sunset Ave.
(410) 482-6758
www.realharrys.net

HURLOCK

Suicide Bridge Restaurant
6304 Suicide Bridge Rd.
(410) 943-4689
www.suicidebridge.com

KENNEDYVILLE

Kennedyville Inn
11986 Augustine Herman
Hwy.
(410) 348-2400
www.kennedyvilleinn.com

OCEAN CITY

Embers
Twenty-fourth and Coastal
Hwy.
(410) 289-3322
www.embers.com

Fager's Island
201 6th St.
410) 524-5500
www.fagers.com

Galaxy 66
66th St., Bayside
(410) 723-6762
www.galaxy66barandgrille
.com

Greene Turtle
11601 Coastal Hwy.
(410) 723-2120
www.greeneturtle.com

Jules
11805 Coastal Hwy.
Suite N
(410) 524-3396
www.julesoc.com

Restorante Antipasti
3101 Philadelphia Ave.
(410) 289-4588
www.ristoranteantipasti
.com

Wharf Restaurant and Lounge (open Mar through Dec)
2801 Coastal Hwy.
(410) 250-1001

OXFORD

Latitude 38 Bistro & Spirits
26342 Oxford Rd.
(410) 226-5303
www.latitude38.org

Masthead at Pier Street Marina
106 West Pier St.
(410) 226-5171
www.latitude38.org/
masthead/masthead.htm

Pope's Tavern at the Oxford Inn
504 South Morris St.
(410) 226-5220
www.oxfordinn.net

ROCK HALL

Inn At Osprey Point
20786 Rock Hall Ave.
(410) 639-2194
www.ospreypoint.com

ST. MICHAELS

208 Talbot
208 Talbot St.
(410) 745-3838
www.208talbot.com

Bistro St. Michaels
403 South Talbot St.
(410) 745-9111
www.bistrostmichaels.com

Sherwood's Landing
(Inn at Perry Cabin)
308 Watkins Lane
(410) 745-5178
www.perrycabin.com

STEVENSVILLE

Big Bats Café
216 St. Clair Place
(410) 604-1120
www.bigbats.com

Hemingway's Restaurant
357 Pier 1
(410) 643-CRAB

Rustico
401 Love Point Rd.
(410) 643-9444
www.rusticoonline.com

TRAPPE

Mitchum's Steakhouse
4201 Main St.
(410) 476-3902
www.mitchumsteakhouse
.com

Places to Stay on the Eastern Shore

BERLIN

Atlantic Hotel Inn and Restaurant
2 North Main St.
(410) 641-3589
www.atlantichotel.com

Merry Sherwood Plantation
8909 Worcester Hwy.
(410) 641-2112
(800) 660-0358
www.merrysherwood.com

BOZMAN

Grandview
6601 Broad Creek Rd.
(717) 392-4876
www.grandviewat
pleasurepoint.com

Harris Cove Cottages Bed 'N Boat
8080 Bozman-Neavitt Rd.
(410) 745-9701
www.bednboat.com

CAMBRIDGE

Cambridge House Bed and Breakfast
112 High St.
(410) 221-7700
www.cambridgehouse
bandb.com

Hyatt Regency Chesapeake Bay Golf Resort, Spa and Marina
100 Heron Blvd.
(410) 901-1234
http://chesapeakebay.hyatt
.com/hyatt/hotels/index.jsp

Lodgecliffe on the Choptank
103 Choptank Terrace
(866) 273-3830
www.lodgecliffeonthechop
tankbandb.com

Mill Street Inn
114 Mill St.
(410) 901-9144
www.millstinn.com

CHESAPEAKE CITY

Inn at the Canal
104 Bohemia Ave.
(410) 885-5995
www.innatthecanal.com

CHESTERTOWN

Brampton Bed & Breakfast Inn
25227 Chestertown Rd.
(410) 778-1860
www.bramptoninn.com

Imperial Hotel
208 High St.
(410) 778-5000
(800) 295-0014
www.imperialchestertown
.com

CLAIBORNE

Claiborne Cottage By the Bay
10449 Claiborne Rd.
(410) 745-6987

CORDOVA

Peaches and Dreams Bed and Breakfast
12824 Peach Lane
(410) 820-5644
(202) 762-3553

CRISFIELD

My Fair Lady Bed and Breakfast
38 West Main St.
(410) 968-0352
www.myfairladybandb.com

DENTON

Bryant-Todd House Inn
119 Gay St.
(410) 310-7817
www.marylandbb.com

EASTON

Bishop's House Bed and Breakfast
214 Goldsborough St.
(410) 820-7290
(800) 223-7290
www.bishopshouse.com

Inn at 202 Dover
202 Dover St.
(866) 450-7600
www.theinnat202dover
.com

Inn at Easton
28 South Harrison St.
(410) 822-4910
(866) 450-7600
www.Innat202Dover.com

John S. McDaniel House Bed and Breakfast
14 North Aurora St.
(410) 822-3704
(877) 822-5702
www.bnblist.com/md/
mcdaniel

OTHER ATTRACTIONS WORTH SEEING ON THE EASTERN SHORE

Academy Art Museum
Easton
(410) 822-2787
www.art-academy.org

Adkins Museum and Historical Complex
Mardela Springs
(410) 677-4740
www.wicomicotourism.org/historical

Avalon Theatre
Easton
(410) 822-0345
www.avalontheatre.com

Barren Creek Springhouse
Mardela Springs
(410) 742-9122
www.wicomicotourism.org/historical

Bazel Methodist Episcopal Church
Cambridge
(410) 288-1000
www.tourdorchester.org

Bucktown Village Store
Cambridge
(410) 901-9255
www.tourdorchester.org

Charles H. Chipman Cultural Center
Salisbury
(410) 860-9290
www.wicomicotourism.org/historical

Chesapeake Bay Maritime Museum
St. Michaels
(410) 745-2916
www.cbmm.org

Chesapeake Classics
Cambridge
(410) 228-6509
http://chesapeake-classics.com

Choptank River Heritage Center
West Denton
(410) 479-4950
www.riverheritage.org

Delmarva Shorebirds
Salisbury
(410) 219-3112
(888) BIRDS-96
www.theshorebirds.com

Double Mills Grist Mill
Mardela Springs
(443) 235-1207
www.wicomicotourism.org/historical

Eastern Neck National Wildlife Refuge
Rock Hall
(410) 639-7056
http://easternneck.fws.gov

Furnace Town Historic Site
Snow Hill
(410) 632-2032
www.dol.net/~ebola.ftown.htm

Geddes-Piper House
Chestertown
(410) 778-3499
www.kentcountyhistory.org/geddes.php

Glass Hill School
Pittsville
(410) 835-2602
www.wicomicotourism.org/historical

Green Hill Church Rd.
Quantico
(410) 749-9064
www.wicomicotourism.org/historical

Historical Society of Talbot County
Easton
(410) 822-0773
www.hstc.org

Janes Island State Park
Crisfield
(410) 968-1565
(888) 432-CAMP
www.dnr.state.md.us

Julia A. Purnell Museum
Snow Hill
(410) 632-0515
www.purnellmuseum.com

Holloway Hall
Salisbury
(410) 543-6000
www.salisbury.edu

Meredith House and Nield Museum
Cambridge
(410) 228-7953
www.dorchesterhistory.org

Milburn Orchards
Elkton
(410) 398-1349
(800) 684-3000
www.milburnorchards.com

Mount Harmon Plantation
Earleville
(410) 275-8819
www.mountharmon.org

Nathan of Dorchester
Cambridge
(410) 228-7141
www.skipjack.nathan.org

Passerdyke Cottage
Allen
(410) 749-9064
www.wicomicotourism.org/historical

Pemberton Hall and Park
Salisbury
(410) 749-0124
www.wicomicorecandparks.org/
pember.htm

Pemberton Historical Park
Salisbury
(410) 860-2447
www.wicomicotourism.org/historical

Pickering Greek Audubon Center
Easton
(410) 822-4903
www.pickeringcreek.org

Pocomoke State Forest
Snow Hill
(410) 632-2566
www.dnr.state.md.us

Poplar Hill Mansion
Salisbury
(410) 749-1776
www.wicomicotourism.org/historical

(James B.) Richardson Maritime Museum
Cambridge
(410) 221-1871
(800) 522-TOUR

Rockawalkin School
Salisburg
(410) 860-0447
www.wicomicotourism.org/historical

Rosenwald School
Sharptown
www.thequintons.org

Sharptown Historical Museum
Salisbury
(410) 883-2269
www.wicomicotourism.org/historical

(continued on next page)

OTHER ATTRACTIONS WORTH SEEING ON THE EASTERN SHORE (CONT.)

Smith Island Museum and Cultural Center
Ewell
(410) 425-3351
www.smithisland.org

Tucker House
Centreville
(410) 604-2100
www.historicqac.org/sites/
tuckerhouse.htm

Washington College
Chestertown
(410) 778-8500
(800) 422-1782
www.washcoll.edu

Waterman's Museum
Rock Hall
(410) 778-6697
(800) 506-6697
www.havenharbour.com

Wicomico Heritage Centre
Salisbury
(410) 860-0447
www.wicomicotourism.org/historical

Wright's Chance
Centreville
(410) 758-3010
www.historicqac.org/sites/
wrightschance.htm

HAMPSTEAD

Hilltop Hideaway Bed & Breakfast
2525 Hanover Pike
(410) 374-0440
www.hampsteadhideaway
.com

OCEAN CITY

There are dozens, if not hundreds, of hotels, motels, boardinghouses, apartments, bed-and-breakfasts, and condo units for rent in Ocean City. They are bayside or oceanside, seasonal and year-round. They are available on a weekly basis (Sat to Sat, Sun to Sun), a full weekend only, or by the night. For your first visit, you might want to contact the Chamber of Commerce (410-213-0552) or one of about a dozen vacation rental establishments and ask for information about this resort area.

The Edge
60th St. in the Bay
(888) 371-5400
(410) 524-5400
www.fagers.com/edge

Fenwick Inn
13801 Coastal Hwy.
(410) 250-1100
(800) 492-1873
www.fenwickinn.com

Inn on the Ocean
1001 Atlantic Ave.
(410) 289-8894
(877) INN-ON-OC
www.bbonline.com/md/
ontheocean

Lighthouse Club Hotel
56th and the Bay
(888) 371-5400
(410) 524-5400
www.fagers.com/hotel

OXFORD

Combsberry
4837 Evergreen Rd.
(410) 226-5353
www.combsberry.net

Robert Morris Inn
314 North Morris St.
(410) 226-5111
www.robertmorrisinn.com

NORTH EAST

Fairwinds Farm Bed and Breakfast
(410) 658-8187
www.fairwindsstables.com/
bandb.htm

POCOMOKE CITY

Littleton's Bed and
Breakfast
407 Second St.
(410) 957-1645
www.littletonsbandb.com

PRINCESS ANNE

Hayman House Bed and
Breakfast
30491 Prince William St.
(410) 651-1107
www.haymanhouse.com

ROCK HALL

Inn at Osprey Point
20786 Rock Hall Ave.
(410) 639-2194
www.ospreypoint.com

Tallulah's on Main
5750 Main St.
(410) 639-2596
www.tallulahsonmain.com

ROYAL OAK

The Oaks
25876 Royal Oak Rd.
(410) 745-5053
www.the-oaks.com

Royal Oak House B&B
10568 Cliff Rd.
(410) 778-5943
www.greatoak.com

SMITH ISLAND

Chesapeake Sunrise B&B
20880 Caleb Jones Rd.
(410) 425-4220
www.smithisland.us

ST. MICHAELS

Bay Cottage Bed and
Breakfast
24640 Yacht Club Rd.
(410) 745-9369
(888) 558-8008
www.baycottage.com

Dr. Dodson House Bed
and Breakfast
200 Cherry St.
(410) 745-3691
www.drdodsonhouse.com

Five Gables Inn & Spa
209 North Talbot St.
(410) 745-0100
(877) 466-0100
www.fivegables.com

Inn at Perry Cabin
308 Watkins Lane
(410) 745-2200
(866) 278-9601
www.perrycabin.com

STEVENSVILLE

Kent Manor Inn
500 Kent Manor Dr.
(410) 643-5757
(800) 820-4511
www.kentmanor.com

TILGHMAN ISLAND

Black Walnut Point Inn
4417 Black Walnut Point
Rd.
(410) 886-2452
www.blackwalnutpoint.com

TYLERTON

Inn of Silent Music
2955 Tylerton Rd.
(410) 425-3541
www.innofsilentmusic.com

VIENNA

Tavern House
111 Water St.
(410) 376-3347
www.tavernhouse.com

WITTMAN

Watermark Bed and
Breakfast
8956 Tilghman Island Rd.
(800) 314-7734
www.watermarkinn.com

DELAWARE

→

The **Delmarva Peninsula** has always been DelMarVa, for DELaware, MARyland and VirginiA. I have not found any reference that indicates it's ever been VaMarDel or MarVaDel. Wade B. Fleetwood, who wrote a column about the people and places of the Eastern Shore, did question it and came to no conclusion. It could be from north to south, or alphabetical, or political. The only definitive thing my research determined was a reference to DelMarVa as early as 1870 when the fourteen counties of the Eastern Shore (three in Delaware, nine in Maryland, and two in Virginia) were discussing separate statehood. Why fight tradition?

So, if the Delaware of Delmarva comes first, why does this book list Maryland first? Because Maryland Off the Beaten Path was here first, and it wasn't until the third edition that it expanded its scope.

Poor Delaware is just too tiny to claim its own volume. I know someone out there is bound to say, "Well, all of Delaware is off the beaten path," and to a great extent that is deliciously true. The late Nancy Sawin, a fifth generation Delawarean and famed Delaware illustrator, has caught the state and the peninsula in many of her 19 books. Most of

DELAWARE

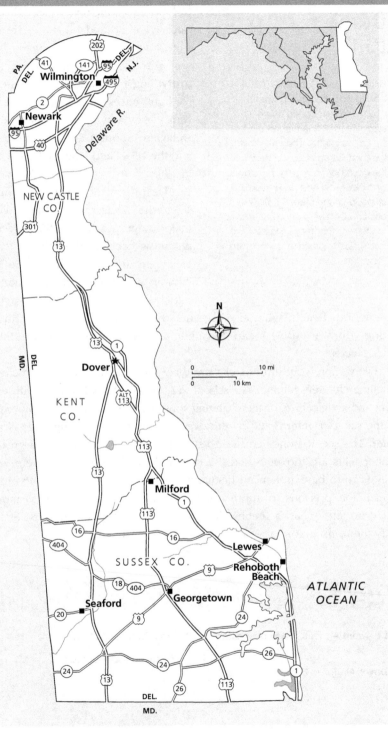

from delawarr to delaware

British captain Samuel Argall landed in a sheltered bay off the Atlantic Ocean during a ferocious storm in 1610. He named the bay De La Warr, after Thomas West, the third Baron of De La Warr and the governor of Virginia, a man who never did and never would step foot in the state. The name became Delaware and was applied to the river that feeds the bay and to the Native Americans who lived there.

her books, which can be difficult to find, were printed on paper from the state's Curtis Paper Company. They are a treasure of information about everything from outhouses to swamps to lighthouses. Yes, she's the same Nancy Sawin who was named to the Delaware Sports Hall of Fame in 1977 and the USA Field Hockey Hall of Fame in 1988.

Despite Delaware's diminutive size, the Delaware Estuary is the major staging area for 80 percent of the snow geese in the Atlantic flyway. Delaware also is known as the state without sales tax, and the number of outlet stores and malls, particularly at Rehoboth Beach (what else are you to do besides shop on a rainy day during your vacation?) mean consumer goods can cost a lot less than in other places.

Everywhere you turn in Delaware there's a delightful treasure, whether it's watching children getting on a school bus, eyes and bodies filled with excitement and anticipation, or the changing song patterns of rain falling pitter patter on the car roof, interrupted by the overhanging trees dropping huge glops of water. The scenic ponds created to supply energy to the dozens of grist- and lumber mills are too perfect to be captured by mere artists or mere words. They have to be experienced firsthand. And the friendliness of everyone you meet is too precious to appreciate in one visit. You may have to move to Delaware and spend a lifetime in this Small Wonder and the First State (to ratify the Constitution).

AUTHOR'S FAVORITES DELAWARE

Delaware Agricultural Museum and Village

Dover Air Force Base

Trap Pond State Park

Zwaanendael Museum

New Castle County

Starting from the north of Delaware, we begin in Wilmington, the largest city in the state, and branch out and then move south. Wilmington was laid out in 1731 by Quakers and was an important shipping center. Early in the 1800s, Eleuthère Irenée du Pont and his two sons moved into the area and, seeing the abundant waterpower potential, started their gunpowder business. Their influence on the development of the city and surrounding area cannot be overstated. Eventually the du Ponts would be responsible for building public schools and creating some of the most incredible museums and museum settings.

runner up

Delaware is the second smallest state in the nation (Rhode Island is the smallest). It is about half the size of Los Angeles County in California.

Draped on either side of the Brandywine Creek that runs from the heart of Wilmington are Brandywine, Alapocas, and Rockford Parks. ***Brandywine Park*** was designed by Frederick Law Olmsted, creator of New York City's Central Park and the National Zoo in Washington, D.C. There's a playground here, a zoo, and the Josephine Garden, with its Japanese cherry trees. The zoo is wheelchair accessible. The park is open daily from 8 a.m. to dusk and the zoo is open from 10 a.m. to 4 p.m. Admission to the park is $3 a day per car for Delaware-registered vehicles and $6 a day for out-of-state registered vehicles from May 1 through October 31. The zoo is located at 41 Adams Dam Rd.; call (302) 655-5740. Zoo admission for the summer is $5 for adults, $4 for seniors, and $3 for children (3 to 11) and in the winter is $4 for adults, $2 for children (3 to 11) and seniors. The park is located at 1001 North Park Dr.; call (302) 571-7788 or visit www.destateparks.com/attractions/brandywine-zoo/index.asp.

A little farther north is the ***Delaware Art Museum,*** with one of the country's most important assemblages of English pre-Raphaelite paintings in the Bancroft collection. American artists also are represented, and a hands-on section is great for children to learn about art. Programs geared toward children or adults are scheduled regularly and traveling exhibits help keep displays new and interesting to encourage your repeat visits. Art camps for children ages 6 to 12 are held in the summer and

treasured location

Delaware is also known as the Diamond State, because it was considered a "jewel" among states due to its strategic location.

awhaleof amural

Downtown Wilmington, near the Amtrak station, is the site of a Wyland mural. Wyland was born in 1956 in Detroit, Michigan, and saw his first grey whales migrating off the California coast when he was fourteen. He started painting whales and dolphins when he was sixteen. By 1974 he had painted his first mural, an Alps mountain scene in Royal Oak, Michigan. The Wilmington painting, called *Whaling Wall XLIV, Marine Mammals*, was done in 1993. It's located between Shipley and Market Sts on Martin Luther King Blvd.

over winter holidays. They include two weeks of learning and fun and an art show for family and friends. The delART café has seating indoors and on the terrace overlooking the sculpture garden. The museum is open Wed through Sat 10 a.m. to 4 p.m. and Sun from noon to 4 p.m. On the first Fri of the month the museum joins Wilmington's Art on the Town program and stays open until 8 p.m. Admission is free from 4 to 8 p.m. Admission is $12 for adults, $10 for seniors over sixty, and $6 for students with ID and children from 7 to 18. There is no admission fee on Sun. Located at 2301 Kentmere Parkway; call (302) 571-9590 or visit www.delart.org.

The *Hagley Museum and Library* is set on 235 landscaped acres at the site of the original DuPont mills. Numerous exhibits show the country's economic growth through industrialization. You can see the mills and community that was created by the DuPonts. The French style garden provided food for the Du Pont family. Exhibits might include a collection of nineteenth-century patent models DuPont's impact on today's science and discovery, or how machines make life easier. Hagley's annual car show in September features more than 500 antique and restored vehicles and is one of Hagley's most popular events. When you consider how explosive gunpowder is, you can look at the architecture and design of the mills with great appreciation. The three side walls farthest from the water were made of heavy stone. The side wall along the creek was made of wood. When the inevitable explosion took place, it would blow out the less-sturdy wooden wall into the creek. This prevented the force of the explosion from blowing out walls that would have otherwise damaged nearby buildings. The Hagley is open daily 9:30 a.m. to 4:30 p.m. from mid-Mar to Dec 30, and weekends 9:30 a.m. to 4:30 p.m. the rest of the year. Admission is $11 for adults, $9 for seniors and students, and $4 for children. Call (302) 658-2400 or visit www.hagley.lib.de.us.

delawaresteelers

Wilmington was a major iron-and steel-working center where the entire suspended superstructure of the Brooklyn Bridge was manufactured.

Climate Overview

Delaware's climate is moderate year-round. Average monthly temperatures range from 75.8 to 32.0 degrees. The average temperature in the summer months is 74.3 degrees. About 57 percent of the days are sunny. Annual precipitation is approximately 45 inches. Temperatures along the Atlantic Coast are about 10 degrees warmer in winter and 10 degrees cooler in summer than the rest of the state. The average growing season varies from 170 to 200 days.

Despite absolute assurances that natural caves do not exist in Delaware, there is a small recess that is 56 feet long with a 24 foot wide, 5 foot high entrance, less than 100 from the Pennsylvania border. Jack H. Speece presented a paper about the cave in August 1977. However, Beaver Valley Cave is on private property and has a "no trespassing" sign posted by the owner. You can see a diorama that depicts Indians at the entrance to the cave at the Hagley Museum.

Visitors to the ***Delaware Museum of Natural History,*** the only natural history museum in Delaware, has been exciting and informing people about the natural world since 1972. This is the place for exploration and discovery without having to trek for days or taking a quick refresher course at the nearby college. Animal Secrets were disclosed as children asked such questions as, "Where do chipmunks sleep?" or "How do mother bats find their babies in a cave?" When it's time to look at life-sized dinosaurs, go face-to-face with a jaguar, or marvel at the diversity of birds. The Larry Scott Nature Trail is a mile-long and meanders through two loops that let you explore the woodlands and wetlands. When you want to

whatareyou pipingupabout?

Old Swedes Church in Wilmington, built in 1698, is the oldest Protestant church still in use in the United States. The pipe organ was built by the Austin Company of Hartford, Connecticut, and has sixteen stops and sixteen ranks of pipe, for a total of 913 pipes. Located at 606 North Church St; call (302) 652-8605 or visit www.oldswedes.org.

share your love of nature to the museum as a volunteer, most positions require that you be at least 16. As a volunteer, you and your immediate family receive free admission to the museum, and discounts on classes and purchases in the gift store. The museum is open Mon through Sat from 9:30 a.m. to 4:30 p.m. and Sun from noon to 4:30 p.m. Admission is $7 for adults, $5 for children (3 to 17), and $6 for seniors (60 plus). Certain events have a small additional fee.

TOP ANNUAL EVENTS IN DELAWARE

FEBRUARY

Cultural Exhibit
Rehoboth Beach
(302) 227-8408

MARCH

St. Patrick's Day Parade
Dover
(302) 678-9112

APRIL

Evening with the Masters
Wilmington
(302) 65-MEALS
www.mealsfromthemasters.com/
evening-with-the-masters.html

Great Delaware Kite Festival
Lewes (Good Friday)
(302) 645-8073

Ocean to Bay Bike Tour
Bethany Beach
(800) 962-SURF
www.TheQuietresorts.com

MAY

Blessing of the Fleet
Lewes
(302) 645-5297

Delmarva Hot Air Balloon Festival
Milton
(302) 684-8404

**Winterthur Point-to-Point
Steeplechase Races**
Winterthur
(302) 888-4994
www.winterthur.org/calendar/point_to_
point.asp

JUNE

Best of the Beach Beebe Art Auction
Rehoboth Beach
(302) 227-8408

Delmarva Chicken Festival
Dover
(800) 878-2449

Sea Glass & Coastal Arts Festival
Lewes
(302) 645-7670
www.historiclewes.org/events/seaglass
.html

Taste of Coastal Delaware
Bethany Beach
(800) 962-SURF
www.thequietresorts.com

JULY

Cottage Tour
Rehoboth Beach
(302) 227-8408

AUGUST

Beach Barbecue
Lewes
(302) 655-4288
www.cbhinc.org

Delaware State Fair
Harrington
(302) 398-3269
www.delawarestatefair.com

**Delaware State News Sandcastle
Contest**
Rehoboth Beach
(800) 441-1329
(302) 227-2233
www.beach-fun.com

Outdoor Fine Art & Fine Craft Exhibit
Rehoboth Beach
(302) 227-8408

SEPTEMBER

Amish Country Bike Tour
Dover
(800) 233-5368
www.visitdover.com/events

Craft Festival at Winterthur
Wilmington
(302) 888-4600
(800) 448-3883
www.winterthur.org

Milton Historical Society Antique Show
Milton
(302) 684-4499

OCTOBER

Celebrity Chefs Beach Brunch
Wilmington
(302) 65-MEALS
(800) 62-MEALS
www.mealsonwheelsde.org

Diamond State BBQ Championship
Dover
(302) 857-2169
(800) 711-5882
www.doverdowns.com

Rehoboth Beach Autumn Jazz Festival
Rehoboth Beach
www.rehobothjazz.com

Restaurant Week Along the Delaware
Various locations
www.delawareriverrestaurantweek.com

Sea Witch Halloween Festival and Fiddlers' Convention
Rehoboth Beach
(800) 441-1329

NOVEMBER

Chocolate Festival
Dover
www.doverdowns.com

Masterpieces in Miniature
Wilmington
(302) 571-9590
(866) 232-3714
www.delart.org

Nemours Mansion and Gardens Tours
Wilmington
(302) 651-6912
www.nemours.org/mansion.html

Rehoboth Beach Independent Film Festival
Rehoboth Beach
(302) 645-9095
www.rehobothfilm.com/festival.html

World Championship Punkin Chunkin Festival
Bridgeville
www.punkinchunkin.com

DECEMBER

First Night Dover
Dover
(302) 734-8228
www2.newszap.com/firstnight

First Night Wilmington
Wilmington
(302) 573-5506

Located at 4840 Kennett Pike, Wilmington; call (302) 658-9111 or visit www .delmnh.org.

A little north of Wilmington is the anomaly of modern government known as **Arden.** It was one of three towns (along with Ardentown and Ardencroft, which would come later) created under the principles conceived by Philadelphia-born economist Henry George and his Theory of Single Tax. Born in 1839, George proposed that land only should be taxed, thereby creating the concept of the "single tax." Thus, in 1895 a group of single taxers from Philadelphia invaded Delaware with their political evangelism. Frank Stephens, a Philadelphia sculptor, with the help of architect Will Price and soap manufacturer Joseph Fels, acquired a Brandywine farm of 160 acres and started the village of Arden. It continues to this day as a single-tax entity.

Utopian in nature, the community also incorporated the artistic ideas of William Morris and the Arts and Crafts Movement, the Garden Cities planning ideas of Ebenezer Howard, and some social theories of Petr Alekseevich Kropotkin (1842–1921). Many of the homes are tiny, for they were summer places, but there definitely is a mix of new and old, fancy and ramshackle, set on lots of various sizes.

The three villages are surrounded by woodlands, including the Naaman's Creek natural area, designated as one of Delaware's Outstanding Natural Areas. Two things seem to drive the residents of Arden: the Arden Club and the Arden Community Recreation Association. Music, dance, theater, visual arts, and such crafts as pottery and ironwork are still highly valued in the three Ardens.

revolutionary battlescene

The only Revolutionary War battle fought in Delaware was the Battle of Cooch's Bridge (east of Newark), on September 3, 1777. It's said that the new thirteen-star flag was first unfurled during this battle, a delaying action to slow the British advance toward Philadelphia. The area in which the Battle of Cooch's Bridge took place can be seen from a 90-foot observation tower in Iron Hill Park, west of State Rte 896 via Welsh Tract Rd. or Old Baltimore Pike in Newark.

Because there isn't a permanent physical display place for all the local artists, they've created a virtual one that features painters, sculptors, photographers, knitters, leather workers, and performing artists. Call (302) 475-0998 or visit www.ardenartists.com for more information.

Hockessin is a delightful little town just outside of Wilmington. As noted earlier, one of the pleasures of the Delmarva is the chance to pick up a Nancy Sawin book; she's written more than a dozen, including Delaware Sketchbook, Backroading Through Cecil (MD) *County*, Between the Bays (Delaware and Chesapeake), and even one on outhouses entitled Privy to the Council Seats

PUBLIC TRANSPORTATION

Philadelphia International Airport, (215) 937-6937; www.phl.org.

Amtrak, (800) USA-RAIL; www.amtrak.com.

Salisbury/Ocean City/Wicomico Regional Airport, (410) 548-4801; www.airnav.com/airport/ksby.

of Yore, with sketches of a variety of "necessary" buildings, from lean-tos and Alpine chalets to one that was fenced and shingled and one that had four columns on its porch.

As you're driving around this area you may want to try the **Back Burner** restaurant. They have delicious seafood and meat entrees and friendly and attentive service. It's a small space, and people from Wilmington make a special drive "to the country" for the food. Located at 425 Old Lancaster Pike, Hockessin; call (302) 239-2314 or visit www.backburner.com.

Old New Castle, a section of New Castle, is filled with Colonial-era homes and buildings that the Rockefeller Foundation initially wanted to restore as a living museum of Colonial America. However, the locals raised such a fuss that the Rockefellers went to Williamsburg, Virginia, instead. Rather than reconstructing the history represented at Williamsburg,

one hill of a vantage point

Iron Hill, just south of Newark, is the home of one of the highest hills in the state (which isn't saying much). On a clear day, from the top of the Iron Hill Tower, you can see four states: New Jersey, Pennsylvania, Maryland, and, of course, Delaware.

New Castle exudes the past from every brick and slather of mortar. It was here that William Penn set foot in North America for the first time. From those Quaker beginnings, the town became a trade center through shipping. A disastrous fire leveled the business area in 1824, but the town was restored when the railroad came through less than a decade later. Eventually, the railroad was rerouted into Wilmington and the town has sat there ever since. Among the houses that are open for your inspection and journey into the past are the Amstel House, the Dutch House, and the George Read II House and garden. You can also tour the restored Court House, or just spend a lazy afternoon on the green.

The **Amstel House,** located at 2 East Fourth St., dates from the 1730s and was the home of colonial governor Nicholas Van Dyke. The furnishings show how life was during the colonial period and include a complete

FAMOUS SONS AND DAUGHTERS OF DELAWARE

Richard Allen, religious leader (1760–1831)

Valerie Bertinelli, actress (1960–)

Dr. Jill Biden, educator, second lady, (1952–)

Joseph Biden, U.S. Vice President (1942–)

Robert Montgomery Bird, author (1806–1854)

Emily Perkins Bissell, social reformer (1861–1948)

Annie Jump Cannon, astronomer (1863–1941)

John Clayton, U.S. Senator (1796–1856)

E. I. DuPont, inventor (1771–1834)

Pierre DuPont, industrialist (1870–1954)

Dallas Green, baseball player and manager (1934–)

Henry Jay Heimlich, physician and developer of Heimlich maneuver (1920–)

Absalom Jones, first black priest of the Protestant Episcopal Church (1746–1818)

John P. Marquand, novelist (1893–1960)

John Bassett Moore, attorney (1860–1947)

Ryan Phillippe, actor (1974–)

Howard Pyle, illustrator (1853–1911)

Jay Saunders Redding, teacher (1906–1988)

Judge Reinhold, actor (1957–)

Caesar Rodney, politician (1728–1784)

Christopher Short, baseball player (1937–1991)

Elisabeth Shue, actress (1963–)

Edward Robinson Squibb, founder of Squibb Pharmaceuticals (1819–1900)

Estelle Taylor, actress (1894–1958)

colonial kitchen. Yeah, we know George Washington was everywhere, and that includes attending a wedding here.

In the *Dutch House,* located at 32 East Third St., you are touring what is thought to be the oldest brick house in Delaware. Constructed in the late seventeenth century, it has been restored and contains wonderful decorative arts and historical items.

Walk-in 40-minute guided tours of both homes are available from Apr 1 through Dec 31, on Wed through Sat from 11 to 4 p.m. and Sun from 1 to 4 p.m. The garden hours are daily sunrise to sunset. Tickets are $4 for adults and $1.50 for children. A combination ticket is $7 for adults and $2.50 for children. Call (302) 322-2794 or visit www.newcastlehistory.org/houses.

George Read was one of the signers of the Declaration of Independence and the U.S. Constitution, and his son's home, called the **George Read II House,** was built over a seven-year period starting in 1797. It's a superb illustration of Federal-style architecture. Note the carved woodwork, fanlights, silver door hardware, and period furnishings as you tour through the twelve rooms (three of which are in the Colonial Revival style). A Philadelphia-style adaptation of a Victorian garden, designed in 1847, decorates the side and back yards. You have a choice of touring this home on your own or calling for an appointment for a guided tour. The house is open Sun and Tues through Fri from 11 a.m. to 4 p.m. and Sat from 10 a.m. to 4 p.m. from spring through fall. It's open on Sat from 10 a.m. to 4 p.m. and Sun from 11 a.m. to 4 p.m. and by appointment in Jan and Feb. The admission is $5 for adults, $4 for seniors (over 65), youngsters (13-21), and military; younger children and garden-only tickets are $2 Located at 42 The Strand; call (302) 322-8411 or visit www.hsd .org/read.htm.

Surely you've noted that the top of the Delaware border, where it meets Pennsylvania, is the arc of a circle. The spire at the top of the **New Castle Court House** is the center point of the 12-mile radius that marks that arc. Although New Castle was the colonial capital of Delaware from 1732 to 1777, the courthouse is now restored to its 1804 appearance. Flags of the Netherlands, Sweden, Great Britain, and the United States represent the various governments that have had jurisdiction over New Castle. Located at 211 Delaware St, between Market and Third Sts, the New Castle Court House is open Tues through Fri 10 a.m. to 3:30 p.m., Sat 10 a.m. to 4:30 p.m., and Sun 1:30 to 4:30 p.m.; closed on state holidays. There is no admission charge. Call (302) 323-4453 or (800) 441-8846 or visit http://history.delaware.gov/museums/ncch/ncch_main.shtml.

If you have time, stop by the hexagon-shaped **Old Library Museum** now home to the New Castle Historical

namethat capital

New Castle was the original state capital of Delaware. In 1777 Dover was named the new capital. Delaware is one of four states in the country in which the initial letter of the capital is the same as the initial letter of the state. The others are Honolulu, Hawaii; Indianapolis, Indiana; and Oklahoma City, Oklahoma.

seizetheday

Welton Academy, the 1950s school that was the setting for the 1989 Oscar-winning film *Dead Poets Society,* starring Robin Williams, was filmed at St. Andrew's School, 350 Noxontown Rd., Middletown. Other locations for the film are in New Castle and Rockland.

Pass the Peas, Please

Fort Delaware, outside of Delaware City, has a calendar full of activities and tours of the site, now a state park, where Confederate soldiers were kept during the Civil War. There's said to be a ghostly sighting every once in a while. The fort is on Pea Patch Island, surely as strange a name as you might find anywhere. Legend has it that the captain of a ship plying the Delaware River didn't realize how shallow the sandbar was in the middle. His ship ran aground and sank. The freight it was carrying was peas—all sizes. They sprouted and thrived and caught silt coming down the river. It started piling up and the peas kept growing. It's now nearly two acres of land.

Visiting Fort Delaware requires a ferry ride (no private boats are allowed to dock at Pea Patch) that cost $11 for adults, $10 for seniors, and $6 for children. Check the Web site for departure times. You must book ahead. Call (877) 98-PARKS or visit www.destateparks.com/park/fort-delaware/ferry.asp.

Society, with regularly scheduled exhibits about the area. Self-guided tours are available May 17 to Dec 31. The museum is open on Sat and Sun from 1 to 4 p.m. There is no admission charge. The building was constructed in 1892 to hold the New Castle Library Company collections. Located at 40 East Third St; call (302) 322-2794 or visit www.newcastlehistory.org/houses/library.html.

Kent County

Kent, the middle of the three Delaware counties, has Dover as its focus. This is the home of the Dover Air Force Base and some Amish families (with their attendant farmers' markets and horse-drawn buggies). It is also the county seat with a hubbub of activity and constant change. Here you'll also find such unusually named places as Slaughter Beach, Seven Hickories, Dutch Neck Crossroads, and Little Heaven and an abundance of protected open spaces where you can explore what nature has left for you and the people of Delaware have protected for you.

The town of **Smyrna,** just off U.S. Hwy. 13 at State Rte 6, has some delightful reasons to visit, besides several thousand friendly residents. The **Smyrna Opera House** was built in 1869 with the first performance staged in 1870. During its lifetime, it has been the town hall, home to police and firefighters, a library, movie house, lodge hall and even a jail. A town fire on Christmas 1948 nearly destroyed the Opera House and surrounding buildings. It was salvaged with the loss of the third floor and the bell tower. With sweat equity and $3.6 million, the Smyrna-Clayton Heritage Association managed to have the building restored, including the bell tower. The building was renewed in 2002 (you can still see the jail's barred windows) and it's now the home to the library, theater, and meeting room with space for an art gallery and other amenities. The Opera House is home to a variety of artists performing throughout the year, including the Chesapeake Brass Band, Tuckers' Tales Puppet Theatre, the music of Simon & Garfunkel, the Brandywine Harps, classes, movies, and summer camp. Locate at 7 West South St; call (302) 653-4236 or visit www .smyrnaoperahouse.org.

On the south side of Smyrna, *Lake Como* (with a freshwater beach) is a beautiful, small lake surrounded by houses with well-manicured yards and the Delaware Home and Hospital. As one local said, "If I focus [into the past], I can see children playing with buckets and shovels in the sand, moms and dads and older kids in striped woolen swimwear walking on the beach, swimming in the cool waters, and diving off the end of the pier."

Stop by the nearly 16,000-acre *Bombay Hook National Wildlife Refuge,* where you're sure to spot plenty of ducks, geese, and shorebirds during migrating season (more than 1.5 million shorebirds traverse Delaware in the annual migration in late May and early June) and other wildlife year-round. More than 256 species of birds, 33 species of animals, and 37 species of reptiles and amphibians inhabit the refuge. You can drive along the 12-mile loop or hike on the nature trails and climb the observation towers for a panoramic view. The refuge is open daily from dawn to dusk, and a visitor center is open daily from 8 a.m. to 4 p.m. throughout the year. Admission to the park is $4 per private vehicle or $2 if you're on foot or coming in by bike.

sealed with state values

The Delaware State Seal was adopted on January 17, 1777, and contains the coat of arms. It also shows a farmer, corn, and a wheat sheaf (signifying the agricultural vitality of the state), a ship (symbolizing New Castle County's ship-building industry), a militiaman with his musket (honoring the role of the citizen-soldier in the maintenance of American liberties), an ox (representing animal husbandry), and water (for the Delaware River).

home sweet home

"Woodburn," the official home of Delaware's governor, was built in 1798 by Charles Hillyard and is considered one of the finest Middle Period Georgian homes in the state. Prior to being purchased by the state in 1965, the home was owned by an abolitionist, two U.S. Senators, three doctors, and a judge. Tours are offered Mon through Fri from 8:30 a.m. to 4 p.m., by appointment only. Located at 151 Kings Hwy., Dover; call (302) 739-5656; or visit www .woodburn.delaware.gov.

just don't call them chicken

The Blue Hen chicken was adopted as Delaware's state bird on April 14, 1939, but its history as a symbol of the state dates from Revolutionary War days. The men of Capt. Jonathan Caldwell's company, recruited from Kent County, brought their fighting game chickens with them, and when the men weren't fighting the enemy they amused themselves with cockfights. The reputation for the tenacity of the cocks in their fights spread throughout the army, and the men of Delaware, equally tenacious, were compared to the fighting Blue Hens.

Those with a Golden Age Passport enter for free. Located at 2591 Whitehall Neck Rd., Smyrna; call (302) 653-6872 or visit http://bombayhook.fws.gov.

The **State House** in Dover is the second-oldest continuously used statehouse (the one in Annapolis, Maryland, is first). This restored 1792 structure has period furnishings and an exhibit of artifacts and historical items. Included in the tour is information about legislative and judicial activities and how these actions affected the population, including slaves and free blacks. Guided thirty-minute tours are available Wed through Sat from 9 a.m. to 4:30 p.m. Located at 25 The Green; call (302) 744-5054 or visit http://history.delaware.gov/museums/sh/visitors.shtml.

If you're at the State House, then you're in the Capital Green, which was laid out in 1722. It is lined with historic buildings and is the ground upon which the U.S. Constitution received its first signature in 1787. From here, Delaware's Continental Regiment mustered for the Revolutionary War, and from here they marched to join Washington's army. Political rallies still are held here, and in May there's Old Dover Days (800-233-5368; www.visitdover.com), with many private homes and buildings open to the public. If you're taking a guided tour, be sure to ask your leader about the woman who sent poisoned candy to her lover's family, resulting in the death of at least one person. This isn't a modern revenge happening; it took place in the 1890s.

MAJOR DELAWARE NEWSPAPERS

Newark Post, 218 East Main St, Suite 109, Newark 19713; (302) 737-0724; www.newarkpostonline.com.

News-Journal, 950 West Basin Rd., New Castle 19720; (302) 324-2700; www.delawareonline.com.

Philadelphia Inquirer, 440 North Broad, Wilmington 19801; (302) 654-6033; www.philly.com/inquirer.

At the **Hall of Records,** near Legislative Hall, is the public archive for the state. This is where you can find the original 1682 charter of King Charles II and William Penn's order for the platting of Dover.

The Hall of Records is at Legislative Ave. and Duke of York St; no charge. It's open Mon through Fri from 8:30 a.m. to 4:15 p.m. Closed on holidays. Call (302) 739-5314.

The **Sewell C. Biggs Museum of American Art,** located behind the statehouse has one of the finest collections of American fine and decorative arts. Biggs, a native of Middletown who died in 2003, collected art from the eighteenth century to modern times and founded this museum in 1993. The collection includes sculptures, early-American furniture, and regional silver. Numerous public programs and events are geared toward students, teachers, families, and adults. The museum is open Tues through Sat from 9 a.m. to 4:30 p.m. and Sun from 1:30 to 4:30 p.m. Located at 406 Federal St, call (302) 674-2111 or visit www.biggsmuseum.org.

sharkattack

According to the Graduate College of Marine Studies at the University of Delaware, there are as many as sixty-two species of shark roaming the eastern waters of North America, including the Delaware and Maryland coasts. Typical mid-Atlantic sharks include the common hammerhead, the Atlantic mako, the sand, the smooth dogfish, the spiny dogfish, and the sandbar shark.

While in Dover, a must stop—if you're a fan of the TV show Homicide: Life on the Street or other police-based shows, or your reading preferences tend toward procedurals—is the **Delaware State Police Museum.** This state-of-the-art educational facility provides an opportunity to learn the history of the Delaware State Police law enforcement methods, a look at a 911 command-and-control console, and a display of uniforms and weapons. Other exhibits cover substance abuse, highway safety efforts, and a variety of other important topics. Talks are presented by specially trained troopers and volunteers. You can also catch a close-up view of patrol cars and motorcycles. The museum is open Mon through Fri from 9 a.m. to 3 p.m. and the third Sat of each month from 11 a.m. to 3 p.m. and by appointment. There is no admission charge. Located at 1425 North DuPont Hwy.; call (302) 739-7700 or visit www.delawaretrooper .com/museum/index.html.

delaware's lincolnlibrary

The Lincoln Collection at the University of Delaware contains more than 2,000 items relating to the public and private life of Abraham Lincoln.

So, your life is filled with CDs—for music, for computer programs, and who knows what else? Your children have never even known an eight-track, much less heard of a Victrola. Now's the time to correct that. Stop by the *John-son Victrola Museum* in Dover to see this tribute to Eldridge Reeves Johnson (a Delaware native who was an inventor, businessman, and philanthropist), the inventor and founder of the Victor Talking Machine Company (1901). Designed to look like a 1920s store, the museum has an extensive collection of phonographs, records, and memorabilia related to the company, including an original oil painting of Nipper, the dog who listened to "His Master's Voice." The museum is open on the first Sat of the month from 9 a.m. to 4:30 p.m. Groups can call for reservations. There's no admission charge (donations are accepted) to 375 South New St; call (302) 739-4266 or visit http://history .delaware.gov/museums/jvm/jvm_main.shtml.

Go north of Dover about 2 miles and you'll see the *Delaware Agricultural Museum and Village,* covering 200 years of the agrarian heritage of Delaware, with dairy and poultry farming objects, horse-drawn equipment, and tractors from 1670 through the 1950s. There's a barbershop, farmhouse, general store, one-room schoolhouse, sawmill, train station, and blacksmith and wheelwright shops, all representing structures from the Civil War to the turn of the twentieth century. Some of the programs that have been featured are A More Abundant Life: Rural Delaware and Culture in New Deal Art, The Ten Ton Tomato Club and Other Tales, and Christmas on the Farm. Special events include Fall Harvest Festival and A Farmer's Christmas. The museum is open Tues through Sat from 10 a.m. to 3 p.m. Admission is $5 for adults, $3 for seniors sixty and older and for children from 6 to 17. Special event admission may vary and group and family rates are available. Located at 866 North DuPont Hwy.; call (302) 734-1618 or visit www.agriculturalmuseum.org.

delaware, inc.

Because of Delaware's liberal incorporation laws, more than half the country's Fortune 500 companies have filed incorporation papers in the state.

Head south of Dover about 4 miles if aviation is your passion. One of the more exciting places to visit is the *Dover Air Force Base.* I know you've seen a lot of historic buildings around here, but this may be the first time you've seen a World War II hangar that's listed on the National Register of Historic Places. Guided tours are available although groups should call for a reservation. It was the site of the Army Air Force's rocket test center and is now the home of the Air Mobility Command Museum. On display at the museum is a collection of vintage planes from 1941, including a C-47 Gooney Bird and a B-17G. Other World War II artifacts also are on display. Programs are available to help complete the Aviation Scout Merit Badge. For those who've always wanted to take flight in one of these magnificent birds, there's a flight simulator open to those who are ten and older. An experienced pilot guides you through takeoff, flying, and landing. The hours are limited by volunteer availability. The museum is open Tues through Sun 9 a.m. to 4 p.m. There is no admission charge. Located at 1301 Heritage Rd. (enter through the State Rte 9 gate); call (302) 677-5938 or visit www .amcmuseum.org.

South of the Air Force base is the *John Dickinson Plantation,* the boyhood home of John Dickinson, who in 1778 drafted the Articles of Confederation, for which he was known as the "Penman of the Revolution." His 1740s brick home and the reconstructed outbuildings are typical of eighteenth-century plantation architecture and lifestyle, with the added benefit that the home is furnished with family pieces and period antiques. Among the topics that are available for group tours are Politics and Plantation, In the Best Manner, Then and Now, and Dickinson Plantation Profiles. The plantation is open Wed through Sat 10 a.m. to 3:30 p.m. Free guided tours are presented by interpreters

veryjumbojet

Each C5A or C-5 Galaxy, the largest cargo airplane in the world, housed at Dover Air Force Base, is big enough to hold several football fields.

Horseshoe Crabs

Horseshoe crabs (*Limulus polyphemus*) are found along the western shores of the Atlantic Ocean, from Maine to the Yucatan, but the Delaware Bay area is home to the largest population of them. The crabs date back 250 million years. One reason for the horseshoe crab's longevity might be because it can go for a year without eating and can endure extreme temperatures. They are more closely related to scorpions, ticks, and land spiders than crabs, although they are not dangerous to humans. They grow when they molt (usually sixteen times over nine to twelve years until they become full-size adults), increasing in size by about one-fourth each time and living for about thirty years. During the high tides of the new and full moon in May and June, thousands of horseshoe crabs descend on the Delaware Bay shoreline to spawn (laying as many as 20,000 tiny eggs). You can view this spectacle at night from an elevated spot using binoculars or field glasses. At the *DuPont Nature Center at Mispillion Harbor Reserve,* 2992 Lighthouse Rd., Slaughter Beach is a great place to see the horseshoe crabs lay eggs and shorebirds eating them. Among the 30 species of birds to visit the area are the Red Knot, Ruddy Turnstone, Semipalmated Sandpiper, Dunlin, and black-necked stilt. Visit www.dupontnaturecenter.org for more information.

dressed in eighteenth-century attire; groups should call for a reservation. There is no admission charge. Located at 340 Kitts Hammock Rd., Dover; call (302) 739-3277 or visit history.delaware.gov/ museums/jdp/jdp_main.shtml.

logon

Swedish immigrants built the first log cabins in America in Delaware, in 1638.

A tribute to agriculture can be found in Harrington at the ***Messick Agricultural Museum,*** with its extensive display of farm implements of the early twentieth century. You'll see automobiles, a covered wagon, various engines, horse-drawn plows and vehicles, tools, tractors, and trucks. There's also an early-twentieth-century kitchen and smokehouse. The museum is open Mon through Fri from 7:30 a.m. to 4:30 p.m., Sat from 7:30 a.m. to noon, and by appointment. There is no admission fee. Located at 325 Walt Messick Rd., Harrington; call (302) 398-3729 or visit http://taylormessick.com/ messick-museum/#anchor.

Sussex County

Even if you've never heard of Sussex County, you've most likely heard of Rehoboth Beach and possibly even Bethany Beach, although both are billed as "quiet resorts." They are primarily residential and have been promoted as great family vacation and residential areas.

The 87-foot-tall white brick ***Fenwick Island Lighthouse,*** with a Third Order Fresnel lens projecting light 15 miles into the ocean, was commissioned on August 1, 1859, to protect ships from venturing onto the treacherous shoals extending 5 to 6 miles out from the Delaware coastline. It

A Nice Salute

The entrance to Bethany Beach, just south of the Delaware Seashore State Park, is marked by a 24-foot Native American totem pole. This greeting to Bethany Beach was sculpted by Peter Wolf Toth and dedicated on July 15, 2002. It's the third pole to grace this site. Toth created the first statue of "Chief Little Owl" and put it in place in 1976. Termites started its demise which was completed by high winds in 1992. The remains are at the Nanticoke Indian Museum in Millsboro. Dennis D. Beach created the second one which lasted until 2000. Toth says the latest version should last for 50 to 150 years. "Chief Little Owl," named for a chief of the Nanticoke tribe, represents an eagle protecting an Indian by clutching him to its breast.

FAST FACTS ABOUT THE FIRST STATE

Area (land): Delaware ranks forty-ninth in the nation, with a total area of 1,982 square miles (5,133 square kilometers)

Capital: Dover

Largest city: Wilmington

Number of counties: three

Highest elevation: 447.85 feet (136.5 meters) above sea level, in New Castle County

Lowest elevation: sea level, along the Atlantic Ocean

Greatest distance from north to south: 96 miles (154.46 kilometers)

Greatest distance from east to west: 35 miles (56.3 kilometers)

Coastline: almost 300 miles (482.7 kilometers)

Population: 885,122 (2009 estimate), forty-fifth among the states

Population density: 401 persons per square mile

Population distribution: 73 percent urban, 27 percent rural

Statehood: December 7, 1787 (first state)

Nicknames: the First State, Small Wonder, Blue Hen State

State flower: peach blossom

State tree: American holly

State motto: Liberty and Independence

State bird: blue hen chicken

State song: "Our Delaware"

State bug: ladybug

State fish: weakfish (aka sea trout, gray trout, yellow mouth, yellowfin trout, and tiderunner)

State beverage: milk

State mineral: sillimanite

State colors: Colonial blue and buff

State marine animal: horseshoe crab

State fossil: belemnite

State butterfly: tiger swallowtail

State soil: Greenwich loam

State herb: sweet goldenrod

State star: Delaware diamond (Ursa major)

State microinvertebrate: stonefly

was automated in 1940, then decommissioned in 1978. A public outcry brought about the reinstallation of the original light, weighing about 1,500 pounds, and it has been in service since then. It's at the eastern terminus of the Mason-Dixon line at the Delaware-Maryland border. There's a cluster of buildings here, the lighthouse, two keepers' dwellings (now in private ownership), storage sheds, and the tower. The light is listed on the National Register of Historic Buildings. The Coast Guard deactivated it in 1978, but the members of the New Friends of the Fenwick Island Lighthouse have been guardian since 2007. Under the guidance of Winnie Lewis (a granddaughter

A Cool Fund-raiser

In 1997 the Bethany-Fenwick Area Chamber of Commerce started a January 1 *Exercise Like the Eskimos* ocean swim. What's involved? About 250 people run into the Atlantic Ocean—which is about forty degrees—to raise scholarship funds for high school seniors! This polar bear stuff has always sounded to me like a cardiologist's heaven, but that's another story. Teams and individuals are invited to participate, with entry fees of $25 for adults (early registration or $30 for late registration) and $15 for students. Everyone registered gets a free hat. The team with the most participants receives a trophy. Hot chocolate and T-shirts are sold. If freezin' for a reason sounds like a lot of fun, then this is your place. Call (302) 539-2100 or visit https://store.bethany-fenwick.org.

of a former lighthouse keeper), Ed Gibson, Donna Schwartz, Tracy Lewis, and Jan Thompson, the fund-raising and public interest has been growing. The lighthouse participates in the United States Lighthouse Society Passport program, so have your passport stamped when you visit. Check the Web site to see which days the lighthouse, the museum, and gift shop will be open. You are not allowed to climb the lighthouse. There's no admission charge, but donations are accepted. Call (302) 539-4115 or visit http://fenwickisland lighthouse.org.

On the south side of the Fenwick Island Lighthouse is one of the original *Transpeninsular Line Markers,* which was erected on April 26, 1751. This stone marked the east end of the 70-mile-long line that connected the Atlantic Ocean to the Chesapeake Bay, denoting what was then the southern border of Pennsylvania. Those three lower counties are now Delaware. A little more than a decade later, Mason and Dixon used the midpoint of the line when they surveyed the border between Pennsylvania and Maryland. The marker is at 146th St. The midpoint marker is on the north side of Rte 54, about halfway between Delmar and Mardela Springs. Call (302) 539-8129 for more information.

DiscoverSea is the place to visit to view hundreds of artifacts recovered from shipwrecks along the Delmarva coastline, dating from colonial days.

here's grist for your mill

The *U.N.O.I. Grain Mill* in Seaford is the former Hearns and Rawlins Mill and is now the last operating flour mill in the state. It was built in 1885 and purchased by the United Nation of Islam (not related to the Nation of Islam) a few years ago to make Dove brand flour and other products from the grain they grow on the Eastern Shore. Located on Rte 13A, Seaford; call (302) 629-4083 or visit www.visit delaware.com.

Dedicated to preserving our maritime heritage, the museum opened in July 1995 after more than seventeen years of research and hard work. Stop by for a visit, a lecture, or a beach tour and travel to the past via this hands-on experience. Open daily Memorial Day through Labor Day from 11 a.m. to 8 p.m. and on weekends from 11 a.m. to 4 p.m. the rest of the year. There is no admission fee to DiscoverSea. Located at 708 Ocean Hwy., Fenwick Island; call (302) 539-9366 or (888) 743-5524 or visit www.discoversea.com.

Think Wyoming and you're thinking the Wild West. This Wyoming is in Delaware, south of Dover and north of Felton. And the Wild West is the **Wicked R. Western Productions, Inc.** Randy and Jennifer Ridgely have sixty acres of countryside and they teach more than three dozen lessons a week and hold four to six birthday and other celebratory parties every weekend in the summer. Regardless of your age or gender, they have something that could be of interest to you. Try an overnight women's ranch retreat, cowboy 101, kids dude ranch camp, spring horse sale, and bull riding clinic. Come fall, there's a corn maze, burlap maze, corn play bin, a straw playground, and more. Located at 2621 Sandy Bend Rd.; call (302) 492-3327 or visit www.wickedr.com.

As one might expect, the southwest Delaware town of **Laurel** (originally Laureltown) was so named because of the abundance of laurel bushes growing along Broad Creek. Settled in 1802, the town was the largest in Sussex County by 1859 and was once a thriving shipping center and port town. With more than 800 buildings on the National Register of Historic Places, it is the largest designated historic district in the state of Delaware. Many properties were destroyed in the Great Fire of 1899, although many survived. A *Walking Tour of Historic Laurel* brochure has

watermelon crazy

The farmers of Delaware produced more than 78 million pounds of watermelon in 2003, making the state eleventh in production in the country.

been created by the Laurel Historical Society to see some of the fascinating moments from the past. Located at 502 East 4th St; call (302) 875-1344 or visit http://laurelhistoricalsociety.com.

As small as Bethel and the area around it are, you can find enough people to see and talk to—and even things to do and learn—that you might find ways to spend an entire day there—even a lifetime. Start with the Laurel-Woodland Ferry, more commonly called the Woodland Ferry that crosses the Nanticoke River just as boats have done since 1793. The cable-operated ferry is the last free river ferry in Delaware. Operated from sunup to sundown, the ferry may make up to 300 trips on a busy day, saving its passengers a road trip of nearly

20 miles. Signs on State Rte 78 in Laurel and Reliance, State Rte 490 south of Blades, and State Rte 80 at Seaford indicate if the ferry is running. The ferry is operated by the Delaware Department of Transportation; located at Woodland Ferry Rd.; call (302) 629-7742 or visit www.deldot.gov.

biggestsale oftheyear

On the Saturday after Labor Day, Miltonians (residents of Milton) clean out garages, attics, and closets, and the Town-Wide Yard Sale takes place.

In Laurel, Milton, Ridgeville, Milford, and other places, you'll see **murals by Jack Lewis** (123 West Lockerman St, Dover; (302) 678-0968; www.raubachergallery.com), a graduate of Rutgers with a master's degree in education. You'll find them on exterior walls, in banks, in the family court in Georgetown, and even in a prison. Lewis taught art in the state for thirty years, and he participated in a Fulbright Scholarship exchange program. Lewis says he's basically a watercolorist, and murals are not his chief interest. Fortunately, he has dabbled in the area of murals, for our enjoyment.

Lewis and **Howard Schroeder** (1910–1995), a nearly life-long friend of Lewis', were fundamental in starting the Rehoboth Art League, the premier art and cultural institution of area. Schroeder (http://howardschroederart.com) came to the area as a military artist during World War II. Look for Schroeder's paintings at the University of Delaware and the Peninsula Gallery in Lewes. He was featured on the CBS *Sunday Morning* show in 1987. Lewis and Schroeder were included in the Artists Biographies program (www.teleduction .com) that also featured artists Mary Page Evans, Helen Farr Sloan, Edward L. Loper, and Charles Parks.

miltonhistory

The town of Milton, settled in 1672 by English colonists, was known by several names over the years, until 1807 when the town was named after the English poet John Milton. With 198 of its homes on the National Register of Historic Places, it's said to have the finest concentration of nineteenth-century architecture in the country. Milton once had a thriving holly industry, providing holiday wreaths to much of the nation. The state tree is the American holly.

The Laurel area is noted for at least one other bit of historical trivia. On June 21, 1904, some signals were crossed and the schooner *Golden Gate*, traveling down the nearby Broad Creek, was struck by a mail train. Luckily the train engine automatically uncoupled, so the rest of the train didn't fall into the creek. This may be the only occurrence of a train and sailing ship colliding.

In a nutshell, or in a potato skin if you will, the life of a sweet potato is not easy. The seeds first must be started indoors in February. Then they must be transplanted to warm beds, then to the outdoors, and then harvested and dried. Sweet potatoes apparently are horrible if eaten when freshly harvested. They'll keep all winter if they're stored at a constant fifty-degree temperature. Specialized buildings were constructed to hold the productive sweet potato cash crop.

The buildings are usually two to three stories tall and are long and relatively narrow. The outer walls are made of three or more layers of wood siding. On the exterior is a horizontal layer, followed by a diagonal layer in the center, and a vertical layer on the inside. All this helped to insulate the building, and sometimes a form of tar paper or sawdust was used between the layers to further insulate it. Inside is a series of bins, about 3 feet by 9 feet, where the potatoes were stored. Sometimes access to the bins was from a central aisle, sometimes from a perimeter walkway. A stove at one end had to be tended morning and night once the first frost had set in. The second and third floors did not butt against the walls; this helped ventilation and ensured an even distribution of the heat to the upper and lower floors.

A blight hit the extremely labor-intensive crop in the 1940s and destroyed the industry. Now, some of the sweet potato or potato houses have been converted into office or living space. The Chipman Potato House, at the junction of DE 465 and DE 465A, was named to the National Register of Historic Places in 1990. It was made of brick, weatherboard, and tin.

earlystamp collecting

Emily P. Bissell (1861–1948) created the first Christmas seals when she drew pictures on stamps in 1907. She sold the stamps to raise funds to aid tubercular children. Emily lived in Delaware and was a cousin of a doctor at a tuberculosis sanatorium in Delaware along the Brandywine River.

There's no telling where you might think you are when you go through ***Trap Pond State Park.*** This 2,000-plus acre park was once part of the large freshwater swampland of southwestern Sussex County. The pond was created in the early 1800s for a sawmill that processed the bald cypress trees from the area. The park has the northernmost publicly owned stand of bald cypress in the country. In the 1930s the federal government purchased the area, and the Civilian Conservation Corps developed the recreation site. Within the park are bald cypress trees, wetlands, wildflowers, wildlife, a nature preserve, a picnic area, a playground, a primitive camping area for youngsters, more than 7 miles of hiking trails, a canoe trail, camping, and a rent-a-camp program that lets you rent equipment to see if you like the experience before investing in all the gear. The 130 family campsites are $24 each for a resident family and

The Oklahoma Connection

When you try to trace Native American bloodlines from the original residents of Delaware, you have to go to Bartlesville, Oklahoma. Yes, that's where you'll locate the headquarters of the Delaware Indians. The Delaware or Lenni Lenape (first people) were a friendly tribe who gradually gave up their lands to the new settlers. They moved westward into Pennsylvania, then Ohio, then Indiana. Some even went to Canada, where they still occupy two small reserves in Ontario province. By 1820 they had crossed the Mississippi River into Missouri, then Kansas, and finally moved into Indian Territory in 1866. An 1867 agreement with the Cherokees allowed them to purchase land where they now reside. The Delawares comprise approximately 10,000 people today.

$28 a day for non-residents. Walk-in tents, secluded walk-in tents, cabins, and yurts can be rented.

Birders can spy on great blue herons, owls, hummingbirds, robins, mockingbirds, cardinals, finches, warblers, bald eagles, and pileated woodpeckers. Pets are permitted in some areas of the park, but they must be kept on a leash and attended to at all times. Bicycles and horses are permitted on designated trails.

Motorboats (electric only) are permitted in some areas of the pond and are limited to a no-wake speed of 5 miles per hour. Rowboats, pedal boats, and canoes may be rented in the summer. The park is part of a trash-free program, which means you carry out everything you carry in. Located at 33587 Baldcypress Lane, Laurel; call (302) 875-5153 or (302) 875-2392 (campground); or visit www.destateparks.com/park/trap-pond.

At **Lewes** (pronounced Lou-iss, not lose) you'll find the Delaware side of the Lewes–Cape May, New Jersey, ferry. The hour-plus ride is a great way to avoid driving up the New Jersey Turnpike and then down to the beach towns of southern New Jersey or Atlantic City. The fare is $36 per car Apr through Oct and $29.50 the rest of the year, plus a peak time fee and a passenger fee (from $3.50 to $10.50, depending on age and time of the year). You can make online reservations ($2 discount) if you're confident about your arrival time. Multi-trip discounts are available. Located at 43 Henlopen Dr. in Lewes. Call (302) 644-6030, (800) 64-FERRY; or visit www.capemaylewesferry.com.

As you drive the 20 miles along the beach from the Maryland border to Lewes, you may notice seven **concrete towers** rising up about 80 feet. They've been there since the days when German U-boats were a threat to our shores. There have been days when people were ready to tear them down. After all, they weren't being used. But there was never enough money, so they still stood. Now, people (perhaps the same ones) have decided the towers are historic. That means you may climb the 115 steps of the *Cape Henlopen State Park tower* to the top for a lovely view that stretches from the Rehoboth boardwalk to Gordons Pond, taking in the Atlantic Ocean, Delaware Bay, and the outlying salt marsh. It's open seven days a week in good weather. Park admission during the season is $4 for Delaware-registered vehicles and $8 for out-of-state vehicles. Tower admission is free with park admission. Located at 15099 Cape Henlopen Dr., Lewes; call (302) 645-8983 or visit www.destate parks.com/chsp/chsp.htm.

Should you need other reasons to come to Lewes, the *Zwaanendael Museum* (Valley of the Swans), a Dutch Renaissance building that is an adaptation of the town hall at Hoorn in the Netherlands should be high on your list. No, it wasn't brought over stone by stone, and it wasn't built three centuries ago. Instead, it was built in 1931 (the tercentenary of the founding of Lewes). Inside are exhibits of historic military and maritime artifacts from 1631 to the

whatadistinct honor

Lewes, known as the "first town in the first state," has had another distinction bestowed upon it: The National Trust for Historic Preservation has named it a Distinctive Destination. Honored in 2006, it joined Prescott, AZ; Monterey and Palm Springs, CA; Waimea, HI; Bowling Green, KY; Arrow Rock, MO; Philipsburg, MT; Saranac Lake, NY; Bartlesville, OK; West Chester, PA; and Milwaukee, WI. It was selected for its parks, historic district, museums, antiques shops, galleries, fine restaurants, and more.

From POWs to Pickles

The Kendzierski family apparently owns the only known privately owned fort in the United States. Fort Saulsbury is six miles east of Milford, near the town of Slaughter Beach, in the northeast corner of Sussex County. The fort was constructed in 1917 and 1918 in a location that would serve to protect the mouth of the Delaware Bay and River during World War I. The fort was named for Delaware's U.S. Senator (1859–71) and attorney general (1850–55) Willard Saulsbury Sr. The casements were 14 feet thick, steel-reinforced concrete, with 6 feet of earth on top for camouflage. Since completion came so close to the November 1918 armistice, the fort wasn't fully staffed as a defensive facility until World War II, and then only until Fort Miles at Cape Henlopen was completed in 1942. The fort then became a POW camp for German and Italian soldiers. The fort was deactivated on January 11, 1946, sold to the Kendzierski family, and then served as a pickle processing and storage operation for the Liebowitz Pickle Company. It later was a storage spot for the Milford Salvage Company. It's unused today, but thought to be the only surviving World War I–era fort that is essentially unchanged. You can take a virtual tour at www.fortsaulsbury.org/Virtual%20Tours.htm.

The Zwaanendael Merman

It's said the first "mermen" (no, not the surfing music group) to reach American shores came from the Japanese in 1822 and that by 1842 P.T. Barnum displayed his first merman as the "Feejee Mermaid." Many fine museums own a merman specimen, but few choose to exhibit it. Therefore, because you get so few opportunities, one of the things you're sure to want to see at the Zwaanendael Museum is the merman. This one is about a foot long, and in 1941 it was loaned to the museum by a prominent local family who received it from a sea captain. The last family member died in 1985, and the museum collected $250 in donations to buy the merman from the estate. Although the museum has tried to provide the best exhibits on maritime history, the public won't allow the removal of the merman from display.

War of 1812 and about the HMB *DeBraak*, a British brig that sank near Lewes in 1798. Guided tours are available throughout the day. Groups should make reservations. The museum is open Tues through Sat from 10 a.m. to 4:30 p.m. There is no admission charge. Located at 102 King's Hwy.; call (302) 645-1148 or visit http://history.delaware.gov/museums/zm/zm_main.shtml.

Also recommended for those interested in nature are the ***Prime Hook National Wildlife Refuge*** in Milton (302-684-8419, http://northeast.fws.gov/de/pmh.htm), and the ***Seaside Nature Center,*** at Cape Henlopen State Park (302-684-8983; www.destateparks.com/chsp/chsp.htm).

At the ***Lewes Historical Society Complex*** is a furnished country store from the early years of this century, the 1798 Burton-Ingram House with period Chippendale and Empire antiques, and other historic buildings that were moved to Lewes. They include the blacksmith shop (now an extension to the gift shop), the Hiram Burton House, a doctor's office, an early plank house (early Swedish-style construction), the Ellegood House (the gift shop), and the Rabbit's Ferry House. Walking tours and trolley tours are offered, usually during the summer season. Reservations are required for groups. The complex is open Mon through Sat from 11 a.m. to 4 p.m. and Sun from 1 to 4 p.m., mid-June until Labor Day; tours are available by appointment. Located at 110 Shipcarpenter St; call (302) 645-7670 or visit www.historiclewes.org.

For curiosity's sake, stop by the ***Cannonball House Museum*** to see a cannonball in the foundation of the building, a souvenir of the attack by the British on April 6 and 7, 1813. Tours are given on Tues, Wed, and Fri at 10:30 a.m. Located at 118 Front St, Lewes; call (302) 645-7670 or visit www.historic lewes.org/museums/cbh.html.

If you're in the area on the first weekend of November, you should stop by the Eagle Crest Aerodrome to witness the ***Punkin Chunkin contest.*** It's just what it sounds like, a contest to see who can hurl pumpkins the farthest distance by the use of catapults and other odd contraptions. Located at the corner of County Rds. 305 and 306 in Long Neck. Admission to the event is $7 per day, plus $2 parking fee. No pets allowed. For information contact the Lewes Chamber of Commerce and Visitor's Bureau at 120 Kings Hwy., Lewes 19958; call (302) 645-8073 or visit www .punkinchunkin.com.

dunebuggy paradise

The sand dunes at Cape Henlopen can reach 80 feet, and the Great Dune is the highest sand dune between North Carolina's Cape Hatteras and Cape Cod in Massachusetts.

While meandering along west of Cape Henlopen on Rte 36, if you get a yen for a little fishing, stop by *Abbott's Mill Nature Center.* It's one of a number of lakes and ponds in the area, but the nature center also has a historic gristmill, trails meandering through pine woods and along a stream, and canoeing and fishing. An Autumn at Abbott's Mill Festival is held the third Saturday in October. Year-round family programs, particularly for children from 3 to 18, but also for adults and families, are highlighted. Located at 15411 Abbott's Pond Rd., Milford; call (302) 422-0847 or visit www.delawarenaturesociety.org.

Chad Moore, Owner and General Manager

Just two blocks from the beach, restaurants, galleries, antiques shops, boutiques, and all that is Rehoboth Beach, the *Bellmoor Inn, Spa and Executive Retreat,* with 78 rooms and suites is a marvelous place for a family getaway, ladies (or men's) weekend, executive retreat, or a nice romantic escape. As a member of Select Registry, Distinguished Inns of North America, the inn, owned and managed by Chad Moore, ranks up there as a delightful place to spend some beach time.

The Jefferson Library is a 500-square-foot snuggle-up place with a wood-burning fireplace and game tables or you can enjoy the Garden Courtyard or even a quiet stay by the adults-only pool. Although equipped with the modern high-tech conveniences of a huge hotel, the Bellmoor feels much more like a bed-and-breakfast.

The Bellmoor Club Floor is an adult-only, all-suite floor with another library, king-sized beds, fireplaces, hydrotherapy tubs, and balconies. A complimentary hearty country breakfast and afternoon refreshments are provided, and the day spa offers a variety of relaxing and rejuvenating spa treatments, massages, facials, manicures and pedicures, and a fitness center. Located at 6 Christian St; call (302) 227-5800 or (800) 425-2355; or visit www.thebellmoor.com.

Places to Eat in Delaware

BETHANY BEACH

Penguin Diner
105 Garfield Parkway
(302) 541-8017
www.penguindiner.com

DELAWARE CITY

Crabby Dick's
30 Clinton St.
(302) 832-5100
www.crabbydicks.net

DOVER

McGlynns Pub and Restaurant
800 North State St.
(302) 674-0144
www.mcglynnspub.com/
mcglynns_pub/Home.html

FENWICK ISLAND

Fenwick Crab House
Coastal Hwy.
(302) 539-2500

LEWES

King's Homemade Ice Cream Shop
201 Second St.
(302) 645-9425
www.kings-icecream.com

Lighthouse Restaurant
Fisherman's Wharf
(302) 645-6271

LONG NECK

Baywood Greens
32267 ClubHouse Way
(302) 947-9800
(888) 844-2254
www.baywoodgreens.com

MILTON

King's Homemade Ice Cream Shop
302 Union St.
(302) 684-8900
www.kings-icecream.com

NEWARK

Deer Park Tavern
108 West Main St.
(302) 369-9414
www.deerparktavern.com/

NEW CASTLE

Arsenal on the Green
30 Market St.
(302) 328-1290

Casablanca Restaurant
4010 North DuPont Hwy.
(302) 652-5344
www.thecasablanca
restaurant.com

REHOBOTH BEACH

Back Porch Café
(open seasonally)
59 Rehoboth Ave.
(302) 227-3674
www.backporchcafe.com

Crabby Dick's
18831 Coastal Hwy.
(302) 645-9132
www.crabbydicks.net

Cultured Pearl Restaurant and Sushi Bar
301 Rehoboth Ave.
(302) 227-8493
www.culturedpearl.us

House of 'shrooms
210 2nd St.
(302) 227-6494
www.theporchinihouse
.com

Nage Rehoboth Beach
19730 Coastal Hwy.
(032) 226-2037
www.nage.bz/rehoboth_
beach/experience.htm

SELBYVILLE

Mr. Bill's Terrace Inn Crab House
37314 Lighthouse Rd.
(302) 436-7500

SMYRNA

Thomas England House
1165 South DuPont Hwy.
(302) 653-1420

WILMINGTON

Gallucio's Restaurant and Pub
1709 Lovering Ave.
(302) 655-3689
www.gallucios.com

Places to Stay in Delaware

Dozens of hotels, condominiums, motels, apartments, houseboats, and other accommodations are along the beaches of Dewey, Fenwick, Bethany, and Rehoboth. Some offer weeklong (Sat to Sat or Sun to Sun) rentals, weekends, or one-night options. Some are open only seasonally. Some are on the ocean, some are several blocks away. Note that accommodations statewide usually are full the first weekend after Memorial Day and the third weekend after Labor Day, due to the NASCAR races at Dover Downs.

BETHANY BEACH

Addy Sea Bed & Breakfast
99 Ocean View Parkway
(302) 539-3707
www.addysea.com

DELAWARE CITY

Olde Canal Inn
30 Clinton St
(302) 832-5100
www.oldecanalinn.com

DEWEY BEACH

Atlantic Oceanside Motel
1700 Hwy. 1
(302) 227-8811
www.atlanticoceanside
.com

Bell Buoy Inn
21 VanDyke St
(302) 227-6000
www.bellbuoyinn.com

Surf Club Hotel
One Read St
(302) 227-7059
(800) 441-8341
http://deweysurfclub.com

DOVER

Dover Inn
428 North DuPont Hwy.
(302) 674-4011

Little Creek Inn
2623 North Little Creek Rd.
(302) 730-1300
(888) 804-1300
www.littlecreekinn.com

Sheraton-Dover
1570 North DuPont Hwy.
(302) 678-8500
www.sheraton.com

FENWICK ISLAND

Atlantic Coast Inn
37558 Lighthouse Rd.
(800) 432-8038
(302) 539-7673
www.atlanticcoastinn.com

Seaside Inn
1401 Coastal Hwy.
(800) 417-1104
(302) 251-5000
www.seasideinnfenwick
.com

GEORGETOWN

Brick Hotel on the Circle
Eighteen the Circle
(302) 855-5800
www.thebrickhotel.com

Master's Manor Inn
22934 Zoar Rd.
(302) 236-5973
www.mastersmanorinn
.com

LEWES

An Inn by the Bay Bed & Breakfast
205 East Savannah Rd.
(866) 833-2565
(302) 644-8878
www.aninnbythebay.com

Blue Water House Bed & Breakfast
407 East Market St.
(800) 493-2080
(302) 645-7832
www.lewes-beach.com

Hotel Rodney
142 2nd St.
(302) 645-6466
www.hotelrodneydelaware
.com

Inn at Canal Sq
122 Market St.
(302) 644-3377
(888) 644-1911
www.theinnatcanalsquare
.com

Savannah Inn Bed & Breakfast
330 Savannah Rd.
(302) 645-0330
www.savannahinnlewes
.com

MILFORD

Causey Mansion Bed and Breakfast
2 Causey Ave.
(302) 422-0979
www.causeymansion.com

Towers Bed & Breakfast
101 Northwest Front St.
(302) 422-3814
www.mispillion.com

NEW CASTLE

Terry House Bed and Breakfast
130 Delaware St.
(302) 322-2505,
www.terryhouse.com

OTHER ATTRACTIONS WORTH SEEING IN DELAWARE

Abbott's Mill Nature Center
Milford
(302) 422-0847

Anna Hazzard Museum
Rehoboth Beach
(302) 226-1119

Bethany Beach History Museum
Bethany Beach
(302) 539-8011
www.townofbethanybeach.com

Bethany Beach Nature Center and Conservation Area
Bethany Beach
(302) 537-7680
www.ecodelaware.com

Brandywine Park Zoo
Wilmington
(302) 571-7747
www.brandywinezoo.org

Cape Henlopen State Park
Lewes
(302) 645-8983
www.destateparks.com/park/
cape-henlopen/

Christiana Skating Center
Christiana
(302) 366-0473
www.christianaskatingcenter.biz

Days Gone By Museum
Seaford
(302) 629-9889

Delaware Center for the Contemporary Arts
Wilmington
(302) 656-6466
www.thedcca.org

Delaware Sports Museum and Hall of Fame
Wilmington
(302) 425-3263
www.desports.org

Fisher-Martin House
Lewes
(302) 645-8073
www.visitdelaware.com

Fort DuPont State Park
Delaware City
(302) 834-7941
www.destateparks.com

Fox Point State Park
Wilmington
(302) 739-9220

The Gallery on Central Ave
Ocean View
(302) 539-4730
www.galleryoncentralave.com

Superlodge New Castle
1213 West Ave.
(888) 711-5544,
www.newcastlesuperlodge
.net

OCEAN VIEW

Cedar Breeze Bed and Breakfast
30680 Cedar Neck Rd.
(302) 537-7015
www.cedarbreeze.com

REHOBOTH BEACH

Abbey Inn Bed & Breakfast
31 Maryland Ave.
(302) 227-7023 (summer)
(239) 652-9107 (winter)
www.amidralrehoboth.com

Indian River Lifesaving Station
Rehoboth Beach
(302) 227-6991
www.destateparks.com/attractions/
life-saving-station

James Farm Ecological Preserve
Ocean View
(302) 645-7325
www.inlandbays.org/cib_pm/james_
farm.php

Loop Canal Centennial Park
Bethany Beach
www.bethany-beach.net/parks.htm

Nanticoke Indian Museum
Millsboro
(302) 945-7022
www.nanticokeindians.org/museum.cfm

Nassau Valley Vineyards
Lewes
(302) 645-9463
www.nassauvalley.com

Nemours Mansion and Gardens
Wilmington
(302) 651-6912
www.nemours.org/mansion.html

Rehoboth Beach Museum
Rehoboth Beach
(302) 227-7310
www.rehobothbeachmuseum.org

Rehoboth Beach Theatre of the Arts
Rehoboth Beach
(302) 227-9310
www.rehobothbeachtheater.com

Trees of the States Arboretum
Georgetown
(302) 856-5400
www.treasuresofthesea.org/other.html

Wilmington Blue Rocks
Wilmington
(302) 888-2015
www.bluerocks.com

**Winterthur Museum, Garden
and Library**
Winterthur
(302) 888-4600
(800) 448-3883
www.winterthur.org

Atlantic Sands Hotels
101 North Boardwalk
(302) 227-7311
(800) 422-0600
www.atlanticsands
hotel.com

Corner Cupboard Inn
50 Park Ave.
(302) 227-8553
www.cornercupboard
inn.com

Henlopen Hotel
511 North Boardwalk
(800) 441-8450
(302) 227-2551
www.henlopenhotel.com

DELAWARE TOURISM OFFICES

Delaware Tourism Office, 99 Kings Hwy., Dover 19901; (302) 739-4271, (866) 2-VISIT-DE; www.visitdelaware.com.

Bethany-Fenwick Chamber of Commerce, 36913 Coastal Hwy., Fenwick Island, 19944; (302) 539-2100, (800) 962-7873; www.bethany-fenwick.org.

Kent County Tourism Corporation, 435 North Dupont Hwy., Dover 19901; (302) 734-1736, (800) 233-KENT; www.visitdover.com.

Lewes Chamber of Commerce and Visitors Bureau, 120 Kings Hwy., Lewes 19958; (302) 645-8073, (877) 465-3937; www.leweschamber.com.

Historic New Castle Visitors Bureau, 220 Delaware St, New Castle 19720; (302) 322-9804, (800) 758-1550; www.newcastlecity.org/visitors/visitor_index.html.

Rehoboth Beach–Dewey Beach Chamber of Commerce, 501 Rehoboth Ave., Rehoboth Beach 19971; (302) 227-2233, (800) 441-1329; www.beach-fun.com.

SOUTHERN DELAWARE TOURISM

Sussex County Convention and Tourism Commission, P.O. Box 240, Georgetown 19947; (302) 856-1818, (800) 357-1818; www.visitsoutherndelaware.com.

Greater Wilmington Convention and Visitors Bureau, 100 West Tenth St, Suite 20, Wilmington 19801; (302) 652-4088, (800) 489- 6664; www.visitwilmingtonde.com

Hotel Rehoboth
247 Rehoboth Ave.
(302) 227-4300
www.hotelrehoboth.com

WILMINGTON

DoubleTree Hotel
700 King St.
(302) 655-0400
www.doubletree.com

Hotel DuPont
100 West Eleventh St.
(302) 594-3100
www.hoteldupont.com/index.cfm

Inn at Wilmington
300 Rocky Run Pkwy.
(302) 479-7900
www.innatwilmington.com

Index

CPSIA information can be obtained
at www.ICGtesting.com
Printed in the USA
LVHW082240140521
687514LV00016B/1271

9 780762 757305